"When all the rivers are used, when all the creeks in the ravines, when all the brooks, when all the springs are used, when all the canyon waters are taken up, when all the artesian waters are taken up, when all the wells are sunk or dug that can be dug in all this arid region, there is still no sufficient water to irrigate all this arid region…

Gentlemen, it may be unpleasant to me to give you these facts…I tell you, gentlemen, you are piling up a heritage of conflict and litigation over water rights, for there is not sufficient water to supply these lands."

— John Wesley Powell addressing the Second International Irrigation Congress, Los Angeles, 1893.

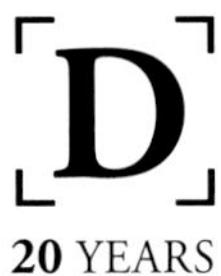

20 YEARS

Cofounders: Taj Forer and Michael Itkoff
Creative Director: Ursula Damm
Copy Editor: Gabrielle Fastman

ISBN: 978-1-954119-31-4

Printed by Ofset Yapimevi, Turkey

Daylight Books
E-mail: info@daylightbooks.org
Web: www.daylightbooks.org

DAMMED

Birth to Death of the Colorado River

DEBBIE BENTLEY

Daylight

DAMS OF THE UNITED STATES

91,807	Total Dams
61 years	Average Dam Age
76%	High Hazard Potential Dams with an EAP
3%	Dams with Hydropower
5%	Regulated Dams
71%	State-Regulated Dams

INTRODUCTION

When John Wesley Powell undertook his first Colorado River expedition in 1869, he encountered a river that today would be unrecognizable. Now dammed and diverted within a complex and interrelated system, the Colorado River provides water for 40 million people and irrigates 5.5 million agricultural acres in the Colorado River Basin and Mexico. Once flowing to the Gulf of Mexico and feeding a robust delta, the river's flow now dries and disappears into the desert sands far short of the Gulf.

Many people do not consider where their water comes from as it flows from faucets, or think about the water used to grow the food on their table. Nor do they consider the electricity that flows to the light switch—electricity generated by the decreasing water levels at dams, such as Hoover and Glen Canyon on the Colorado River. They are removed from the origin of these waters, and their increasing scarcity. Unfortunately, data presented in the news and on television is often complex and difficult to visualize. This project sought to provide that visual connection so often lacking—a view of the entire interconnected and complex system to further understanding—coupled with background information to raise awareness.

To deliver such large amounts of water, the Colorado River has become one of the most controlled rivers in the world, with fifteen, soon to be sixteen, dams to impound and divert its waters on the main stem alone. Unbridled growth in the arid West and Southwest (Phoenix and its suburbs, for example, have ballooned from a population of 65,000 residents in 1940 to 4.6 million in 2021) coupled with legally mandated water deliveries required by the 1922 Colorado River Compact have stretched the water supply to its limit. Added stress on the system comes from aridification, increasing dust within the basin, reservoir evaporation, and transit losses. Each one of these issues brings the river system closer to crisis.

To understand the system, it is helpful to start at the beginning. The basis for all current water delivery in the system are series of compacts, federal laws, court decisions and decrees, contracts, and regulatory guidelines collectively known as the "Law of the River." The cornerstone of these agreements is the Colorado River Compact of 1922. This agreement was negotiated by the seven Colorado River basin states and the federal government. It laid out the relationships between the Upper Basin states and the Lower Basin states. Most of the water demands were in the Lower Basin, primarily as a result of growth and agriculture.

The Upper Basin states were concerned that the Lower Basin's plans for Hoover Dam and other projects would deprive them of the river's water in the future, under the Western water law doctrine of prior appropriation. The states could not agree on how the Colorado River's waters should be allocated. Ultimately, Herbert Hoover, who was secretary of commerce at the time, suggested the basin be divided into upper and lower halves, with each basin having the right to develop and use 7.5 million acre-feet (maf) annually. In addition, the Upper Basin was to deliver a definite quantity of 75 maf every ten years, as measured at Lee Ferry. An acre-foot is roughly 360,000 gallons of water, or enough to cover an acre of land with water one foot in depth. The Compact was based on flawed assumptions placing the annual flows in excess of 15 maf, even though more accurate data was available at the time, as presented by E.C. LaRue of the USGS. Ranges during historically low runoff periods were more in the 12 maf to 13 maf range, with many years below that mark.

This 1922 apportionment did not end the disagreements over the control of the Colorado River. Modifications were made in 1928 with the Boulder Canyon Project Act, the Mexican Water Treaty of 1944, the Arizona v. California US Supreme Court decision of 1964, the Colorado River Basin Project Act of 1968, the Colorado River Water Delivery Agreement of 2003 (a.k.a. the Federal Quantification Settlement Agreement), and the Colorado River Interim Guidelines for Lower Basin Shortages and the Coordinated Operations for Lake Powell and Lake Mead of 2007.

Notably missing from the Compact of 1922 were all rights due the thirty Indigenous tribes located in the basin. Numerous nations have begun to assert claims for water rights, which now amount to as much as 30% of the Colorado River's waters. But most of this water is "paper water," meaning rights are owned on paper, but there is no access to it. Often, rights haven't been legally quantified and set, or the water is designated as single use and can't be utilized for any other purpose. Often, there simply is no infrastructure in place to provide physical access to the water.

Currently, a new proposal generated by California, Arizona, and Nevada is under discussion but has not been ratified to date. California plans to contribute 1.6-maf savings over three years, with Nevada pledging to conserve 285,000 acre-feet, and Arizona 1.1 maf. In exchange, affected entities would receive $1.6 billion in federal grants. This proposal would end in 2026. By that time, theoretically, a completely new operating agreement will be in place, taking effect in 2026. The Bureau of Reclamation has said that the states need stop using 2 to 4 maf of water. This is about one third of the river's flow.

What are some of the factors creating the need to regulate the basin states' access to Colorado River waters? One of the primary issues is the trend of aridification, not just in the Colorado River Basin, but also across the US. More than a megadrought, aridification is described by experts as the result of a "hot drought" due to increasingly higher global temperatures. The increase in temperatures in turn creates more evaporation from water bodies and soil, and more evapotranspiration from plants and sublimation from snow. This creates an increasingly water-scarce environment and is permanent.

Does a wet year with heavy snowpack mean there is no problem? No. For example, 2011 was one of the wettest years on record for the Colorado River. This was followed by two of the driest years on record (2012 and 2013). The continuing aridification of the area is based on trends, not the occasional wet year.

Increasing temperatures affect water lost to evaporation. In 2022, the Southern Nevada Water Authority produced an analysis indicating about 1.5 maf of water is lost to evaporation and other losses, such as transit, each year in the Lower Basin alone. This amount is more water than the state of Utah uses from the river on an annual basis. The analysis examined where water loss occurs downstream of the measuring station at Lee Ferry to the northern boundary of the US-Mexico border.

Additional losses come in the form of dust. Increasing amounts of dust in mountain snowpack is occurring on a worldwide basis. Winds carry fine sediment particles from arid regions, sometimes hundreds or thousands of miles. This dust can be caused by eroded soil, earth disturbed by human construction activities, land disturbed by grazing and farming, and fine debris from wildfires.

When this airborne dust lands on snow, it darkens the surface. Dark surfaces absorb more sunlight than light surfaces. This speeds snowmelt, which causes multiple issues. It creates faster snow retreat, which increases soil exposure and adds to evaporation. The faster snowmelt reaches rivers sooner each year, overwhelming river systems in the spring and early summer. And lastly, earlier and faster runoff can leave rivers drier in late summer.

While the Colorado River may be the poster child for poor water-management practices, overuse, and the effects of aridification, it is hardly the only river at risk in the US, and indeed the world. Sustainability is key. And for our endangered rivers to be sustainable, despite existing dams and diversions, we must all be willing to learn, be aware, and accept that we are responsible for our own water use. We must be willing to make our concerns about proposed dams known on the local, state, and national level. Most importantly, we all must be willing to accept a future with less water, and to come to terms with what that might mean for our current way of life.

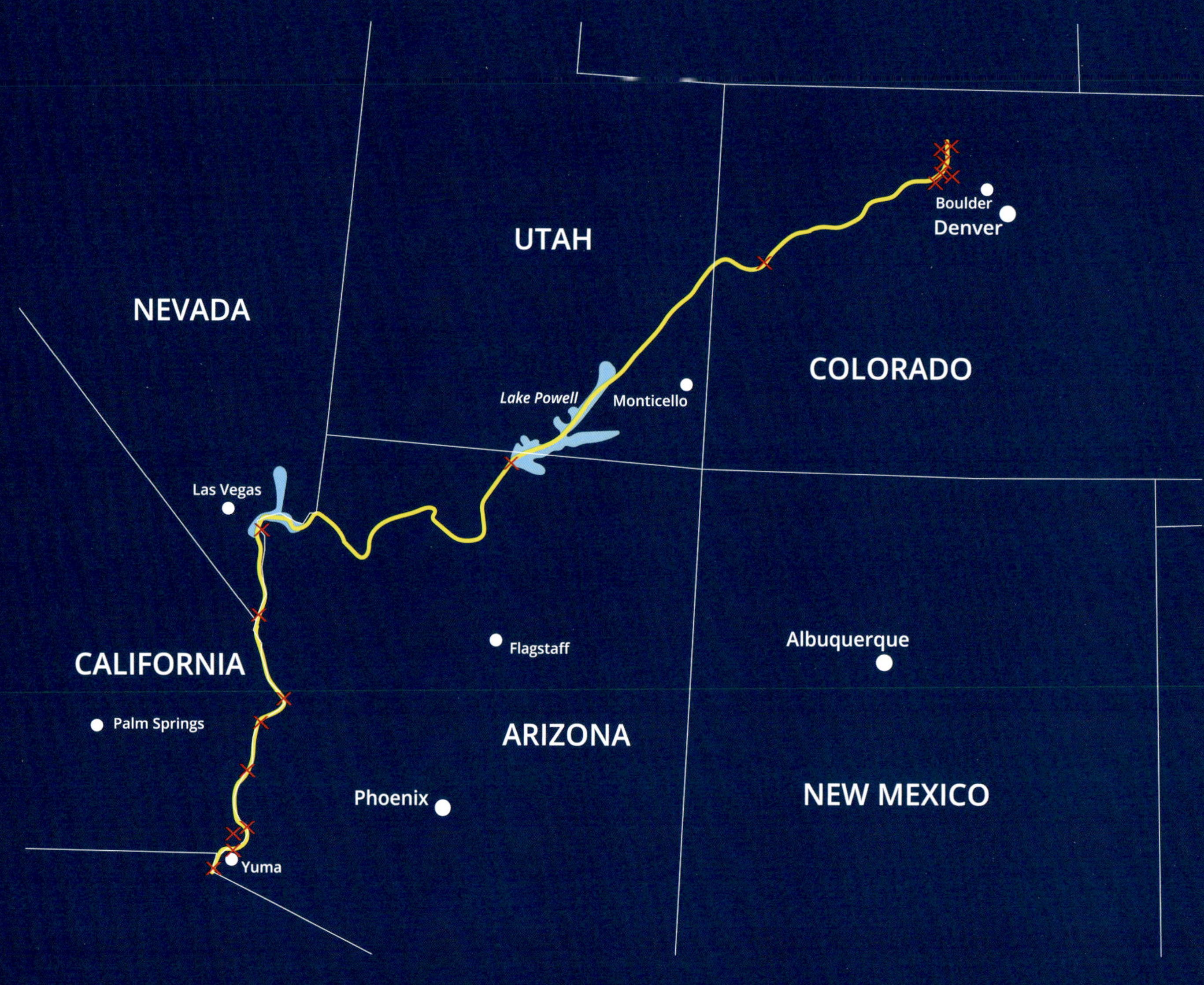

*Map is for illustrative purposes only

THE COLORADO RIVER

The Colorado River has been known by many names. Among these are the Grand, Big Red, the American Nile, and the River of Law. Whatever its name, the river has become a lifeline to the burgeoning populations and agricultural areas of the West and Southwest.

The main stem of the Colorado River runs approximately 1,450 miles from its headwaters at La Poudre Pass in Colorado to the border of Mexico. Along the route, the river is impounded and diverted by sixteen dams. These dams work in complex tandem to control the river and provide water deliveries to nearly 40 million people and roughly 5.5 million acres of agricultural land in the Western and Southwestern US and Mexico. In fact, 80% of the water diverted from the river is for agricultural purposes.

The river is divided into the Upper Basin and the Lower Basin. Each basin is allocated 7.5 maf of water per year, in compliance with the 1922 Colorado River Compact, known as the "Law of the River." The combined total of both basins, at 15 maf, translates to 1.9 trillion gallons of water used in a typical year.

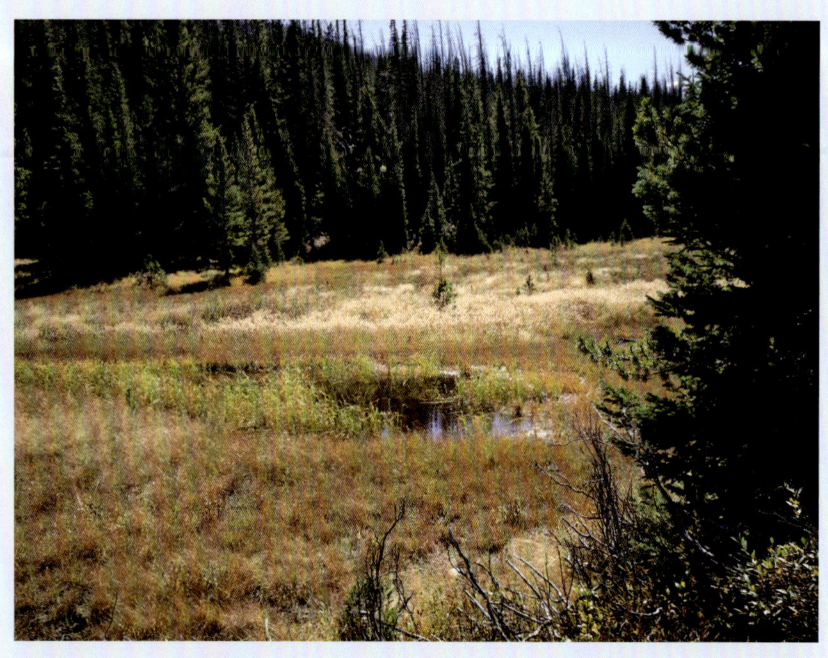

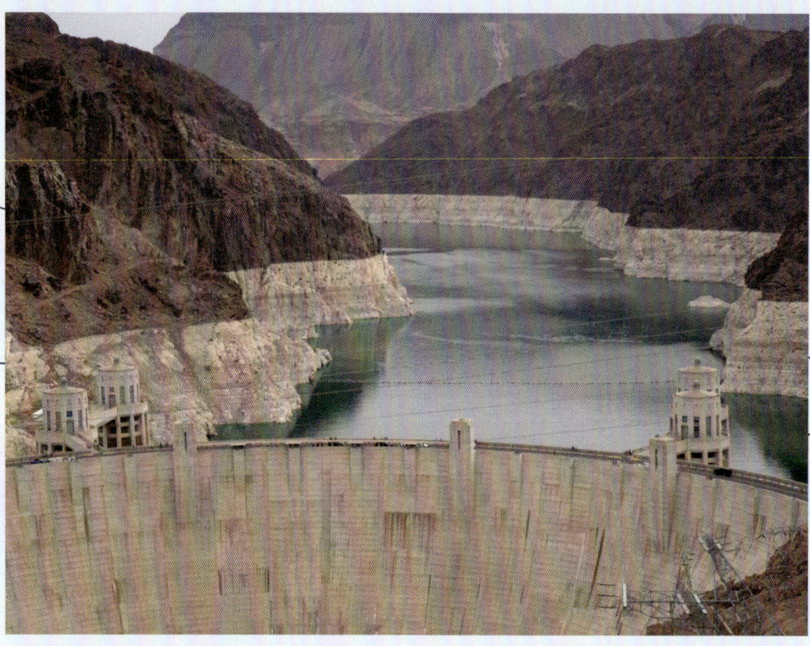

Top:
La Poudre Pass Lake.

Bottom:
Hoover Dam.

THE HEADWATERS

40.4738N 105.8257W

Headwaters of the Colorado River are at La Poudre Pass, elevation 10,184 feet above sea level, in Colorado. As the river travels through Rocky Mountain National Park, creeks such as Specimen and Lady add to its flow.

From this beginning, the river is fed by numerous major tributaries, such as the Gunnison, White, Yampa, San Juan, Delores, Green, Little Colorado, Gila, and Virgin. It makes its way though mountains, canyons, and deserts to its termination in Mexico. Sometimes referred to as the American Nile, the Colorado supplies water for nearly 40 million people and irrigates roughly 5.5 million acres throughout the west and southwest United States.

The Colorado River is one of the most controlled and endangered rivers in the world.

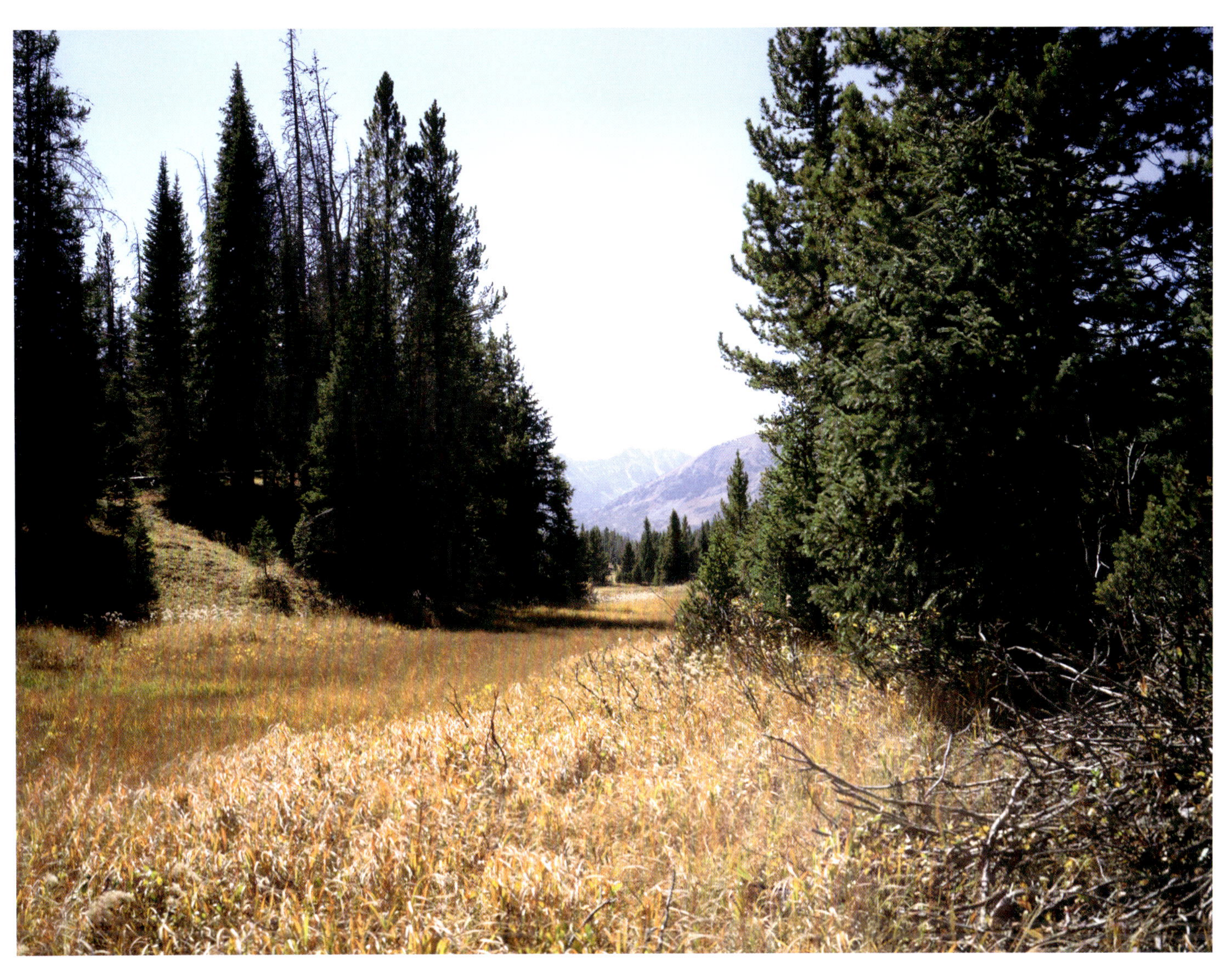

The headwaters
in Colorado at
40.4738N 105.8257W.

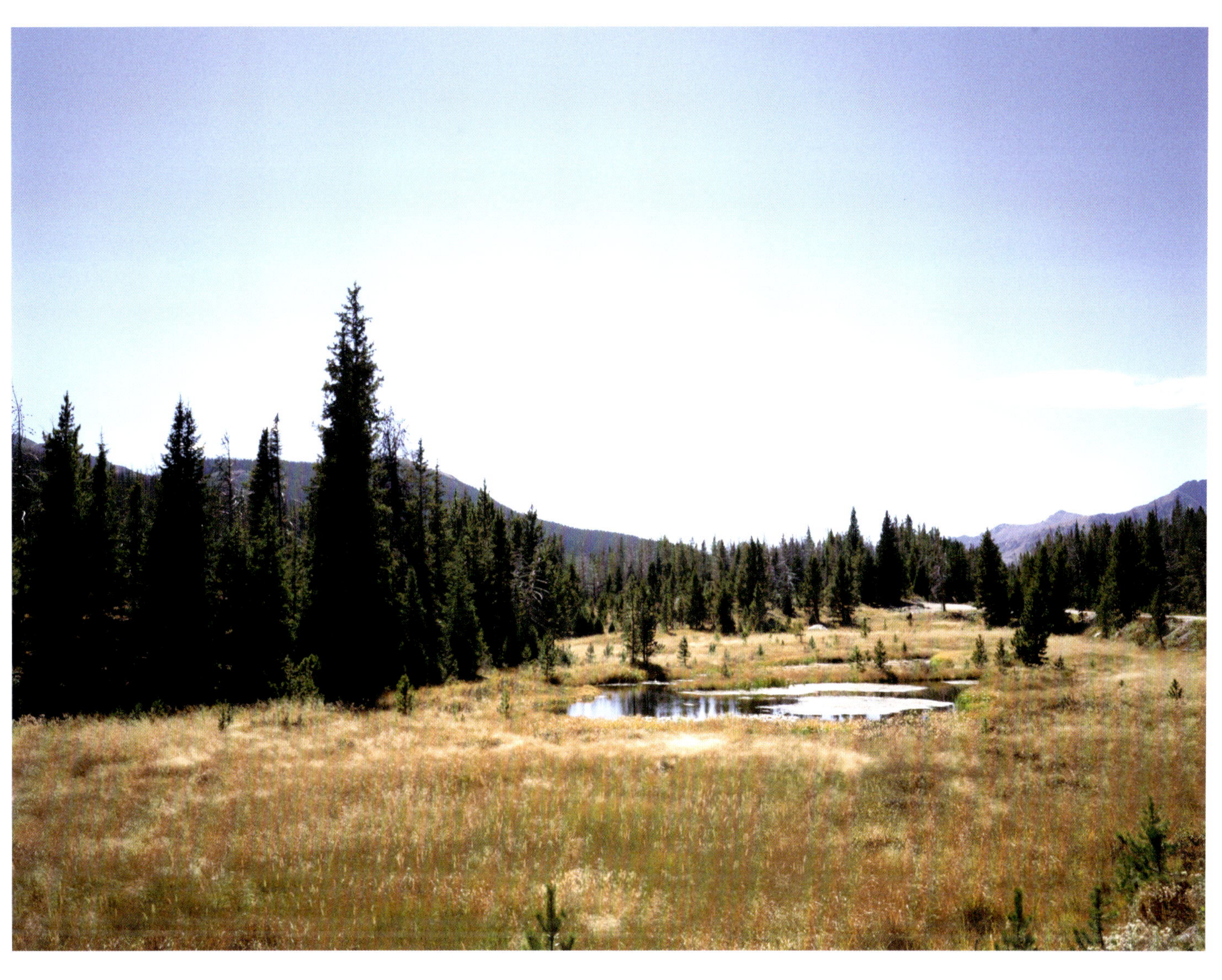

La Poudre Pass
Lake at headwaters.

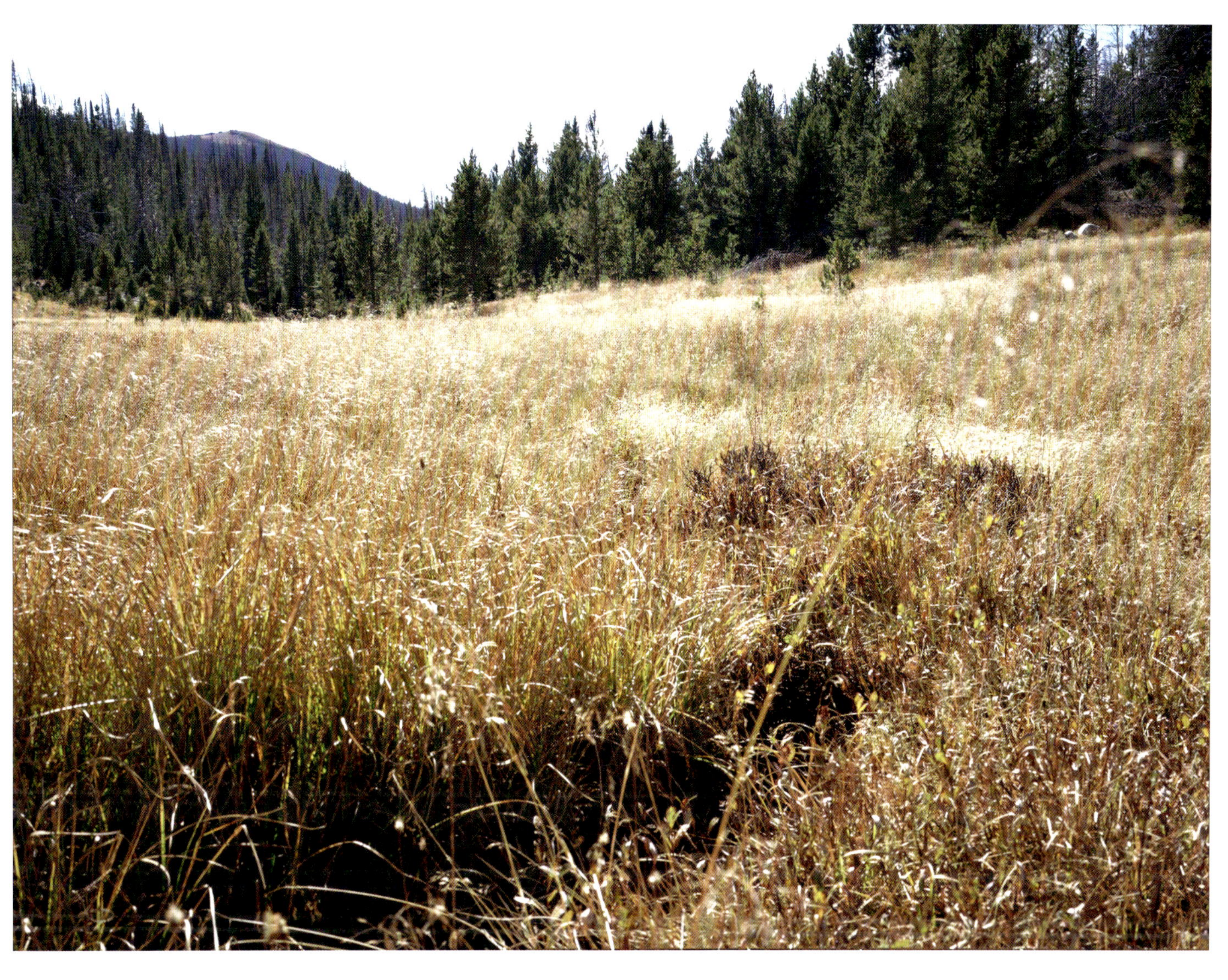

Beginning of
Colorado River flow
at headwaters.

GRAND DITCH

The Grand Ditch is a more-than-century-old diversion project located in the northwestern corner of Rocky Mountain National Park, Colorado. Begun in 1896, this hand-dug canal didn't reach its full fifteen-mile length until the 1930s.

The Grand Ditch diverts an average of 29% of the runoff from the Never Summer Mountains, which would otherwise feed the headwaters of the Colorado River. Water levels in associated peatlands drop by as much as twenty inches when snowmelt is diverted. The diversion siphons off approximately 20,000 acre-feet of water per year, when flows from the Specimen Ditch are combined. The Specimen Ditch enters the flow of the Grand Ditch near the newly reconstructed pump house.

In addition to water from peatlands, eleven headwater tributaries of the river are captured by the ditch between May and September each year. These waters are carried through Rocky Mountain National Park and across the Continental Divide at La Poudre Pass, ultimately captured in Long Draw Reservoir.

From Long Draw Reservoir, the diverted water is then released to the Cache La Poudre Creek, and ultimately to the eastern plains of Colorado for agricultural use.

The Grand Ditch is operated by the Water Supply and Storage Company.

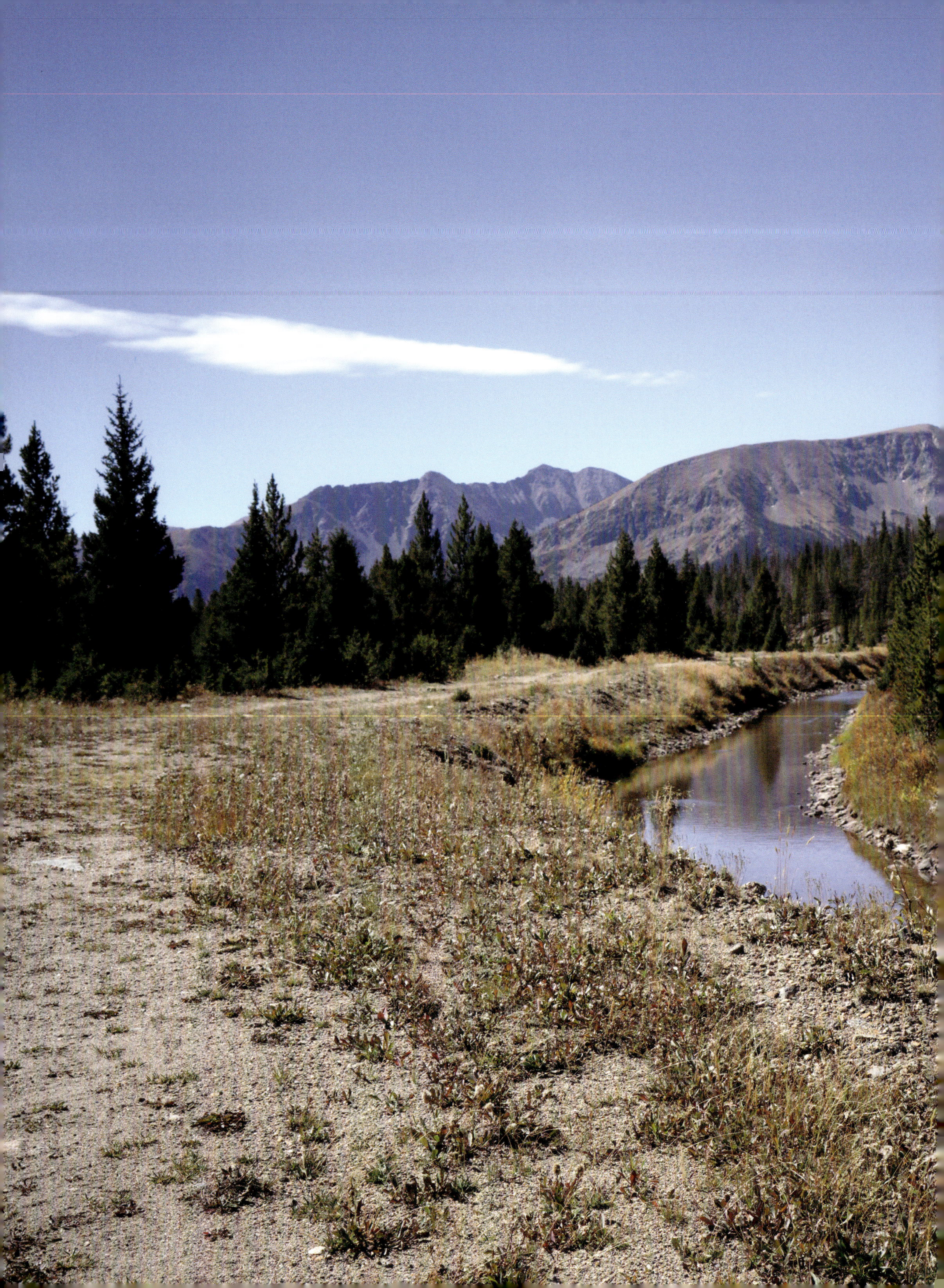

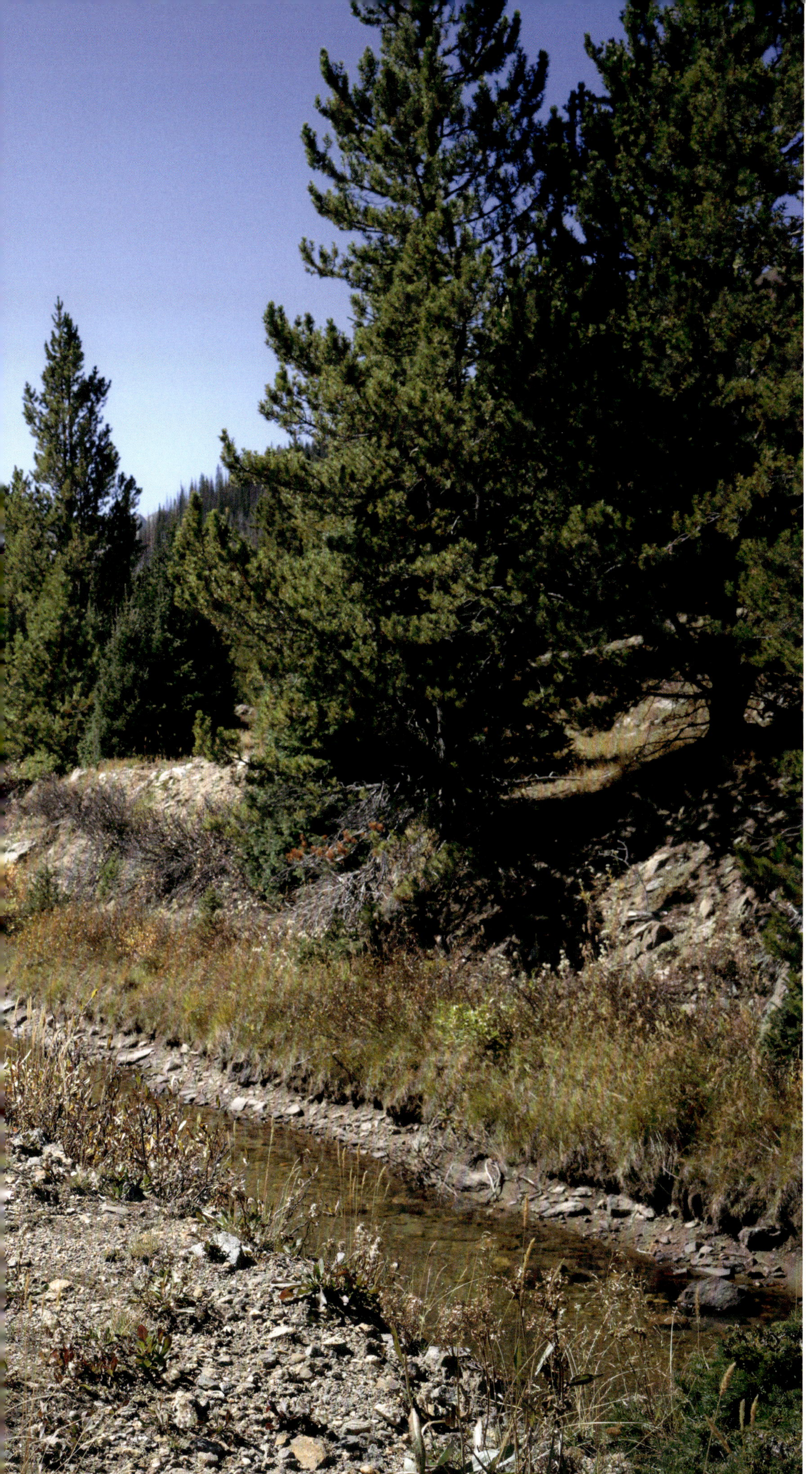

Grand Ditch across
from headwaters,
Colorado.

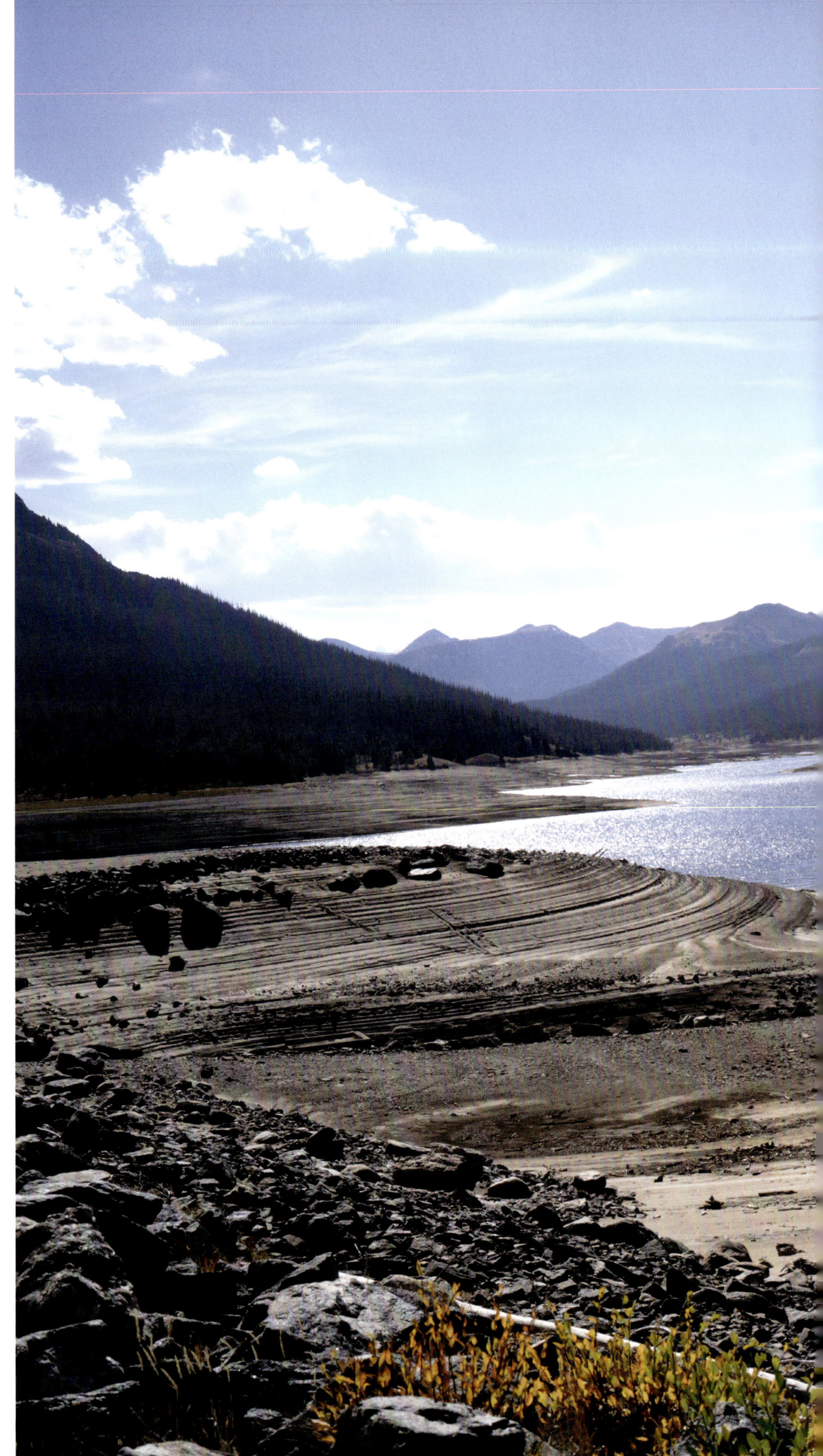

Long Draw
Reservoir, Colorado.

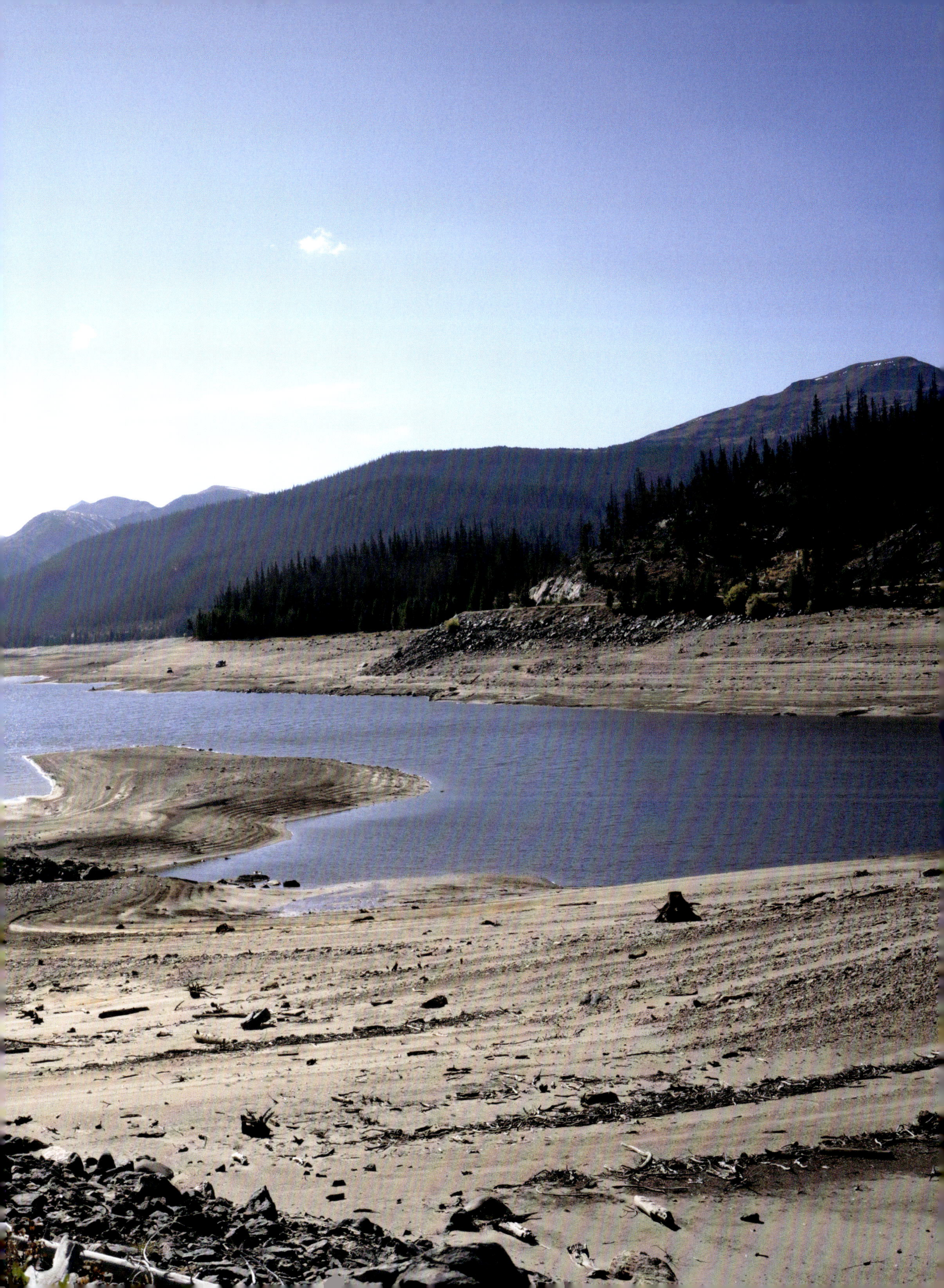

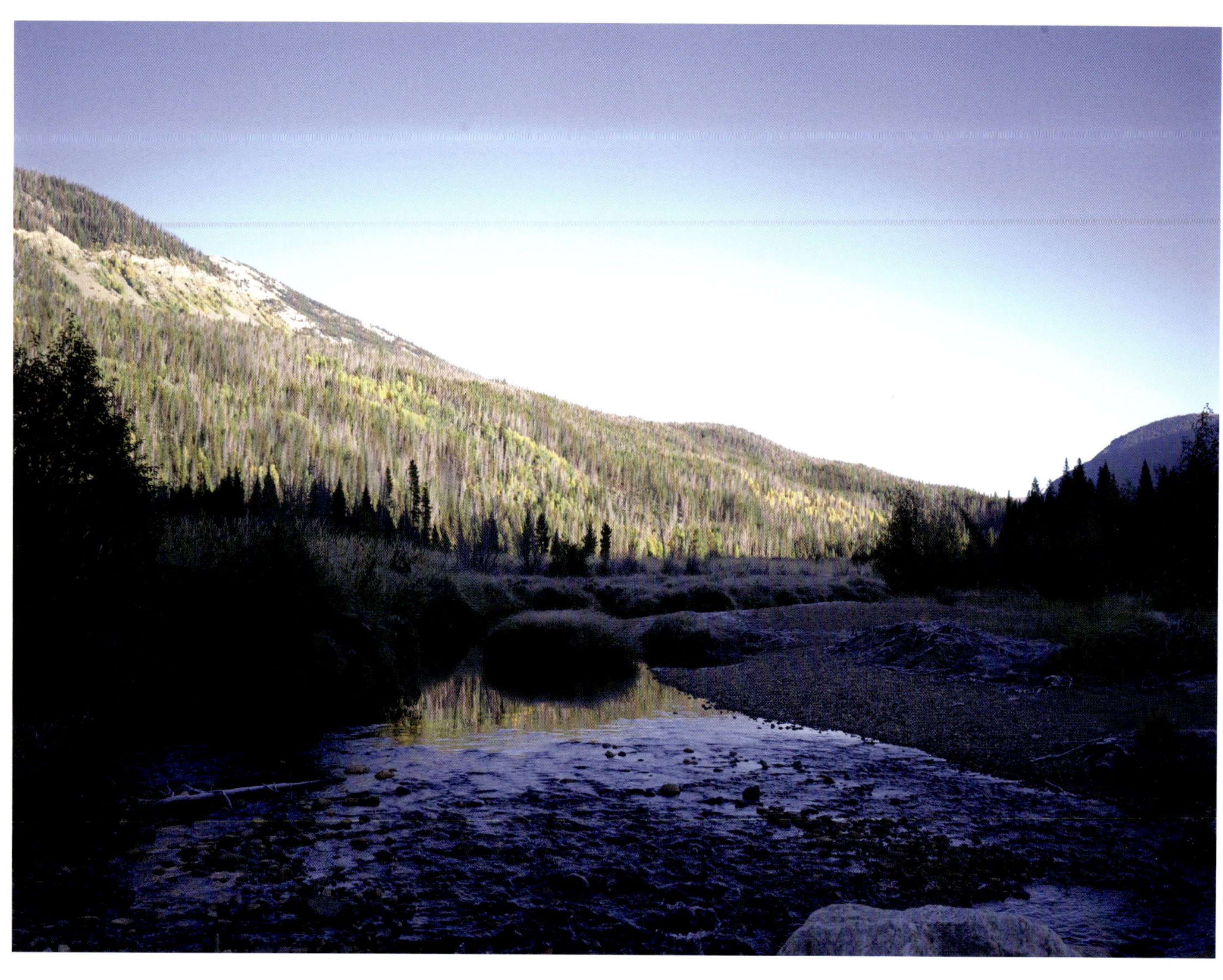

Colorado River at
early morning in
Rocky Mountain
National Park,
Colorado.

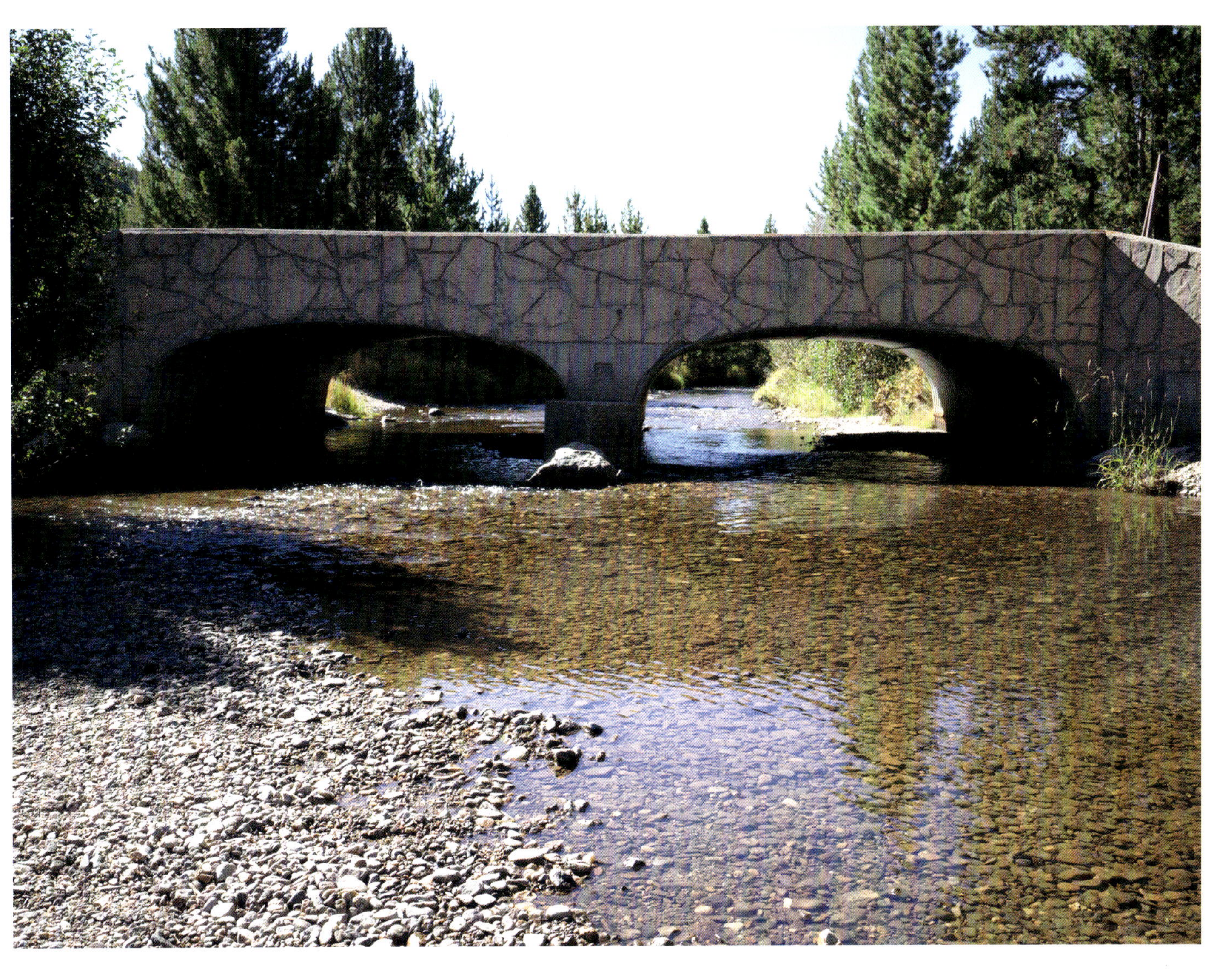

The river in Rocky
Mountain National
Park.

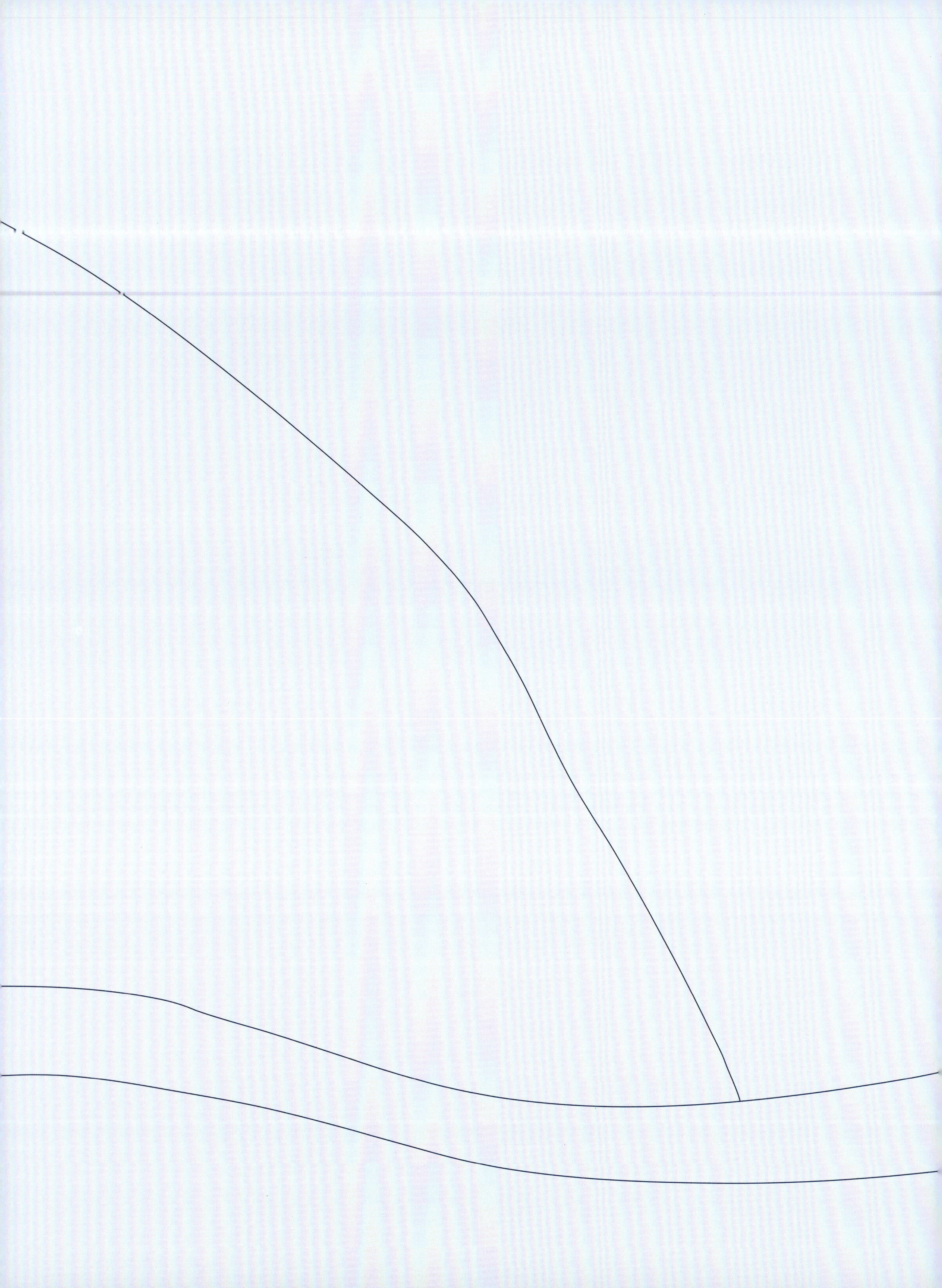

SHADOW MOUNTAIN DAM

Shadow Mountain Dam and Reservoir is located between Lake Granby and Grand Lake, on the western slope of Colorado. It acts as a conduit to transport water pumped from neighboring Lake Granby to Grand Lake and the Adams Tunnel via the Granby Pump Canal. Small boats can navigate the connecting channel between Shadow Mountain Reservoir and Grand Lake.

The north fork of the Colorado River enters Shadow Mountain Reservoir near Pine Beach. The Colorado River then emerges through release from Shadow Mountain Dam, flowing toward Granby Dam—the next dam on the system.

The dam itself was built between 1944 and 1946 and has a capacity of 17,354 acre-feet of water.

Shadow Mountain Dam and reservoir along with Lake Granby and Willow Creek Reservoir, are components of the Colorado–Big Thompson Project (C-BT), easily the largest trans-mountain water diversion in the state of Colorado. The C-BT diverts water, via the thirteen-mile-long Alva B. Adams Tunnel, underneath the peaks of Rocky Mountain National Park to the eastern slope of Colorado. Two pump plants, Farr and Willow Creek, send collected water upslope before it enters the Alva B. Adams tunnel.

The Adams Tunnel is nearly ten feet in diameter, lined in concrete, and cuts under the Continental Divide as much as 3,800 feet beneath the earth's surface. Once water leaves the tunnel, it passes through a distribution system of canals, pipelines, small reservoirs, and hydroelectric plants. The water is stored in three terminal reservoirs: Horsetooth, Boulder, and Carter Lake. Recipients include residents in Boulder, Broomfield, Larimer, Logan, Morgan, Sedgwick, Washington, and Weld counties in Colorado.

The C-BT contains seven hydropower plants that generate approximately 770 million kilowatt-hours of energy per year.

Shadow Mountain Dam is operated by the Northern Colorado Water Conservancy District (Northern Water).

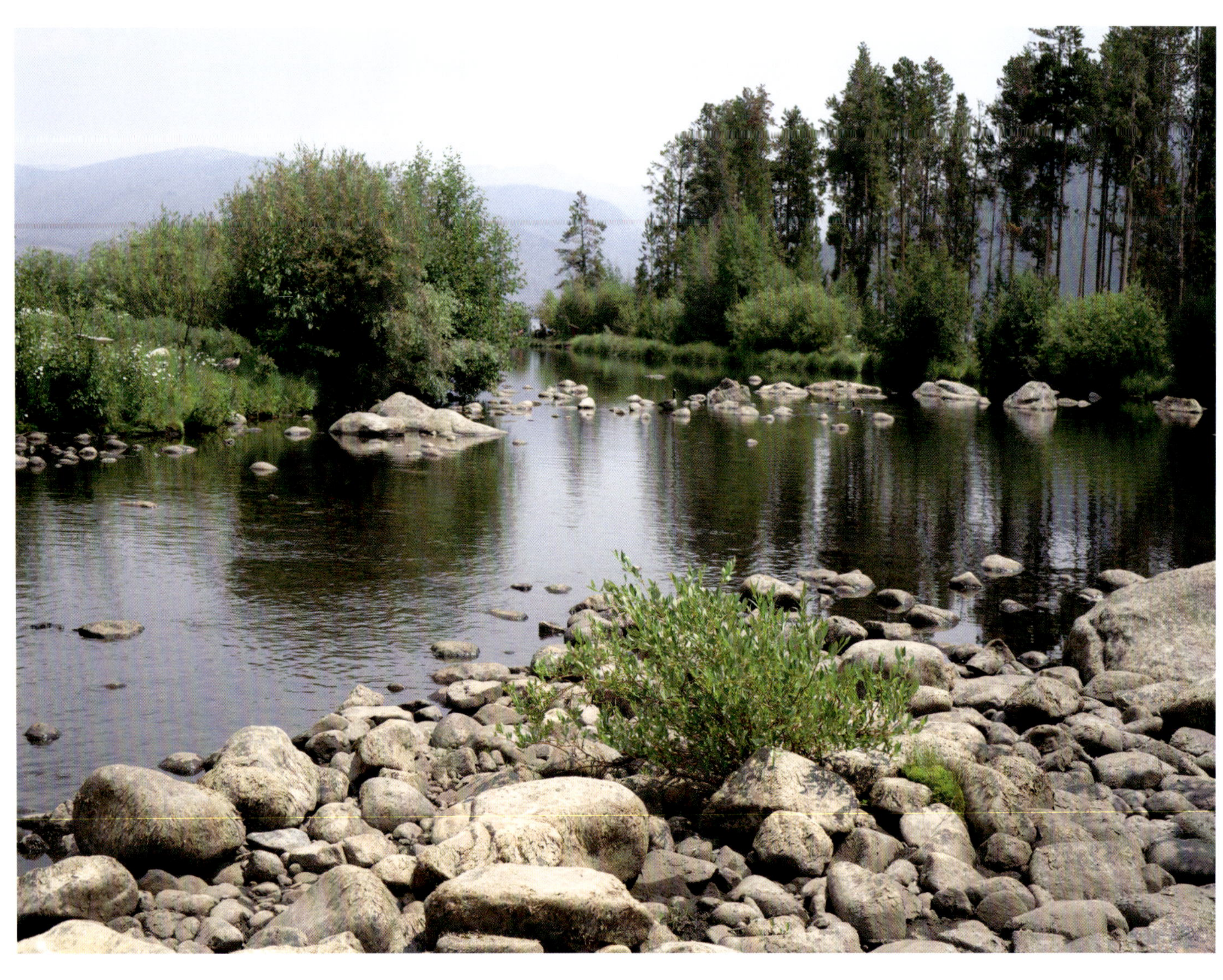

Colorado River
upon entering
Shadow Mountain
Dam.

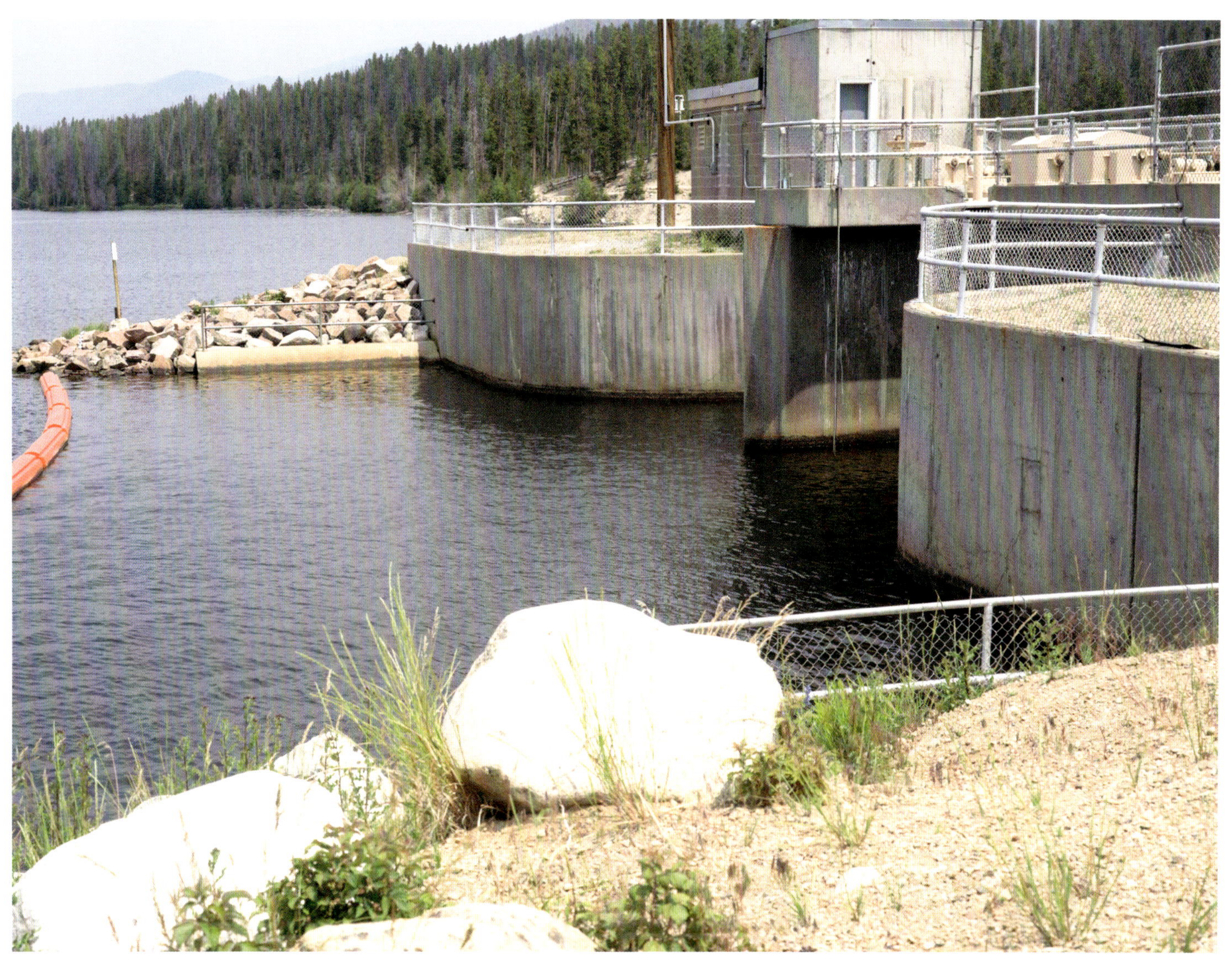

Shadow Mountain
Dam, Colorado.

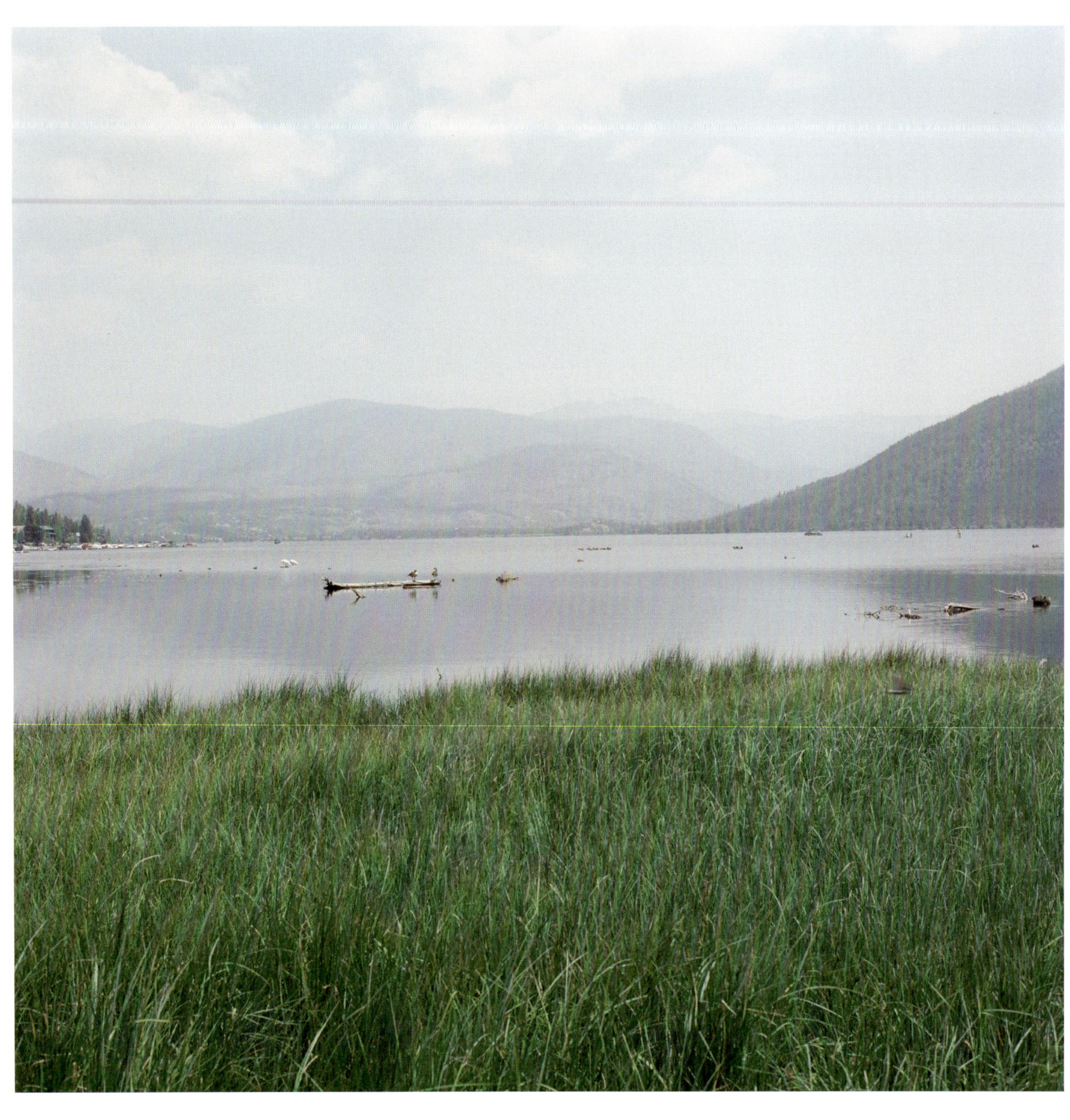

Shadow Mountain
Reservoir.

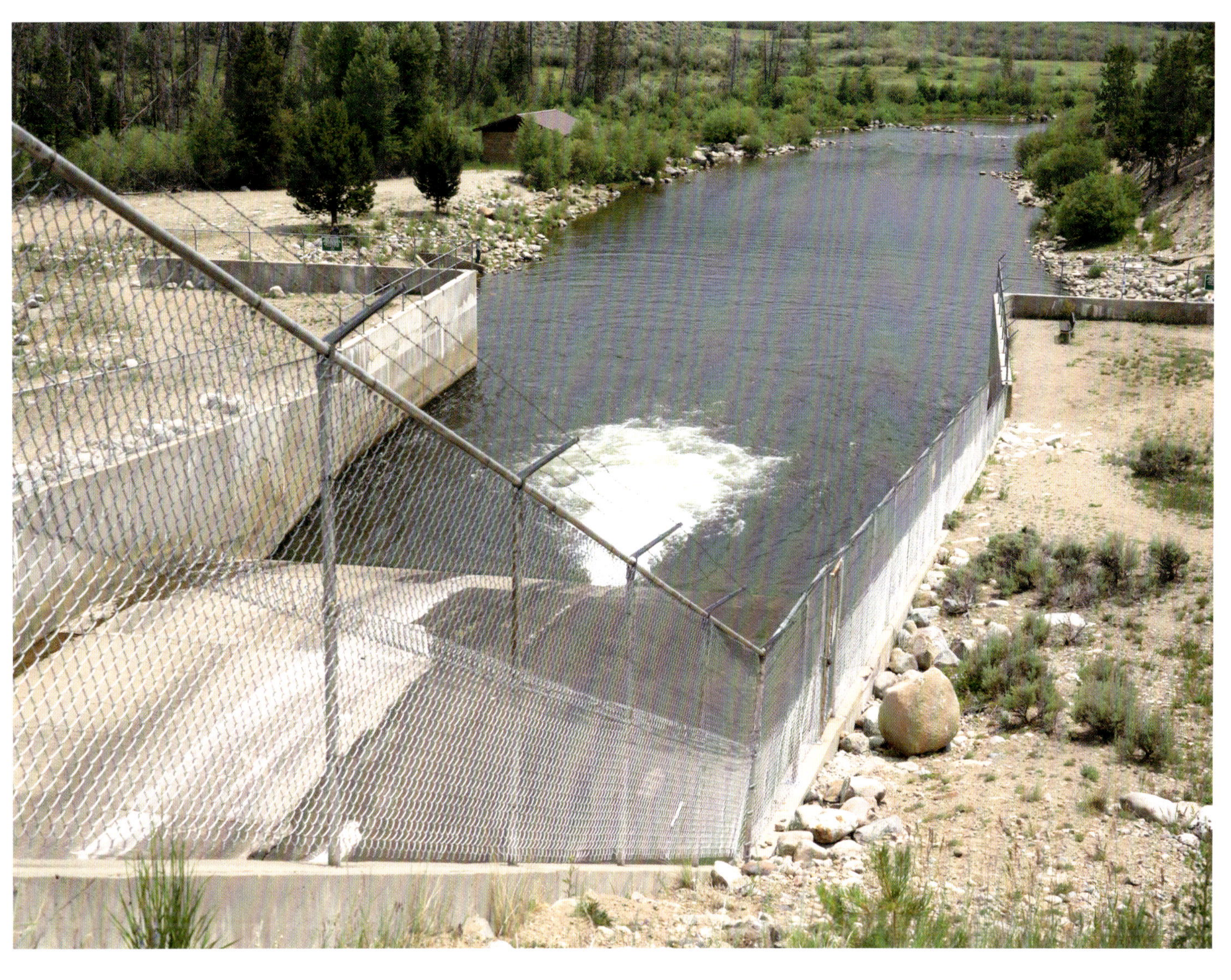

Colorado River
released from
Shadow Mountain
Dam.

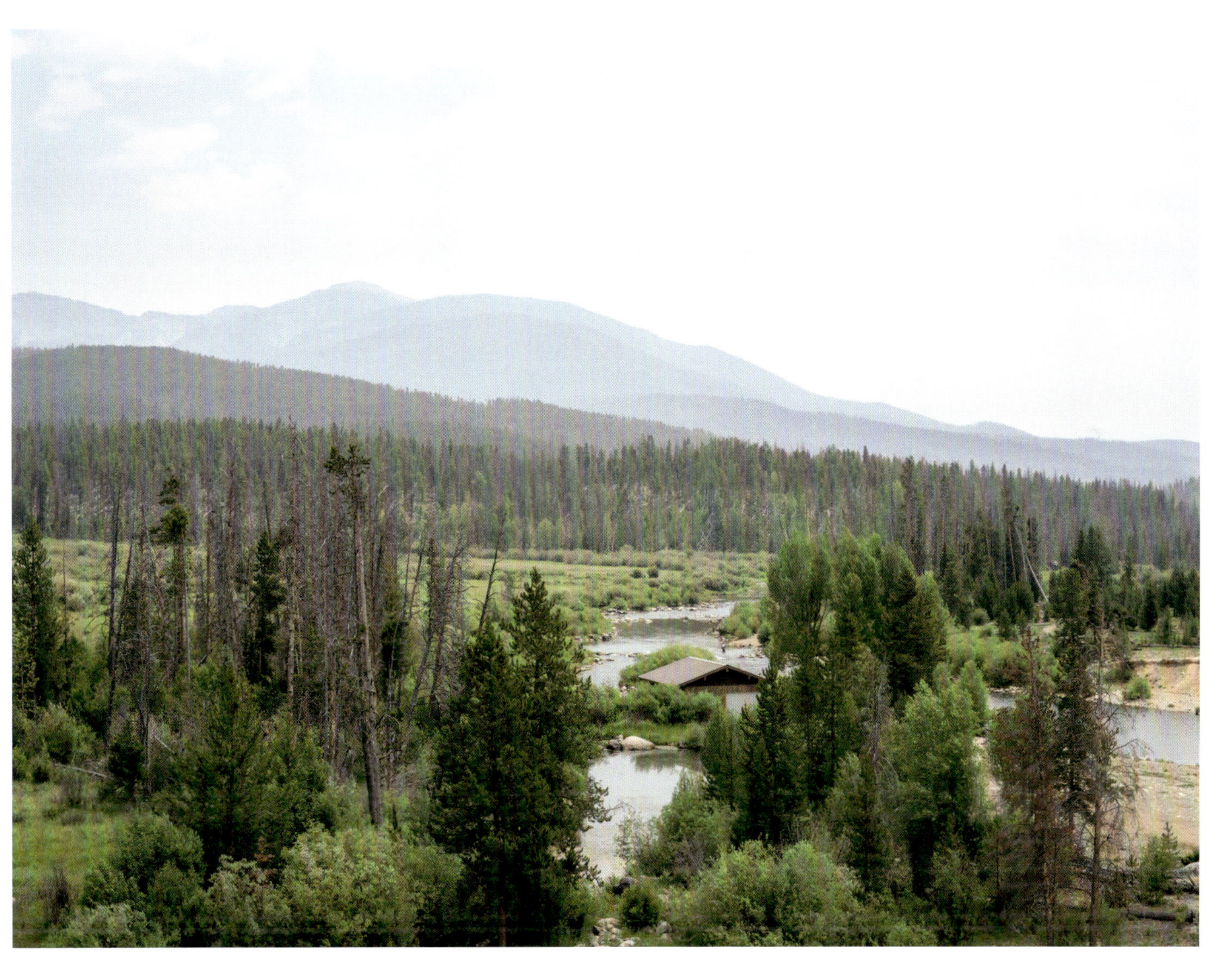

The river flowing
postrelease from
Shadow Mountain
Dam.

GRANBY DAM

Lake Granby is the largest storage reservoir on the C-BT and the second largest body of water in Colorado, impounding a maximum of 539,758 acre-feet of water. Water is pumped from Lake Granby via the Farr Pump Plant to the Granby Pump Canal. From there, it flows to Shadow Mountain Reservoir. Once it has reached Shadow Mountain Reservoir, the water flows through a connecting channel to Grand Lake, then into the West Portal of the Alva B. Adams Tunnel.

Lake Granby is located on the Colorado River, approximately five miles northeast of the town of Granby, Colorado. The Colorado River flows from the Shadow Mountain Reservoir into Lake Granby on the northeast side and exits at Granby Dam.

Construction of the dam began in late 1942, with water first stored in the reservoir in 1949.

Granby Dam is operated by Northern Water.

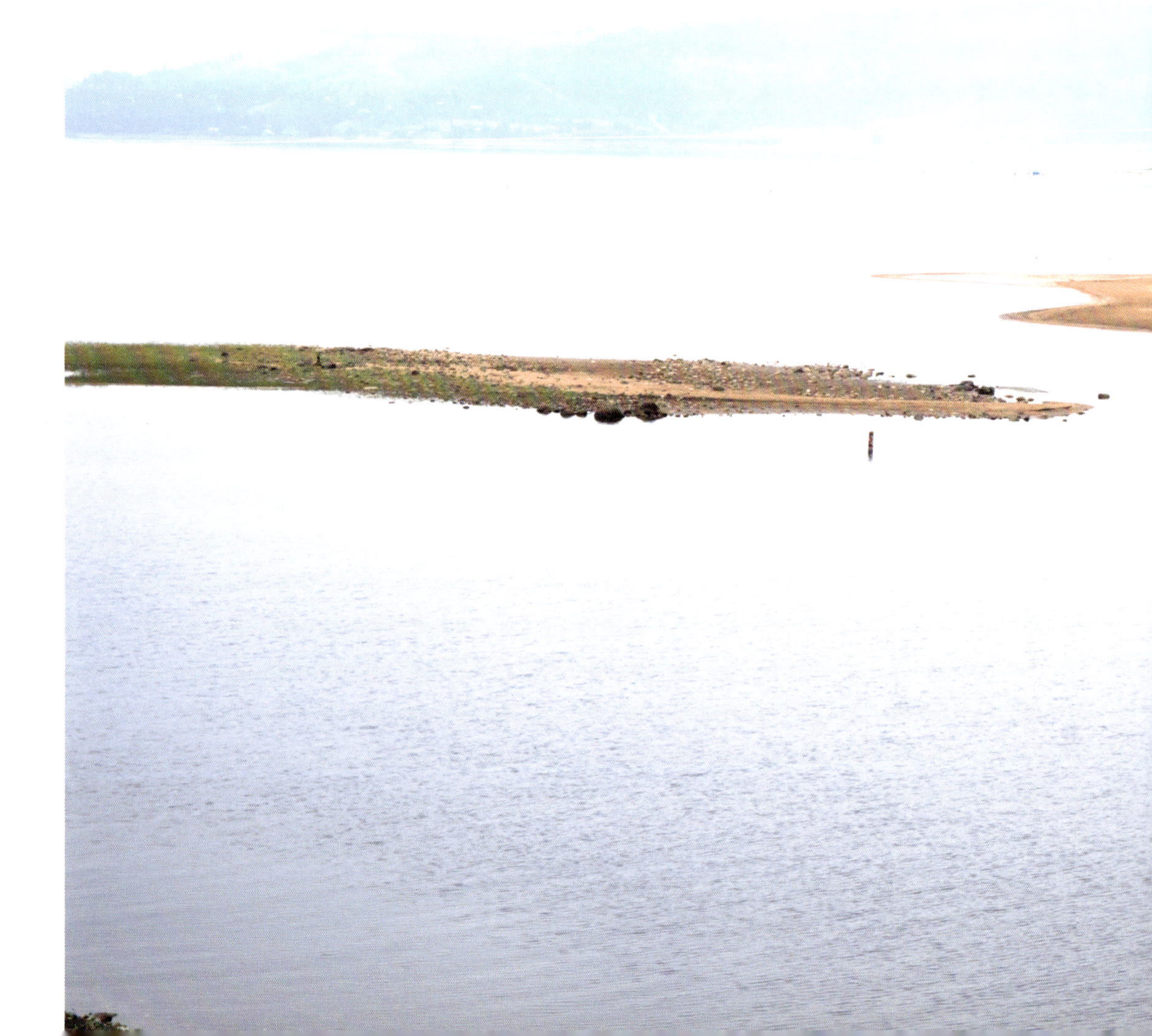

The river
impounded in Lake
Granby.

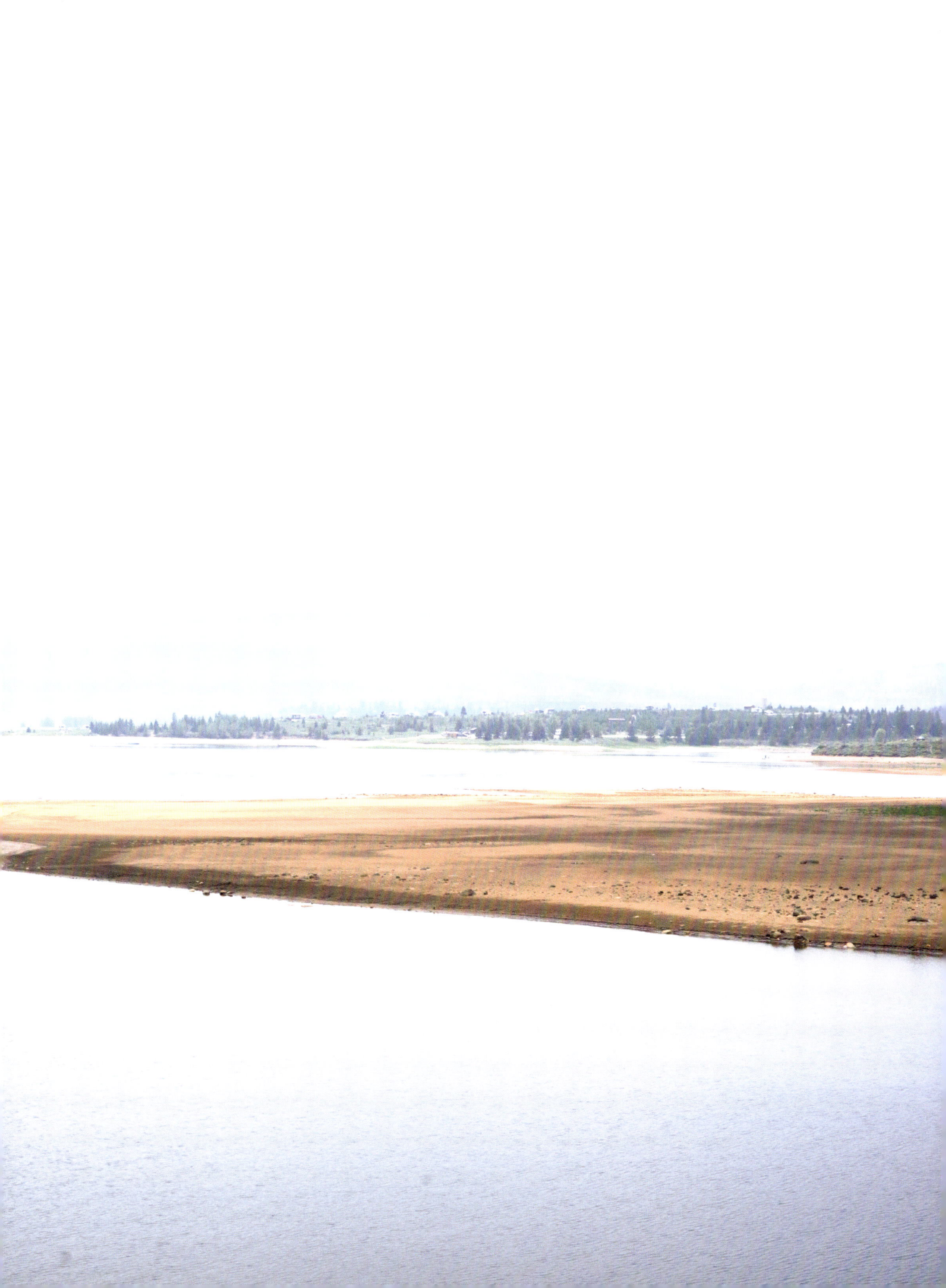

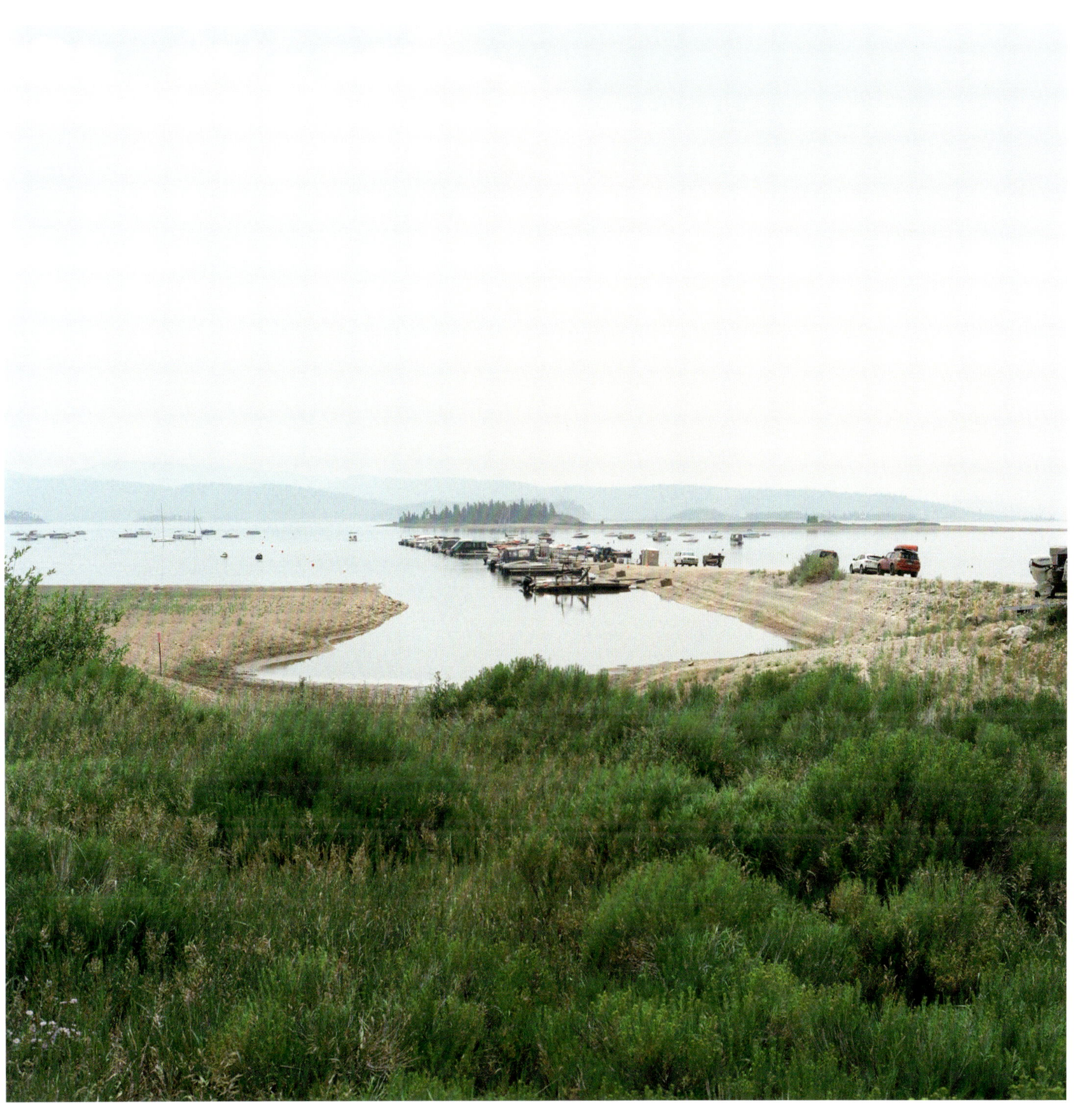

Marina at Lake
Granby.

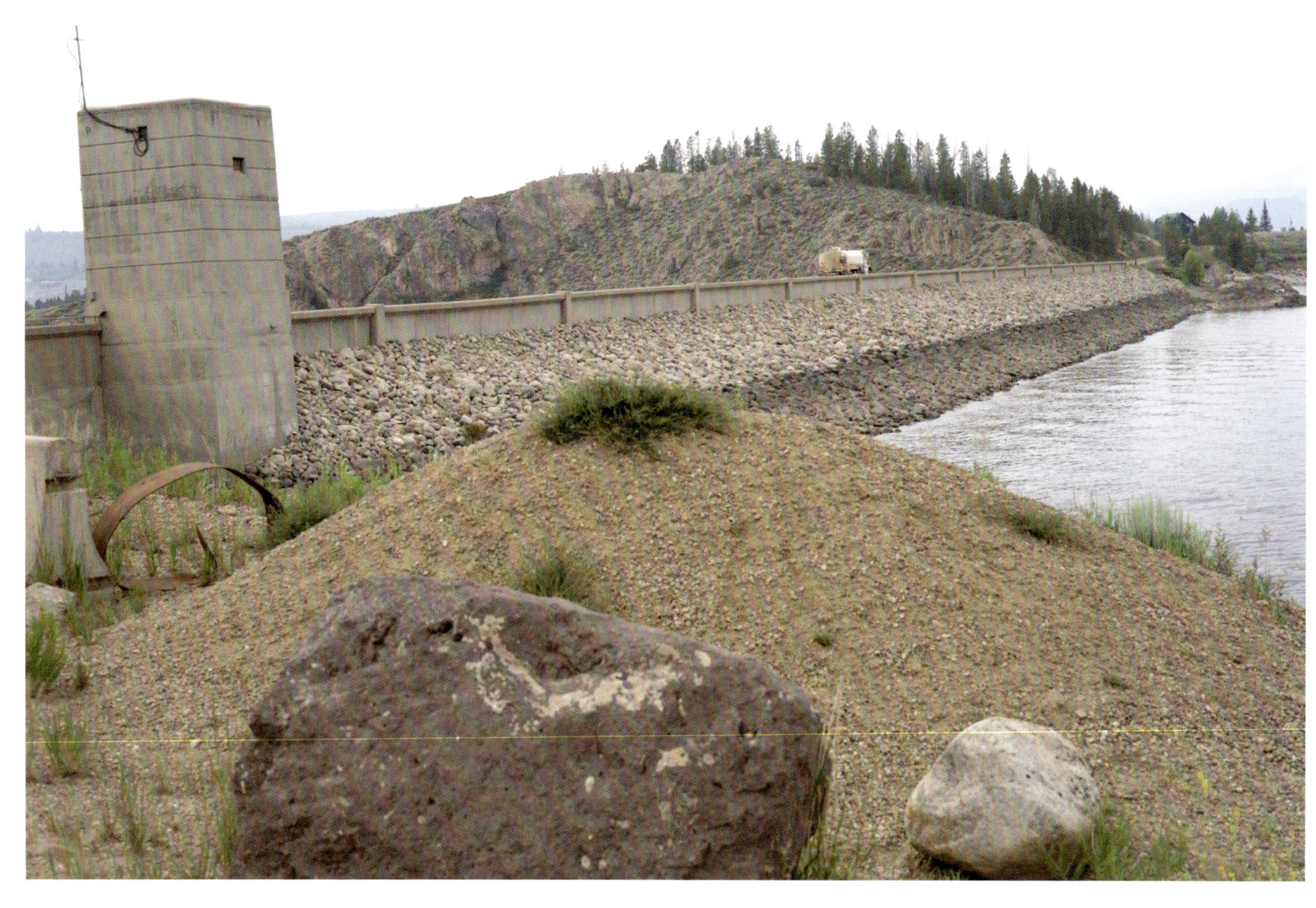

Granby Dam,
Colorado.

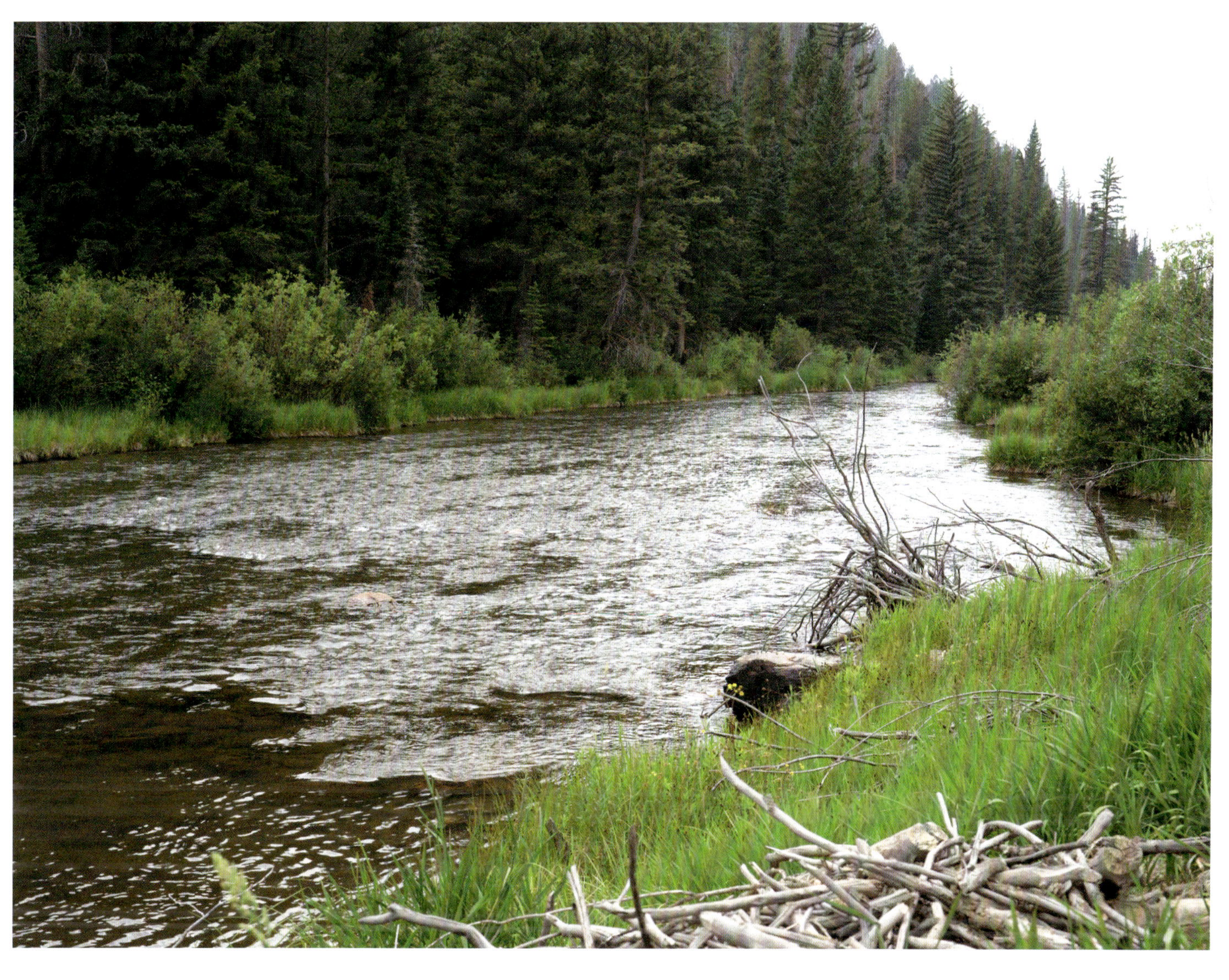

Release from
Granby Dam.

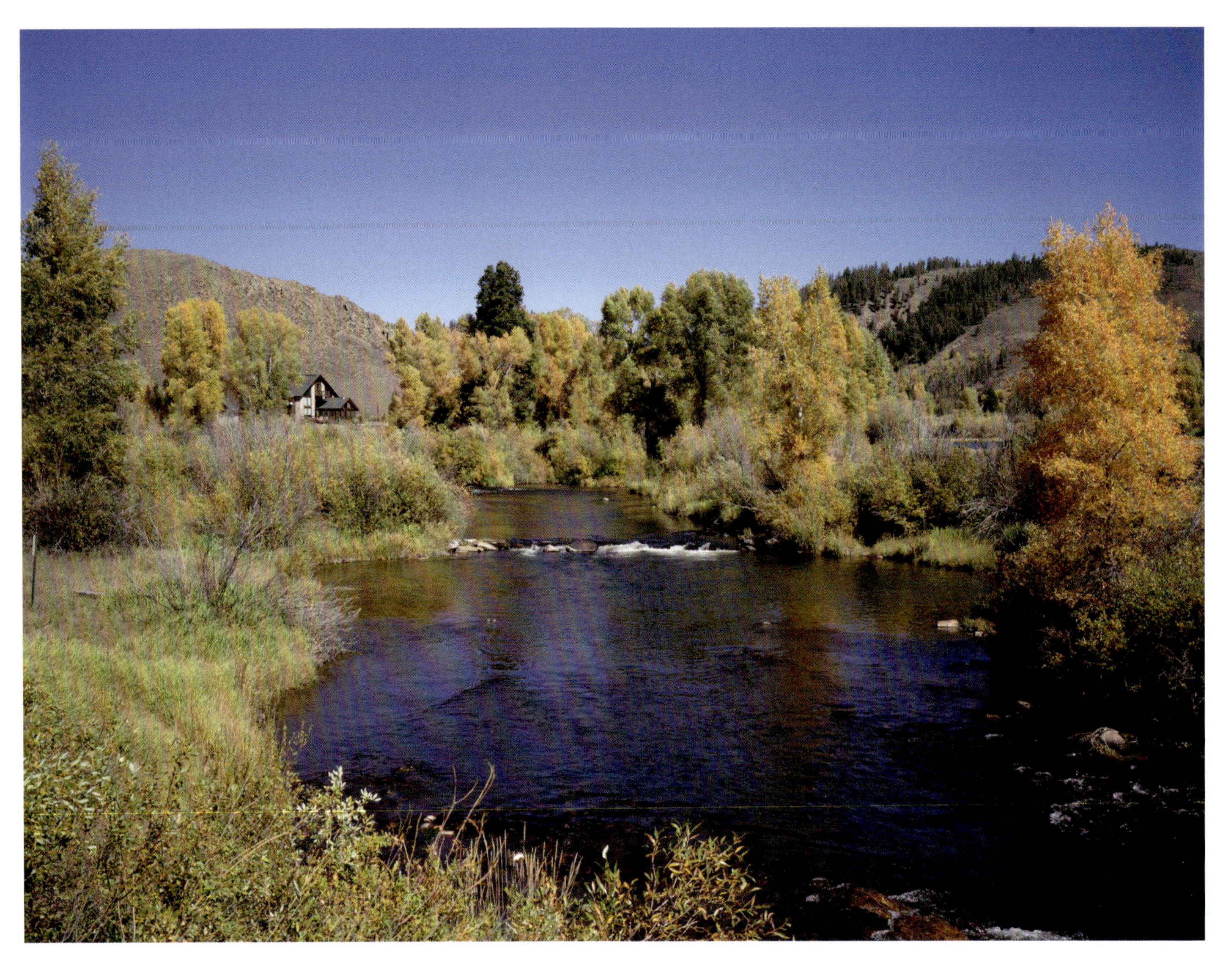

The river prior to
entry at Windy Gap
Reservoir.

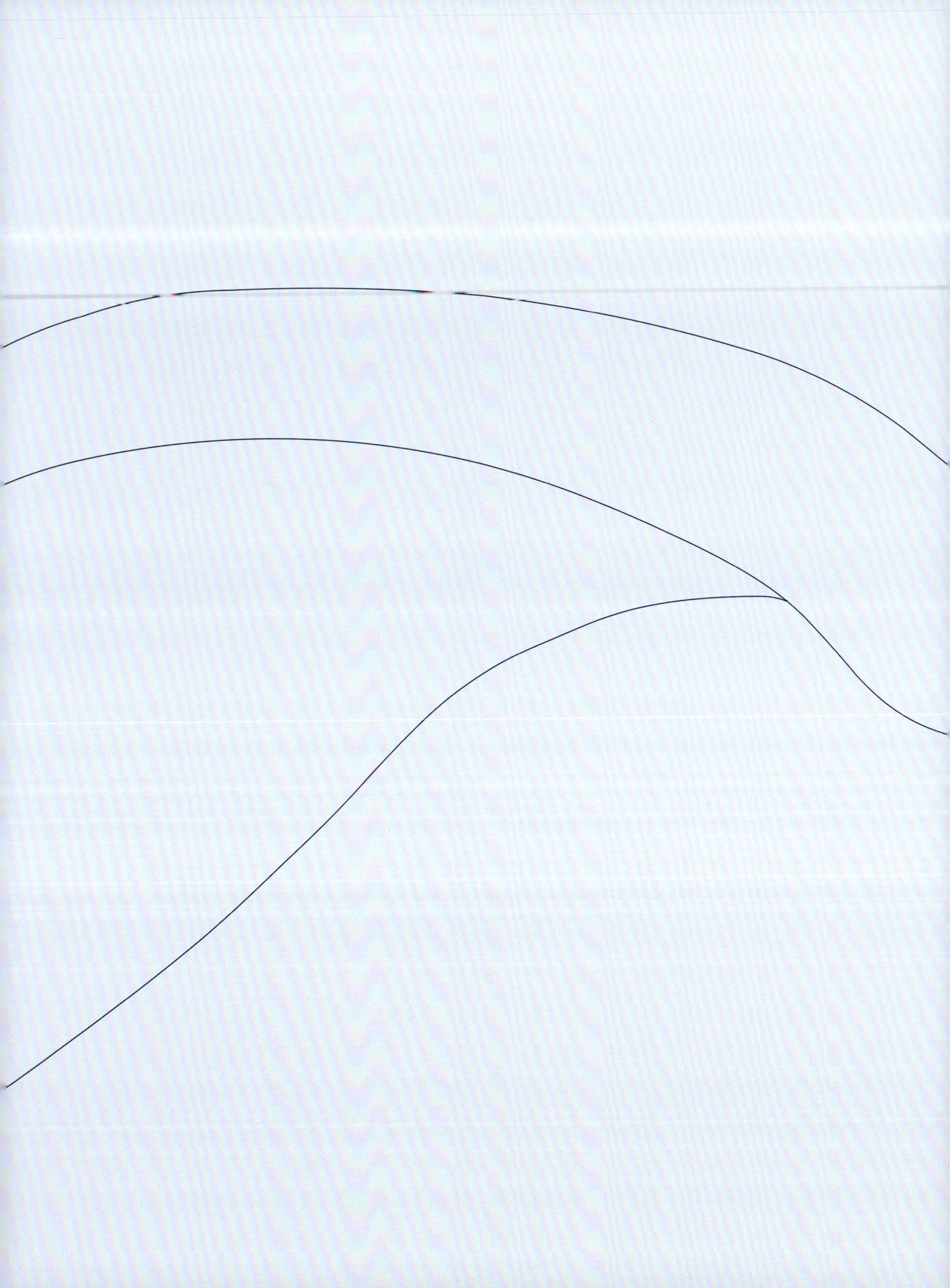

WINDY GAP

Windy Gap Project water is pumped from Lake Granby via the Farr Pump Plant to the Granby Pump Canal, into Shadow Mountain Reservoir and through a connecting channel to Grand Lake.

At Grand Lake, water then enters the Adams Tunnel and flows beneath Rocky Mountain National Park. The water is then distributed to Windy Gap Project participants via a series of C-BT reservoirs, canals, and pipelines.

During periods of high flows in the Colorado and Fraser rivers, water is pumped from Windy Gap Reservoir via the Windy Gap Pump Plant into Lake Granby, where it is stored for delivery. Operated from a control center at the Farr Pump Plant, the Windy Gap Pump Plant pumps water through a six-mile pipeline to Lake Granby.

The Windy Gap Project construction began in July 1981, and was completed in 1985. The original capacity of the Windy Gap Reservoir was 445 acre-feet. Windy Gap was never popular, as it cuts the Colorado River in half, preventing unrestricted flows and impacting trout populations. Additionally, it has severely impacted a thirty-mile stretch of the Colorado River stretching from Windy Gap to its confluence with the Blue River.

Windy Gap is managed by Northern Water.

Colorado River Connectivity Channel

As part of the Windy Gap Firming Project, the historical impacts of the original Windy Gap Project were evaluated, including the loss of river connectivity following construction of the Windy Gap Reservoir dam on the Colorado River. To minimize the dam's impact on aquatic habitat and species, municipalities agreed to decrease the reservoir's footprint and construct a connecting channel around the reservoir capable of passing water, fish, and sediment, effectively reconnecting two segments of the Colorado River.

The goal of the Colorado River Connectivity Channel is to establish a natural river channel around Windy Gap to reconnect the river and eliminate the reservoir's negative impacts. The project will also divert water to Chimney Hollow Reservoir, which is currently under construction.

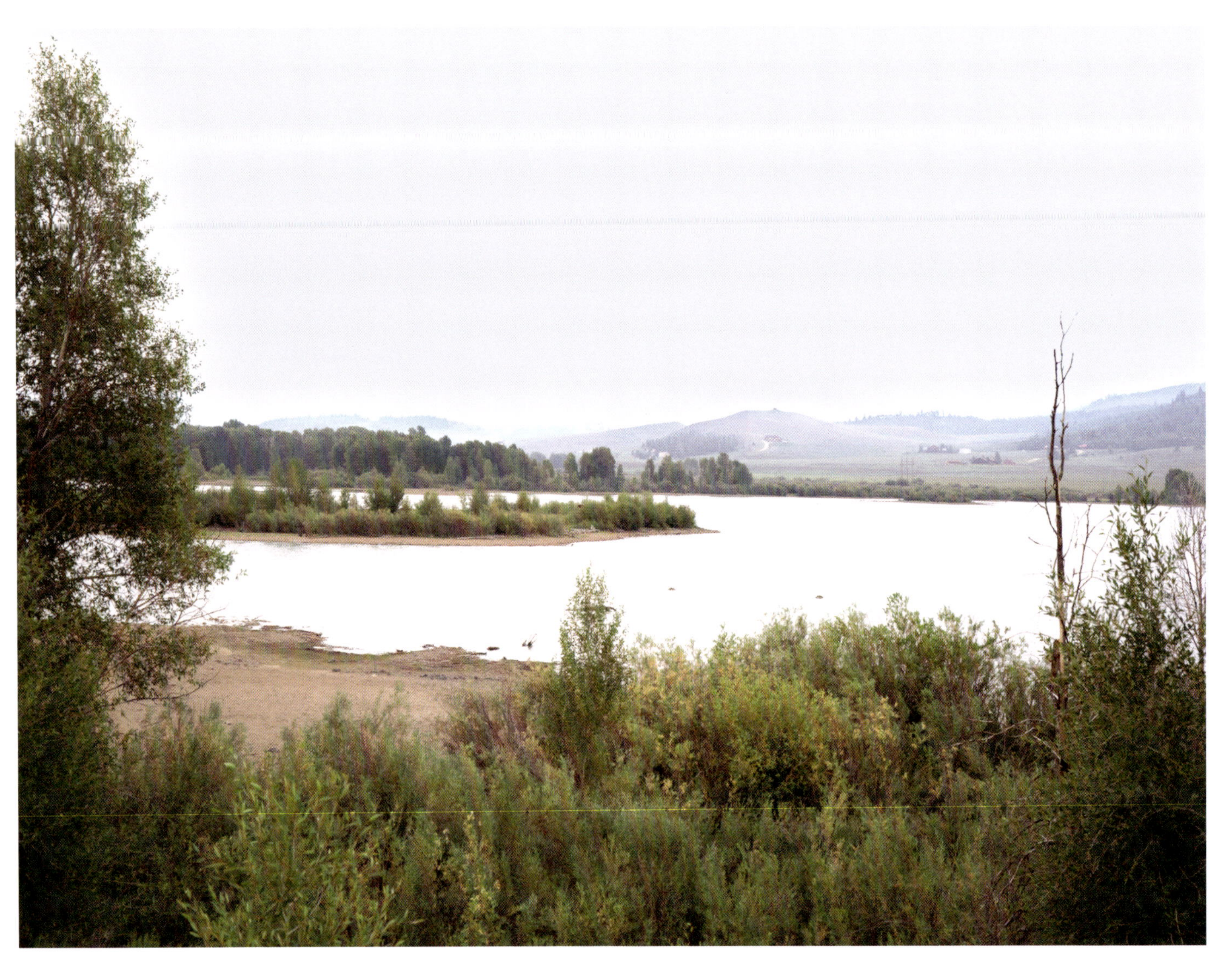

Windy Gap
Reservoir, 2021,
Colorado.

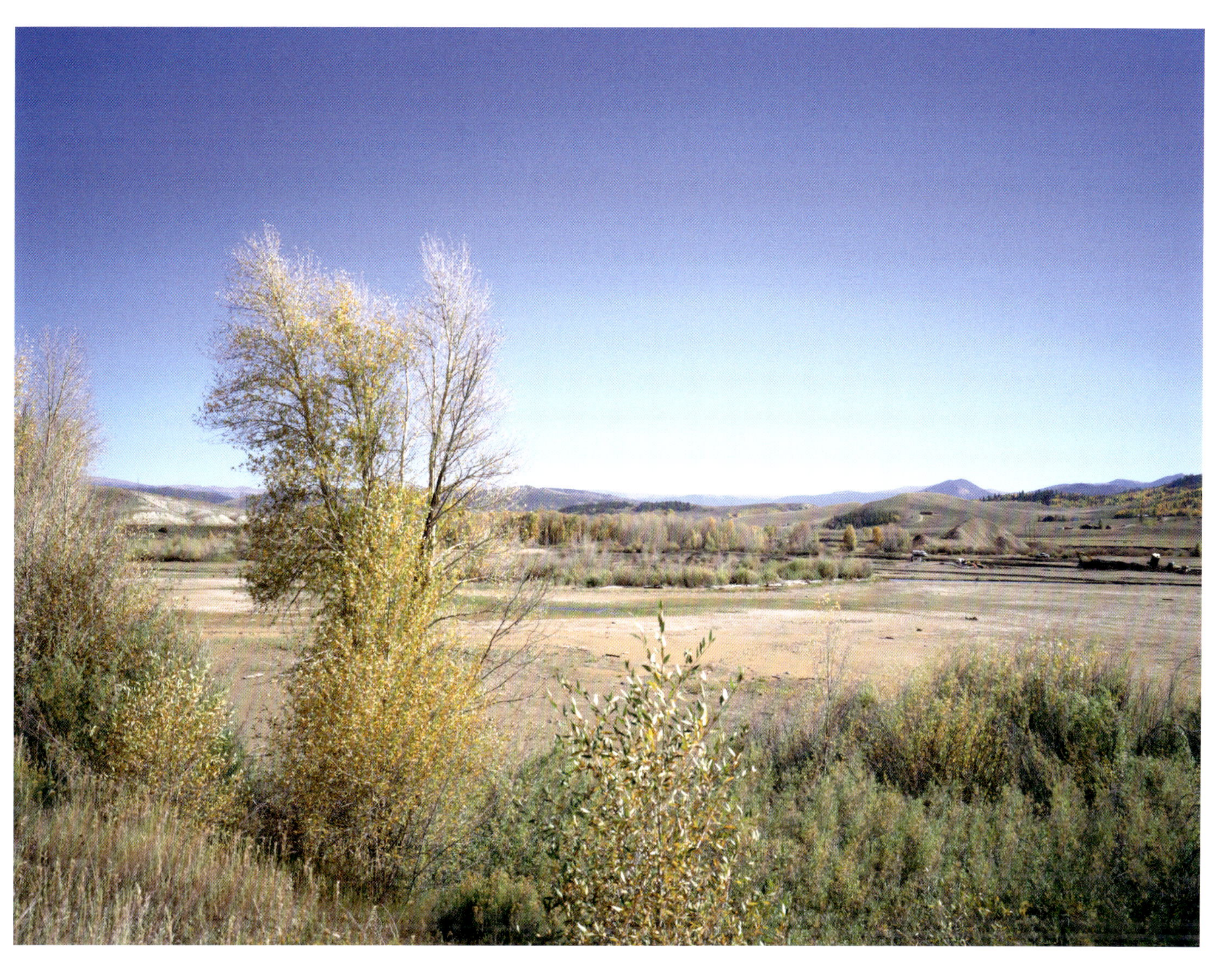

Windy Gap, 2022.

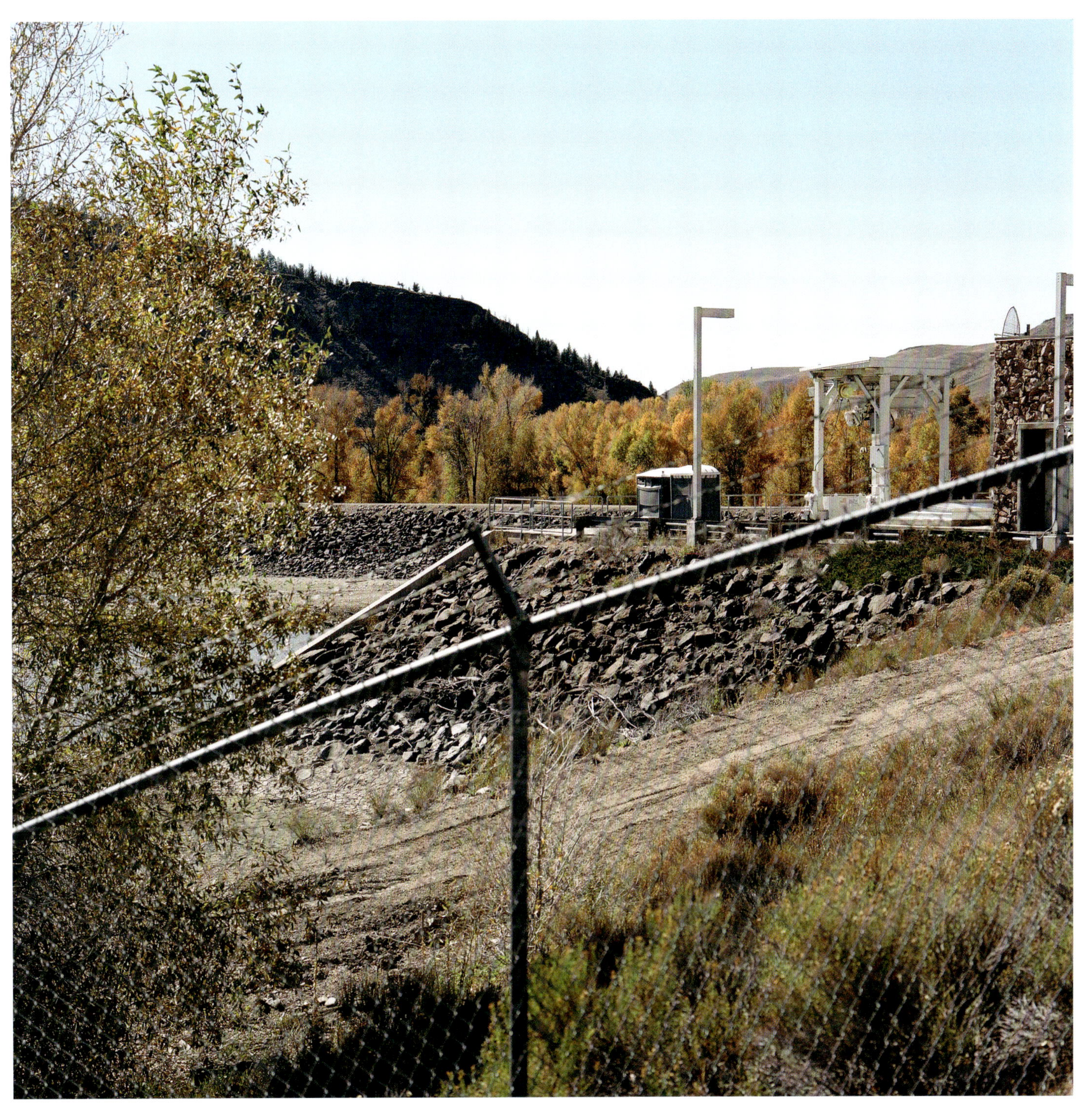

Windy Gap Dam,
2022.

CHIMNEY HOLLOW DAM

The Windy Gap Project was designed to deliver an average of 48,000 acre-feet of water per year to its participants. However, during wet cycles Lake Granby is often full, leaving little or no space for Windy Gap water. Participants in water-delivery agreements were unsatisfied with these varying water-delivery amounts.

This variance gave rise to the Windy Gap Firming Project (of which Chimney Hollow Reservoir is the major component) along with a collaboration of nine eastern-slope municipalities, two water districts, and a power provider. The project will provide a "firm" yield of 30,000 acre-feet annually, with a dedicated storage capacity of 90,000 acre-feet.

The reservoir connects to existing infrastructure by storing water diverted into Windy Gap Dam's system, which pumps water into Lake Granby and uses C-BT facilities for delivery to participants. The firming project would fill Chimney Hollow Reservoir using original Windy Gap water rights.

Construction on Chimney Hollow Dam began in August of 2021, with completion slated for 2025.

The Chimney Hollow Reservoir Project is operated by Northern Water.

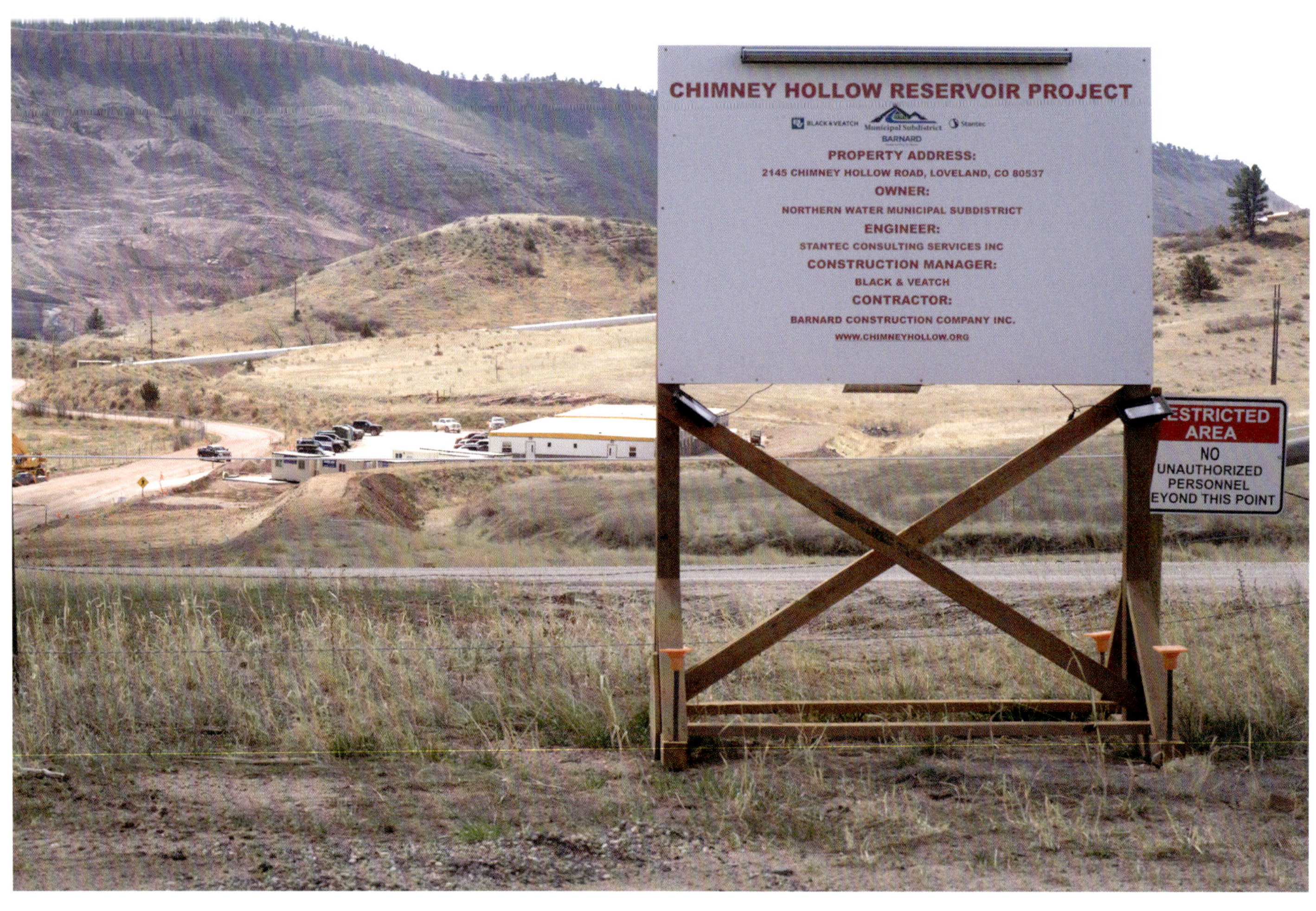

Chimney Hollow
Dam, Colorado,
under construction.

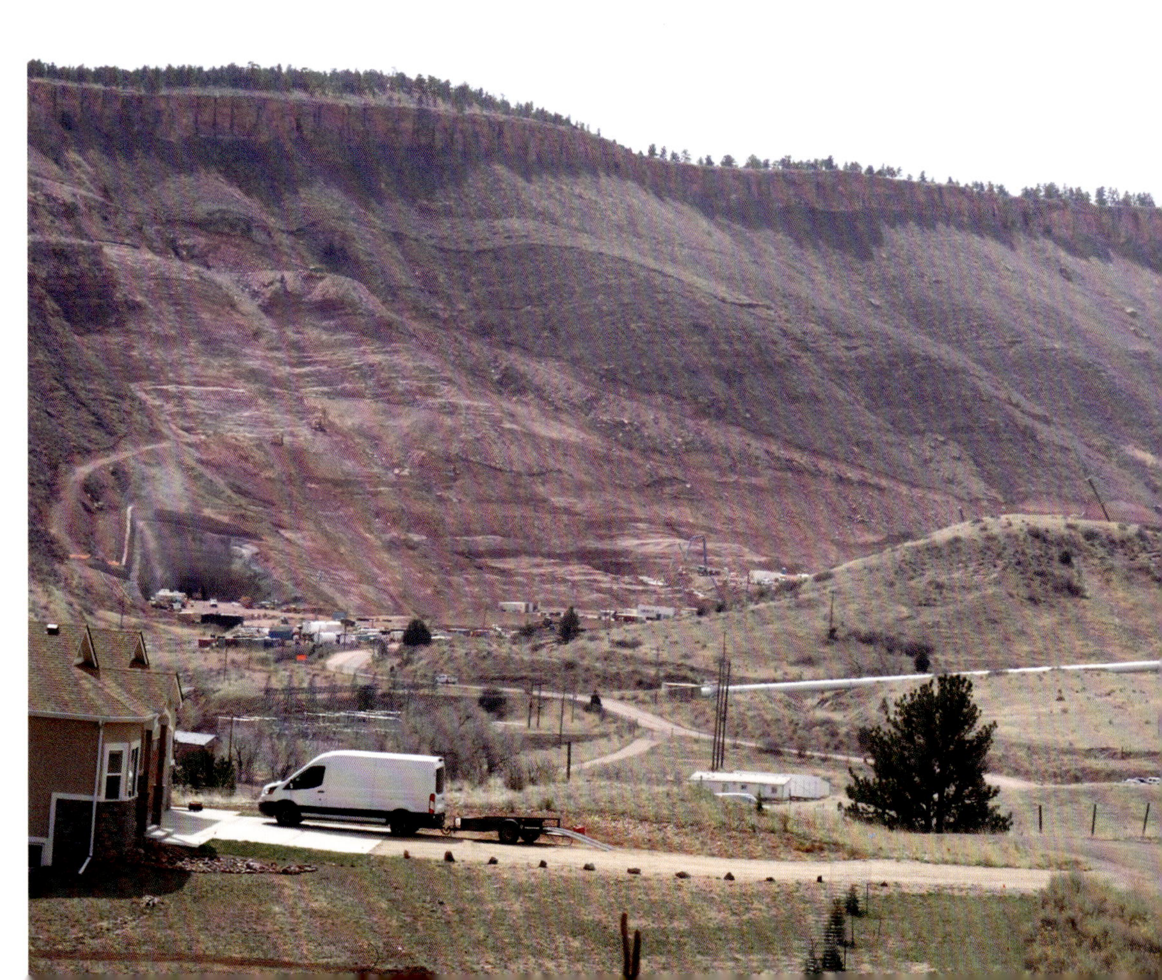

Site of Chimney
Hollow Dam.

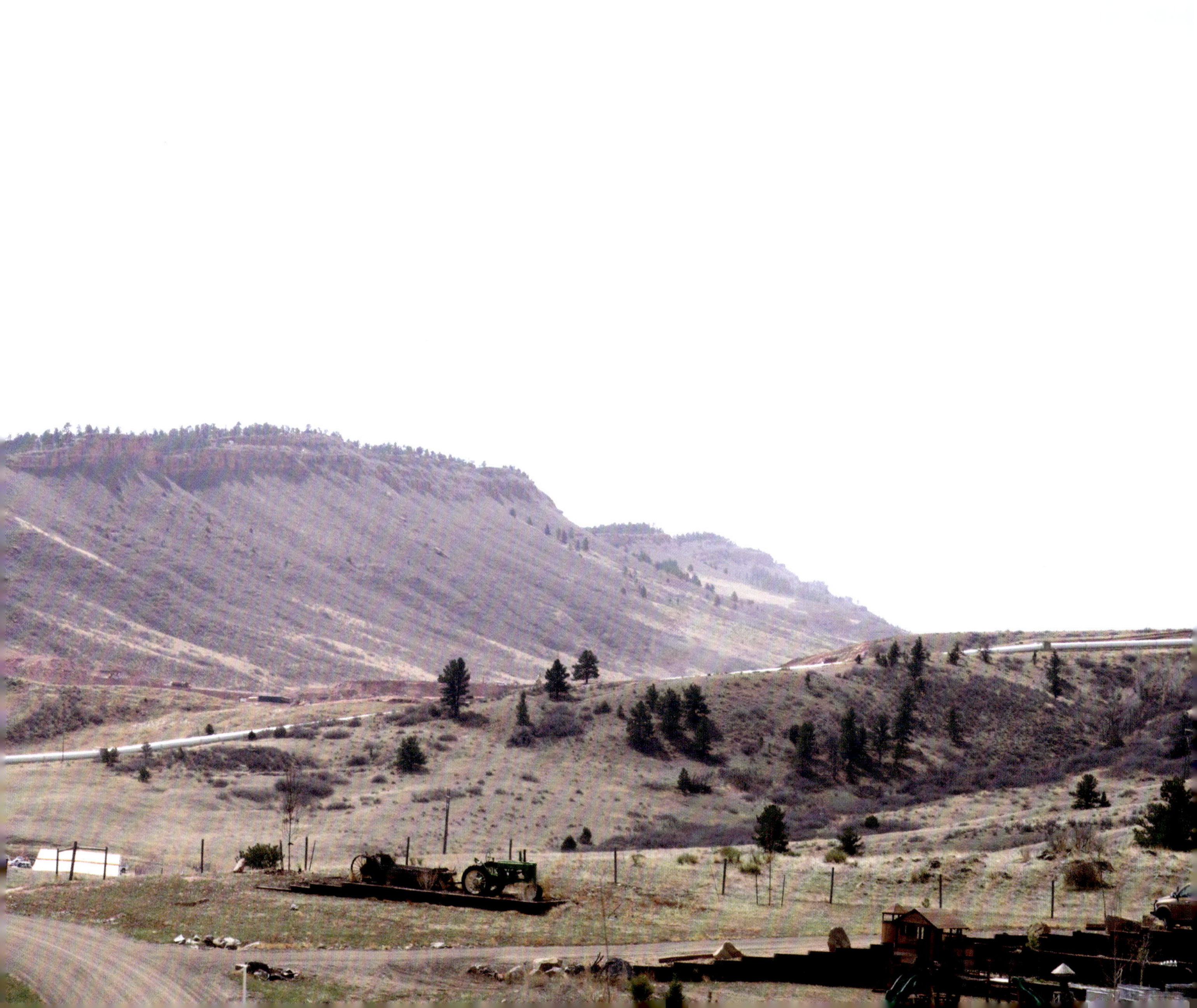

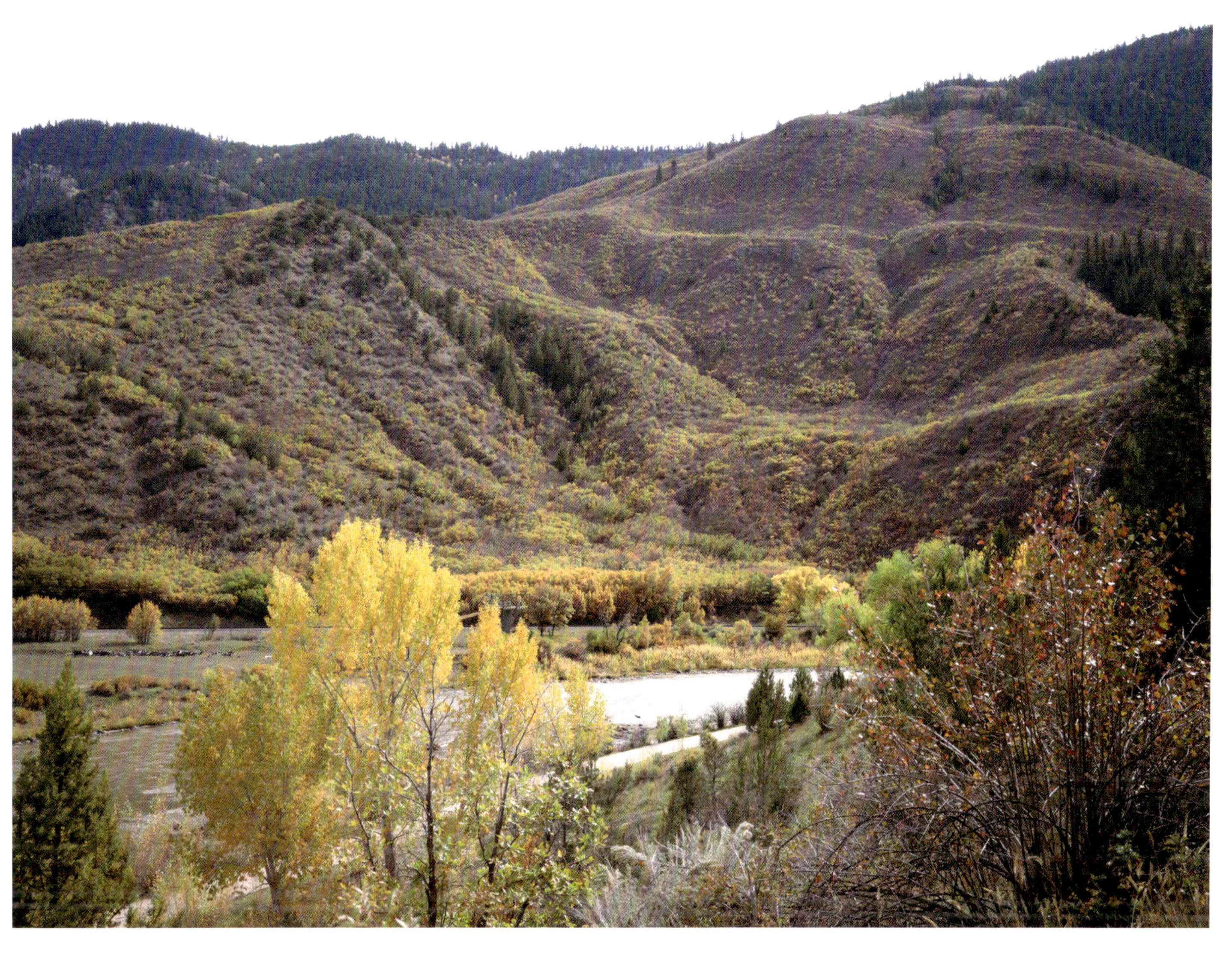

The river near De
Beque, Colorado.

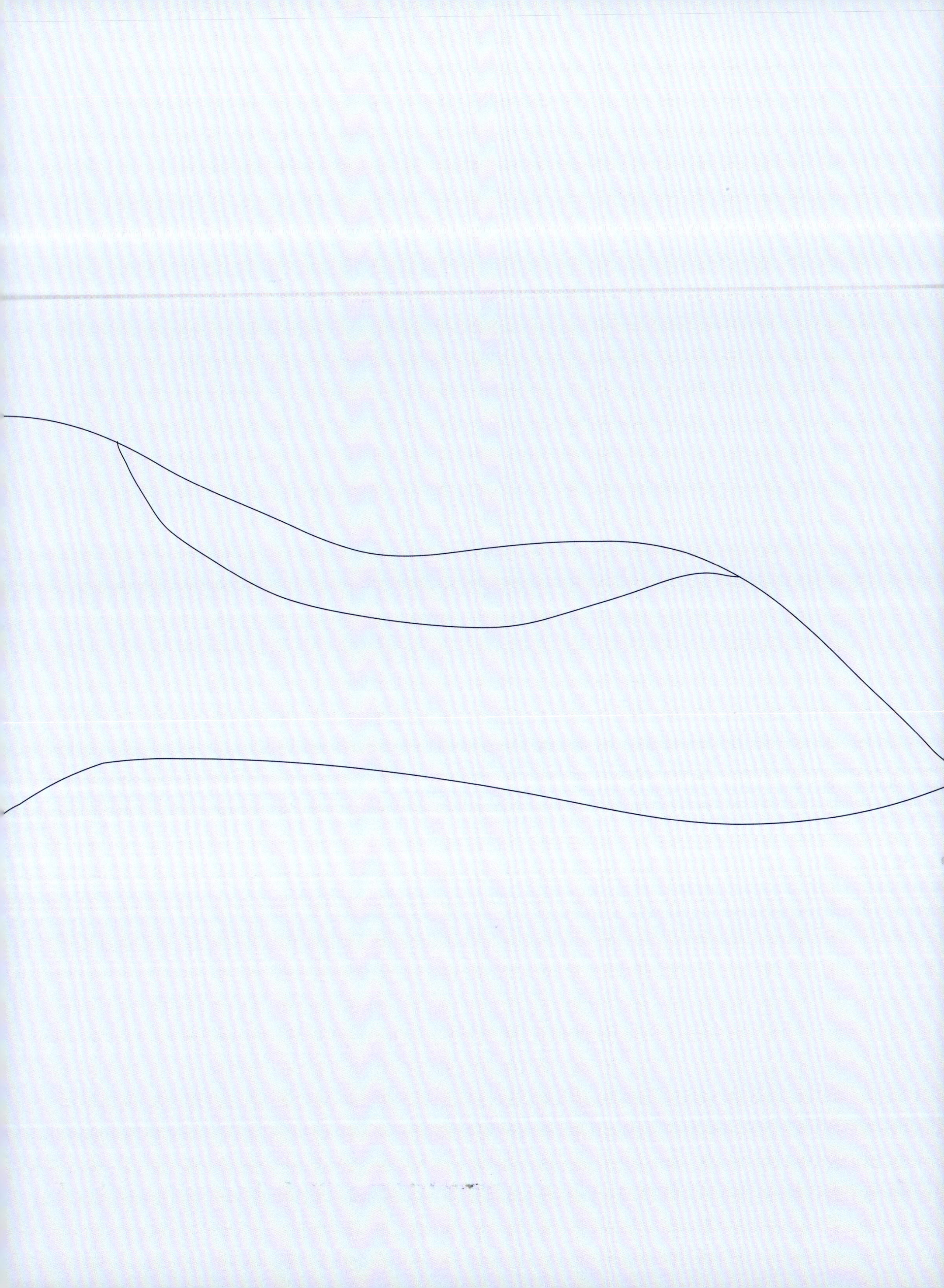

GRAND VALLEY DIVERSION DAM

Soon after their arrival in the Grand Valley of Colorado in 1881, settlers began work on ditches to irrigate lowlands adjacent to the north side of the Colorado River. By 1886, the Grand Valley Canal (not part of the Grand Valley Project and the Grand Valley Dam) was completed and the canal system expanded to serve approximately 45,000 acres of land.

The present Grand Valley Project and Grand Valley Dam is in west-central Colorado. In 1905, the Colorado General Assembly authorized the formation of local water associations. These associations then entered into repayment agreements with the Reclamation service for the construction of irrigation infrastructure. In that same year, the Grand Valley Water Users Association (GVWUA) was organized as a not-for-profit corporation and continues to operate under this structure.

The GVWUA and Reclamation worked together to develop the Grand Valley Project and Dam. The Grand Valley Diversion Dam spans the Colorado River in De Beque Canyon, Colorado. Diverted waters are transported via the 55-mile-long Government Highline Canal. The flow travels through three tunnels before entering the Grand Valley northeast of the town of Palisade, Colorado. The Government Highline Canal supplies irrigation water to approximately 25,000 acres in the GVWUA service area, and an additional 15,000 acres in other irrigation districts.

The Grand Valley Diversion Dam can remove up to 1,675 cfs (cubic feet per second) from the Colorado River, and the project includes a small hydroelectric plant with a capacity of 3,000 kilowatts. It is operated by the Grand Valley Water Users Association.

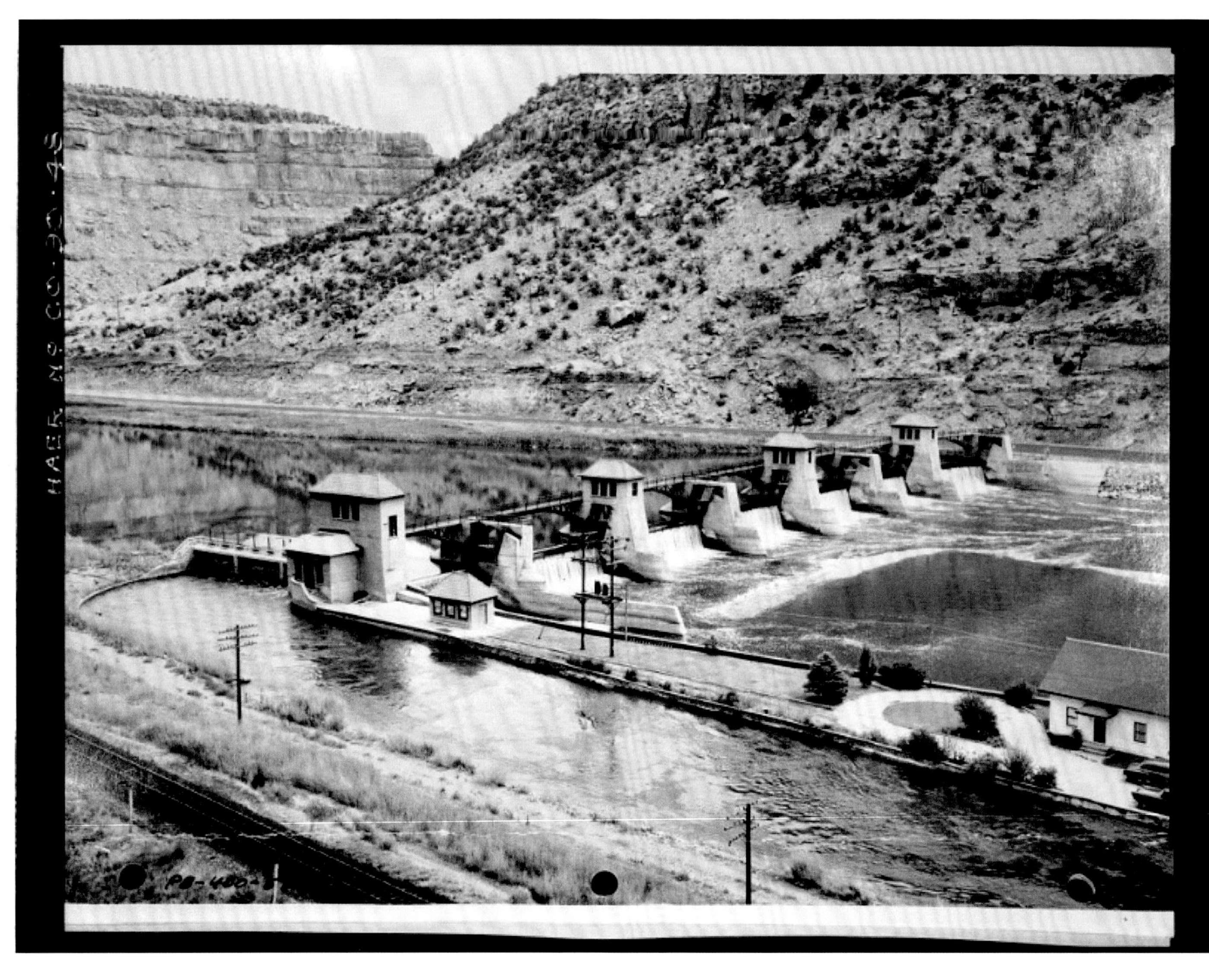

Historical view of the Grand
Valley Dam, 1958, *Historic
American Engineering Record*,
Creator, et al., photograph by
Archimede, Gianfranco.

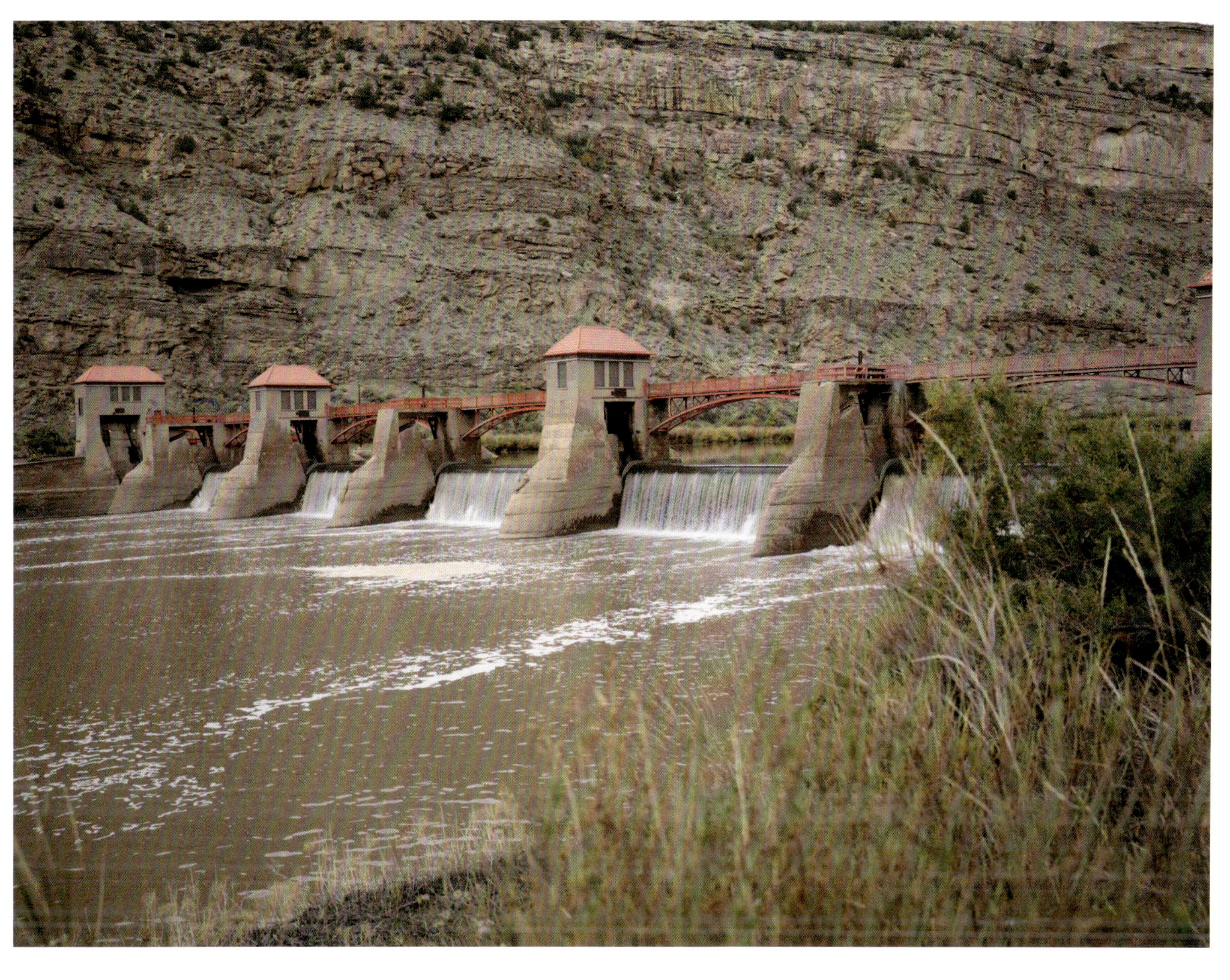

Grand Valley Diversion Dam.

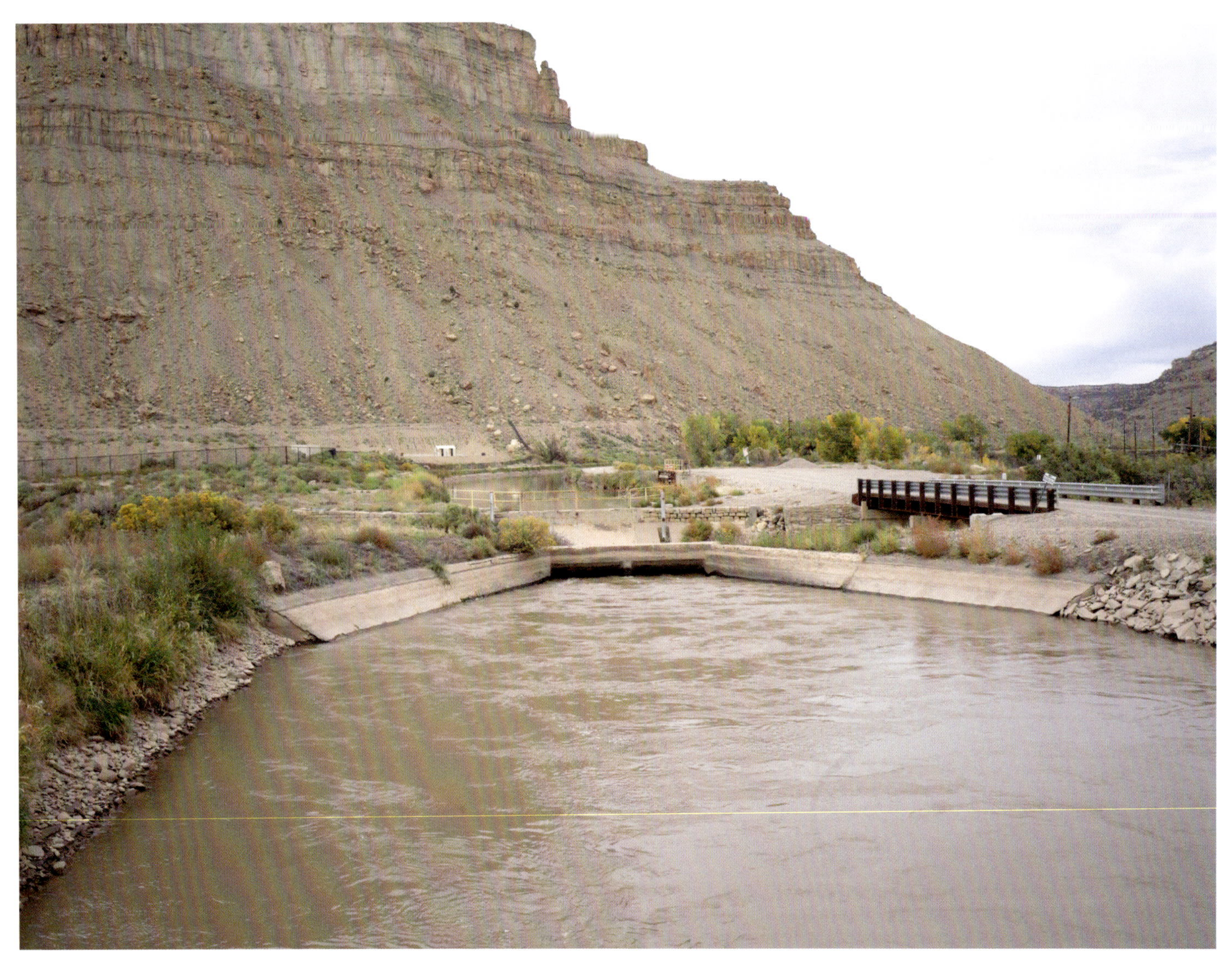

Government
Highline Canal,
Colorado.

I was brick-red, mud-laden:

Big Red, the River Colorado:

Trickle or flood at Nature's whim

Since time began.

To the sea my waters wasted

While the lands cried out for moisture.

Now man controls me

Stores me, regulates my flow.

The wild red outlaw river

Tamed.

Now flowing clean and blue

Unmaimed.

—from "Lake Powell: Jewel
of the Colorado," US Department of the
Interior and Bureau of Reclamation
publication. US Printing office, 1965.

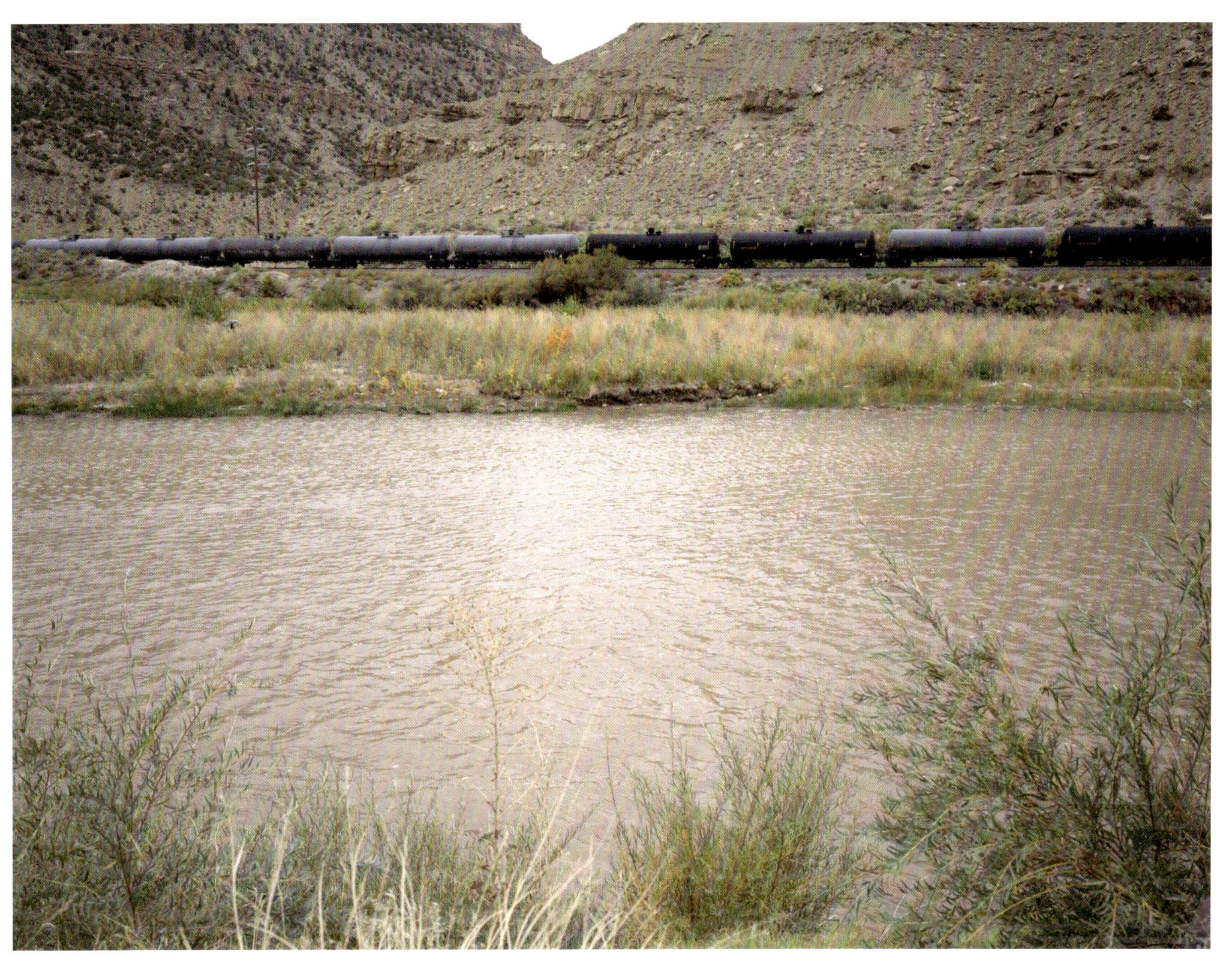

Downstream
of Grand Valley
Diversion Dam.

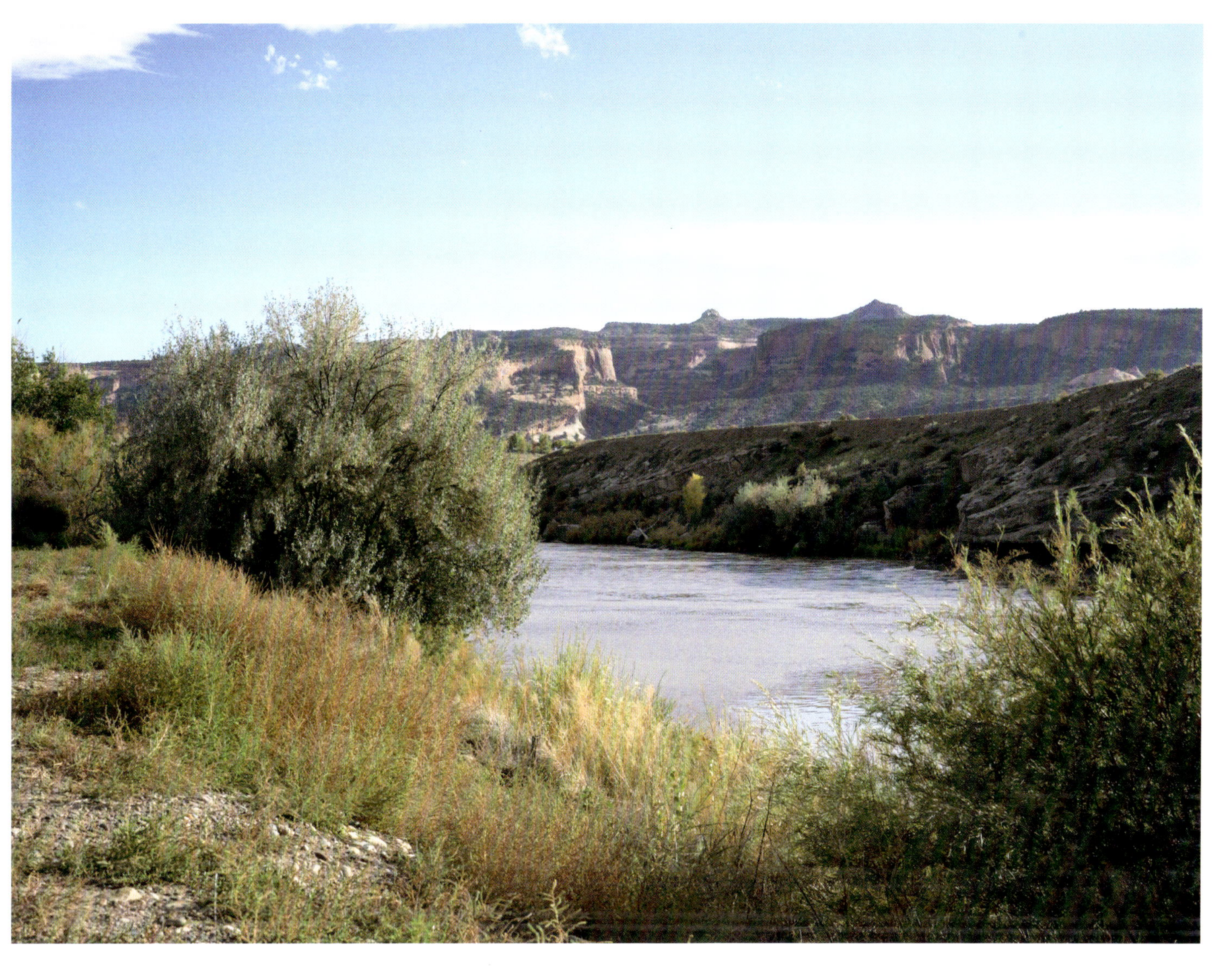

River near Grand
Junction, Colorado.

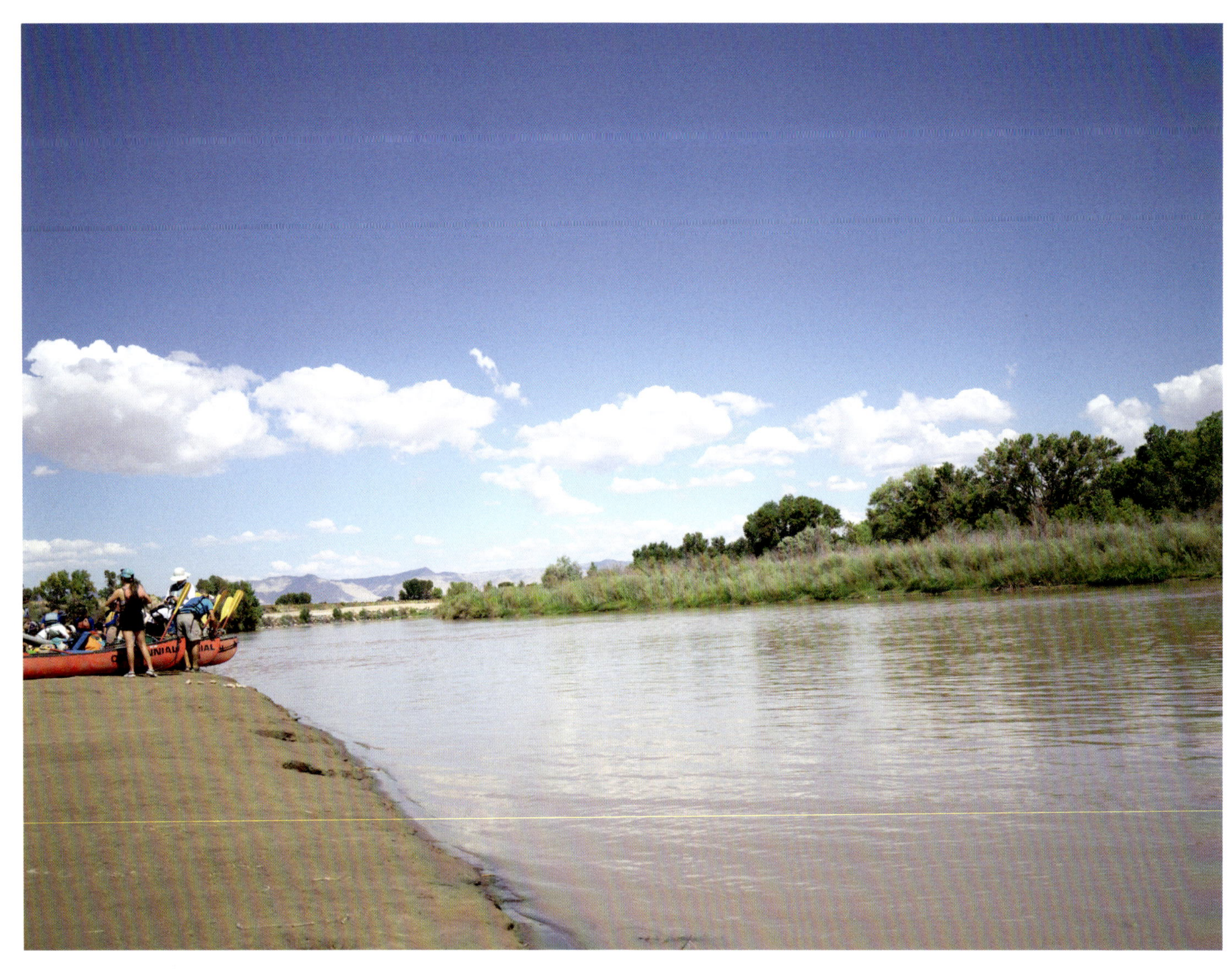

Launching into the
Colorado at Fruita,
Colorado.

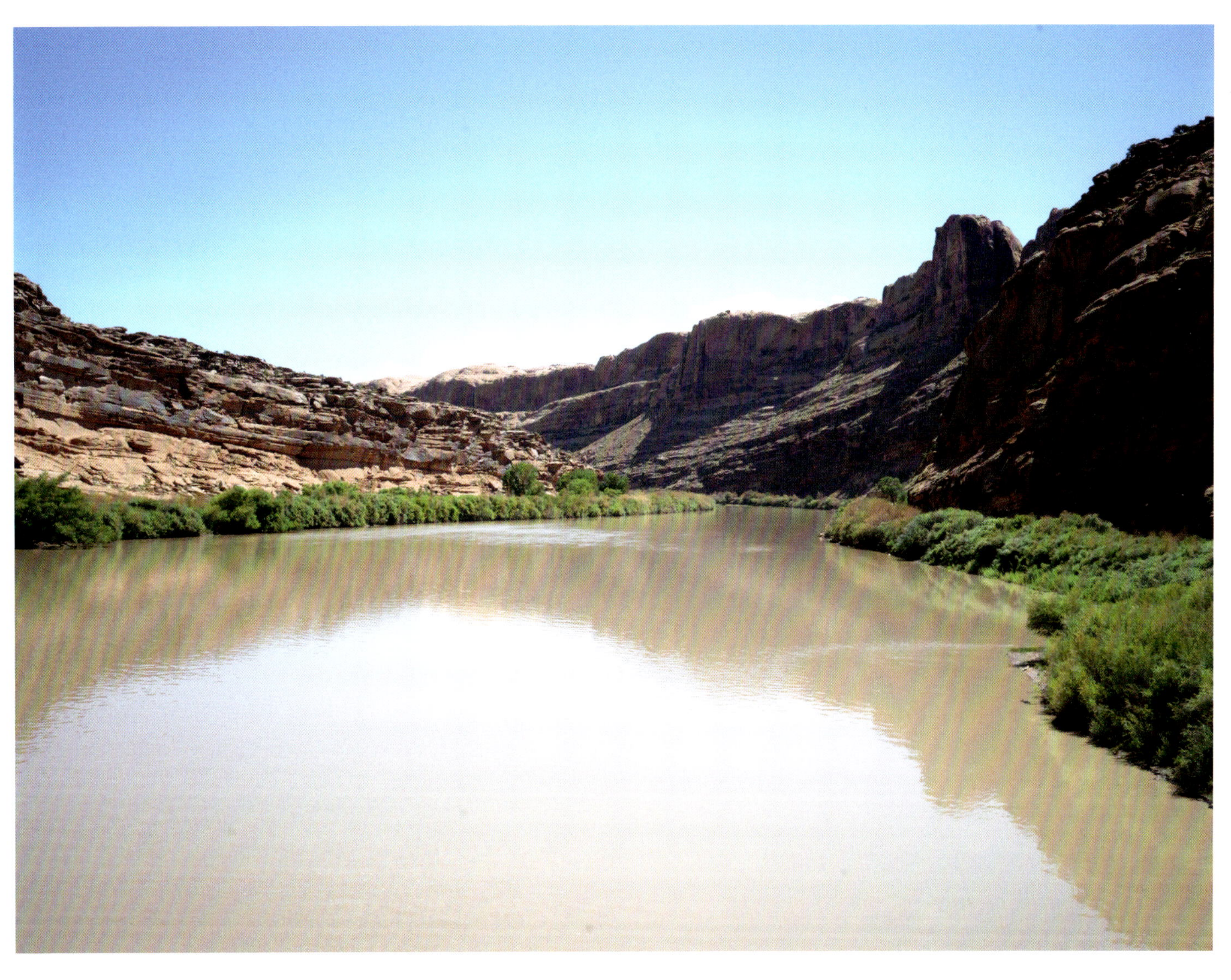

The river near
Moab, Utah.

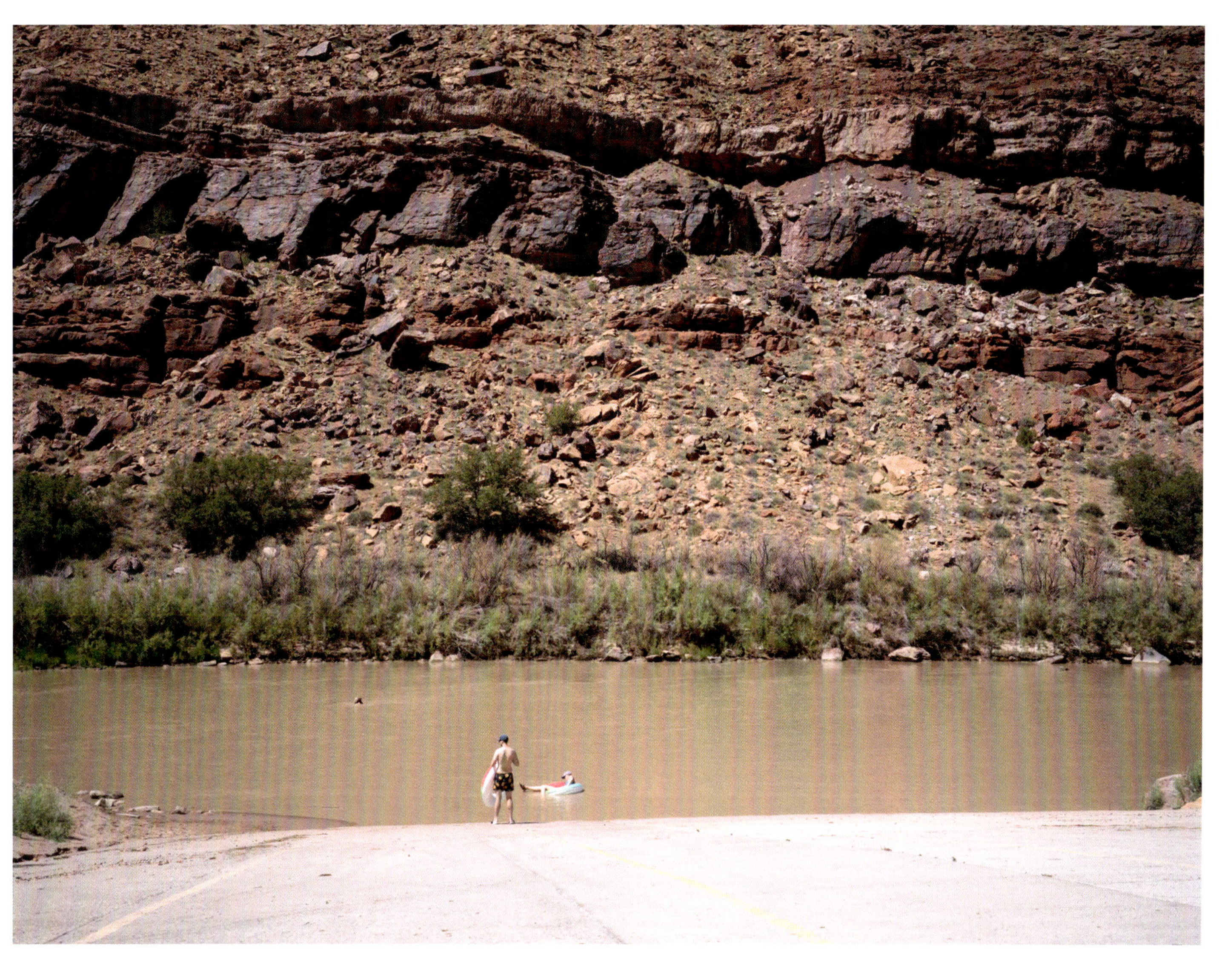

Tubing near Moab,
Utah.

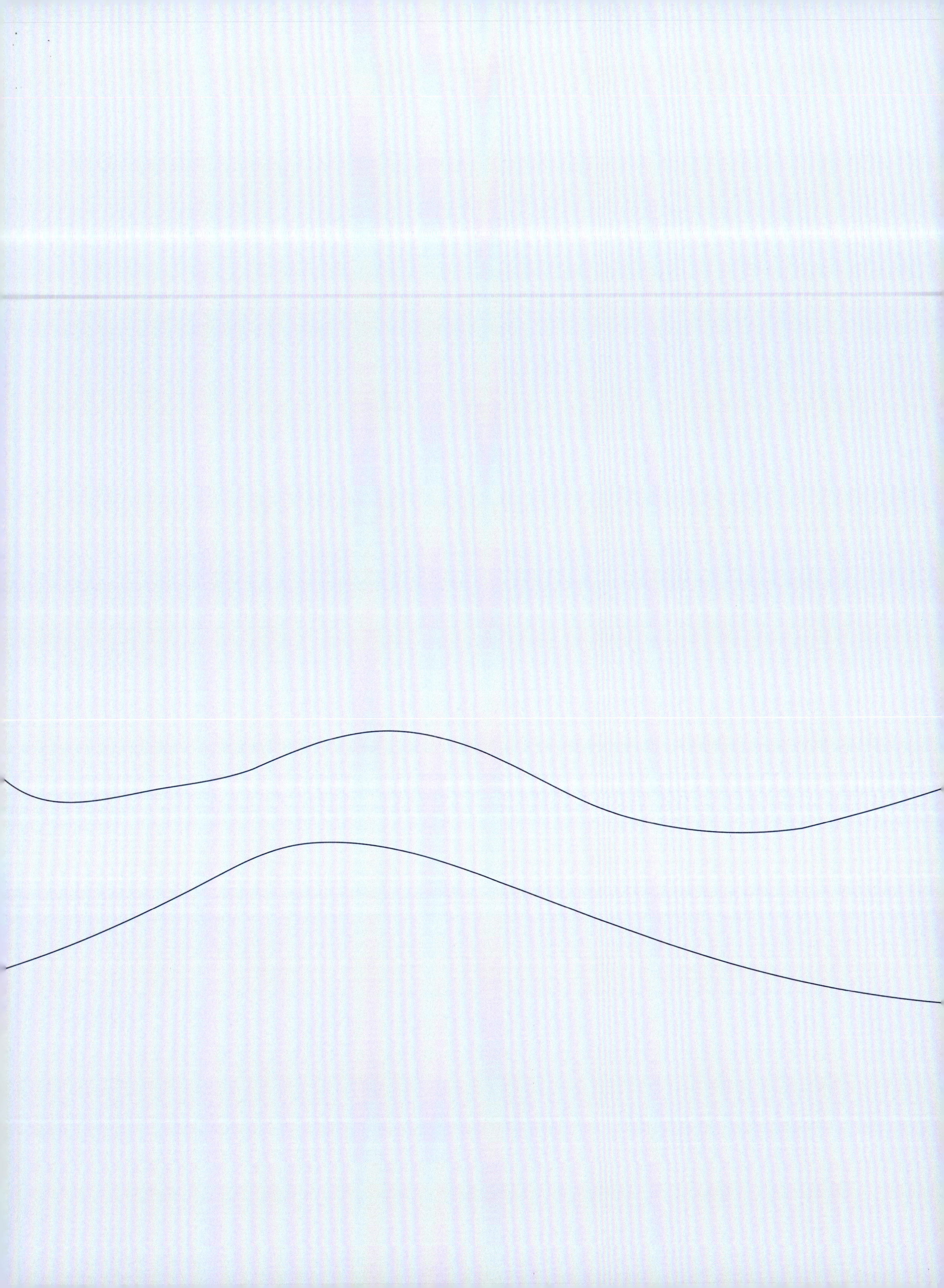

GLEN CANYON DAM

Glen Canyon Dam is the second highest concrete-arch dam in the United States, at 710 feet, second only to Hoover Dam, which stands at 726 feet. The 26.2 maf of water-storage capacity in Lake Powell, created by Glen Canyon Dam, was touted as a "bank account" of water to be drawn on in times of drought. Hydroelectric power is produced by the dam's eight generators.

With a total capacity of 1,320 megawatts, Glen Canyon Powerplant can produce around 5 billion kilowatt-hours of hydroelectric power annually, which is distributed by the Western Area Power Administration to Wyoming, Utah, Colorado, New Mexico, Arizona, Nevada, and Nebraska.

The original goal of Glen Canyon Dam was water security, ensuring delivery to the Lower Basin, and protecting the water dowry of the Upper Basin states. Under the Colorado River Compact of 1922, the Upper Basin is required to deliver 8.23 maf of Colorado River water to the Lower Basin and Mexico every year.

However, it has been determined that annual delivery requirements were based on flawed projections of annual river flows of 16.5 maf. More than one hundred years since the Compact was signed, the average annual flow has proven to be closer to 13.5 maf.

Currently, Lake Powell's water level is approximately 23% of capacity.

Due to its high-desert location and huge surface area, Lake Powell loses an average of 860,000 acre-feet of water annually to evaporation and bank seepage. In fact, the reservoir loses more than 6% of the Colorado River's annual flow, which is more than three times Nevada's annual allotment.

Since the dam was completed, more than 34 maf of stored water has been lost to evaporation and bank seepage.

Glen Canyon Dam and Lake Powell are managed by the Department of the Interior and the National Park Service.

Lee Ferry

Lee Ferry lies on the Arizona-Utah border and is the dividing point between the Colorado River's Upper and Lower basins. This dividing line is important when it comes to determining how much water will be delivered from the Upper Basin to the Lower Basin.

Under the 1922 Colorado River Compact, the Upper Basin is committed to deliver 7.5 maf to the Lower Basin, on average, every ten years. The deliveries occur at Lee Ferry, which is located one mile below the mouth of the Paria River.

After the Lower Basin states (Arizona, California, and Nevada) and Mexico have received their respective allotments, the Upper Basin states (Colorado, New Mexico, Utah, and Wyoming) retain the remaining water supply. The Upper Basin may not "unreasonably" withhold water from the Lower Basin States, regardless of the actual available water supply.

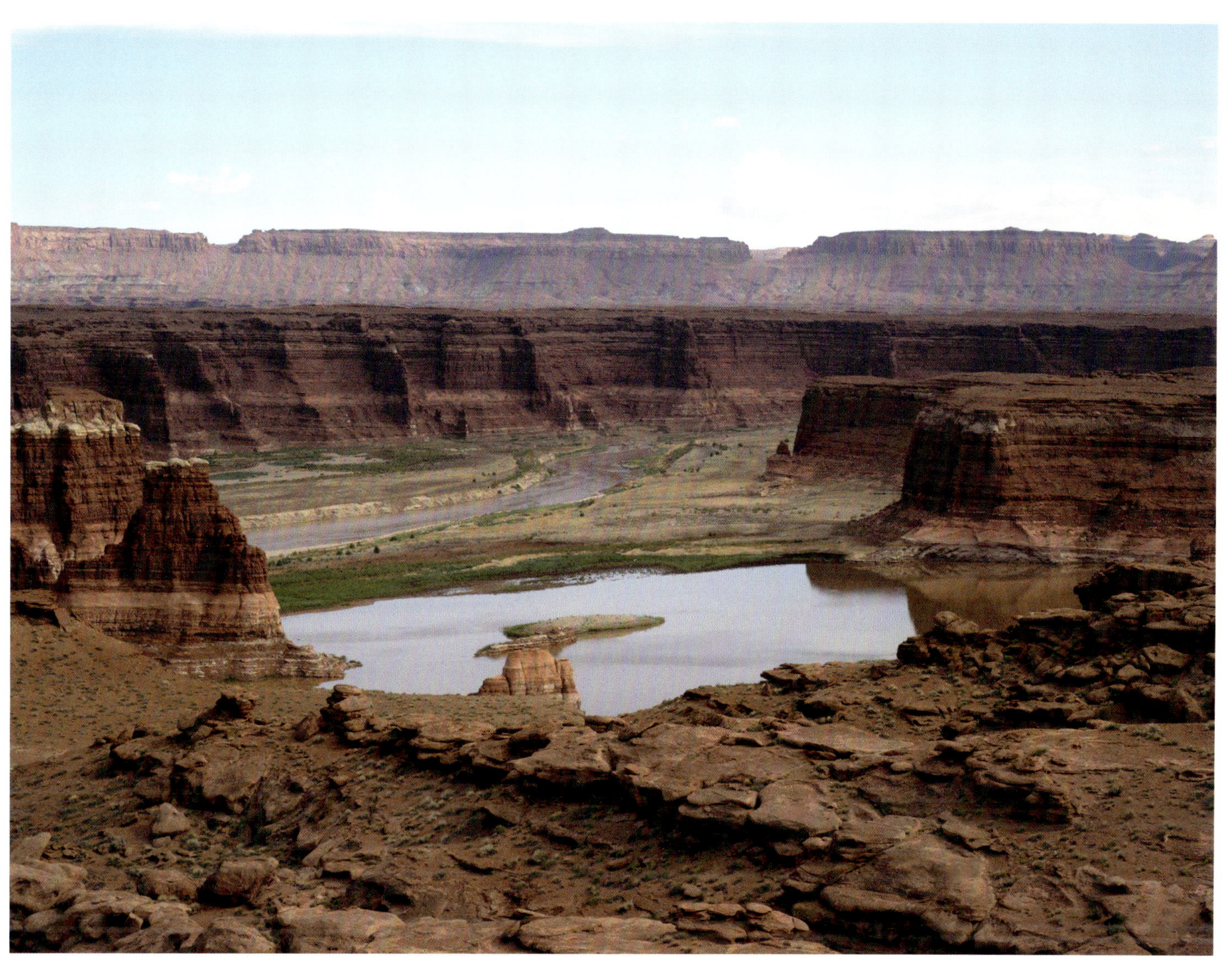

Confluence of
Colorado River and
Dirty Devil River,
Utah.

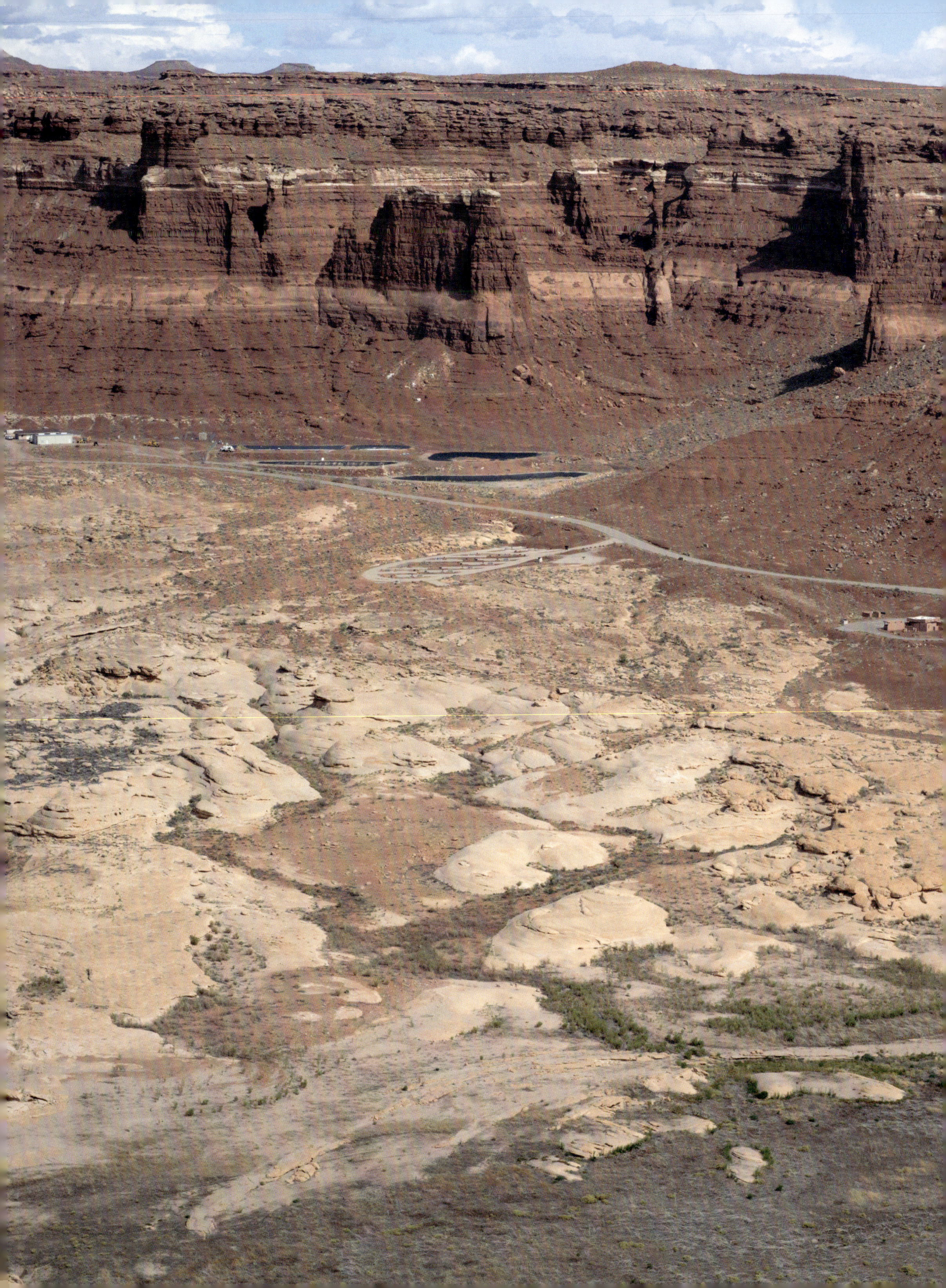

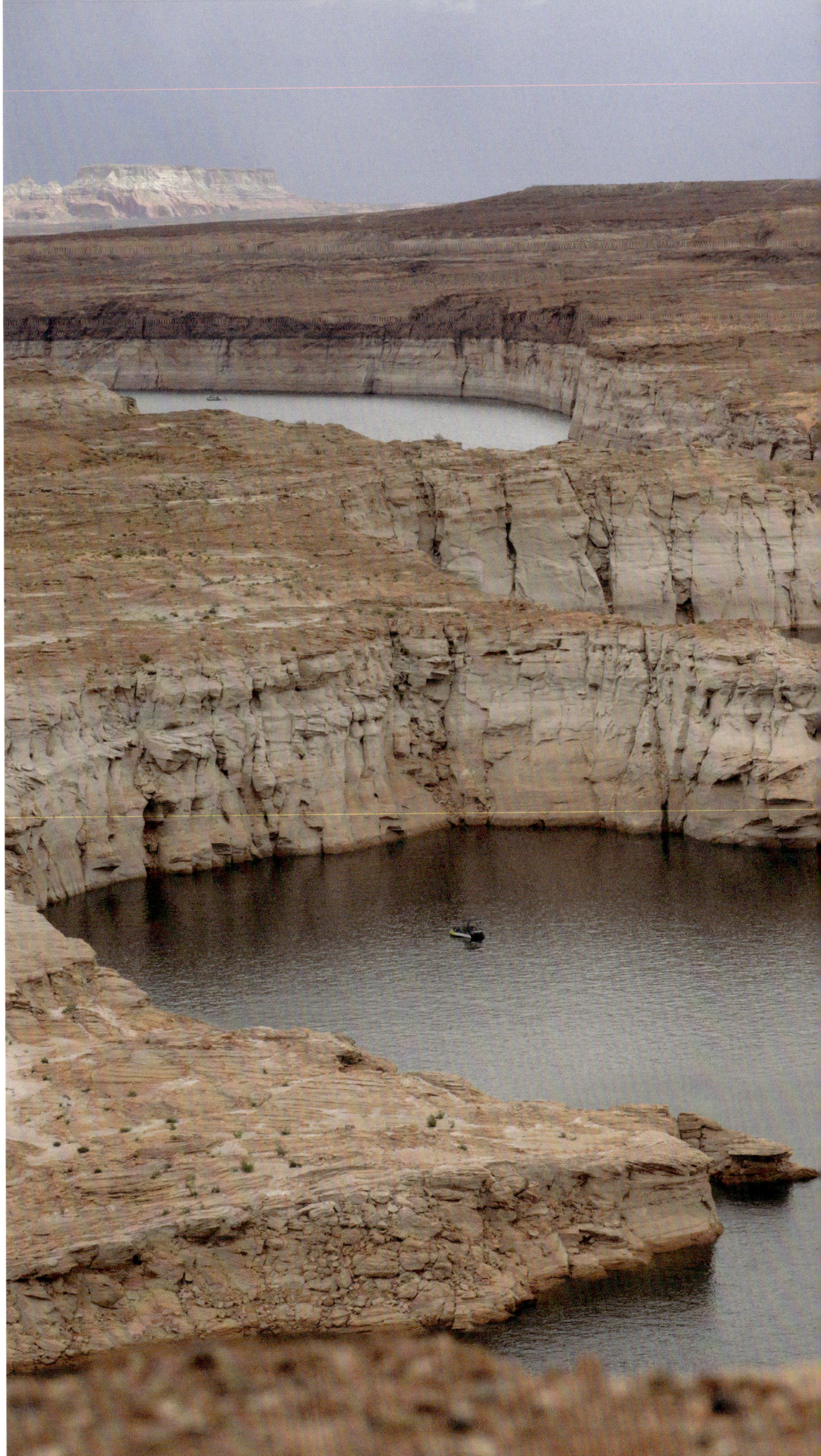

Lake Powell,
Arizona.

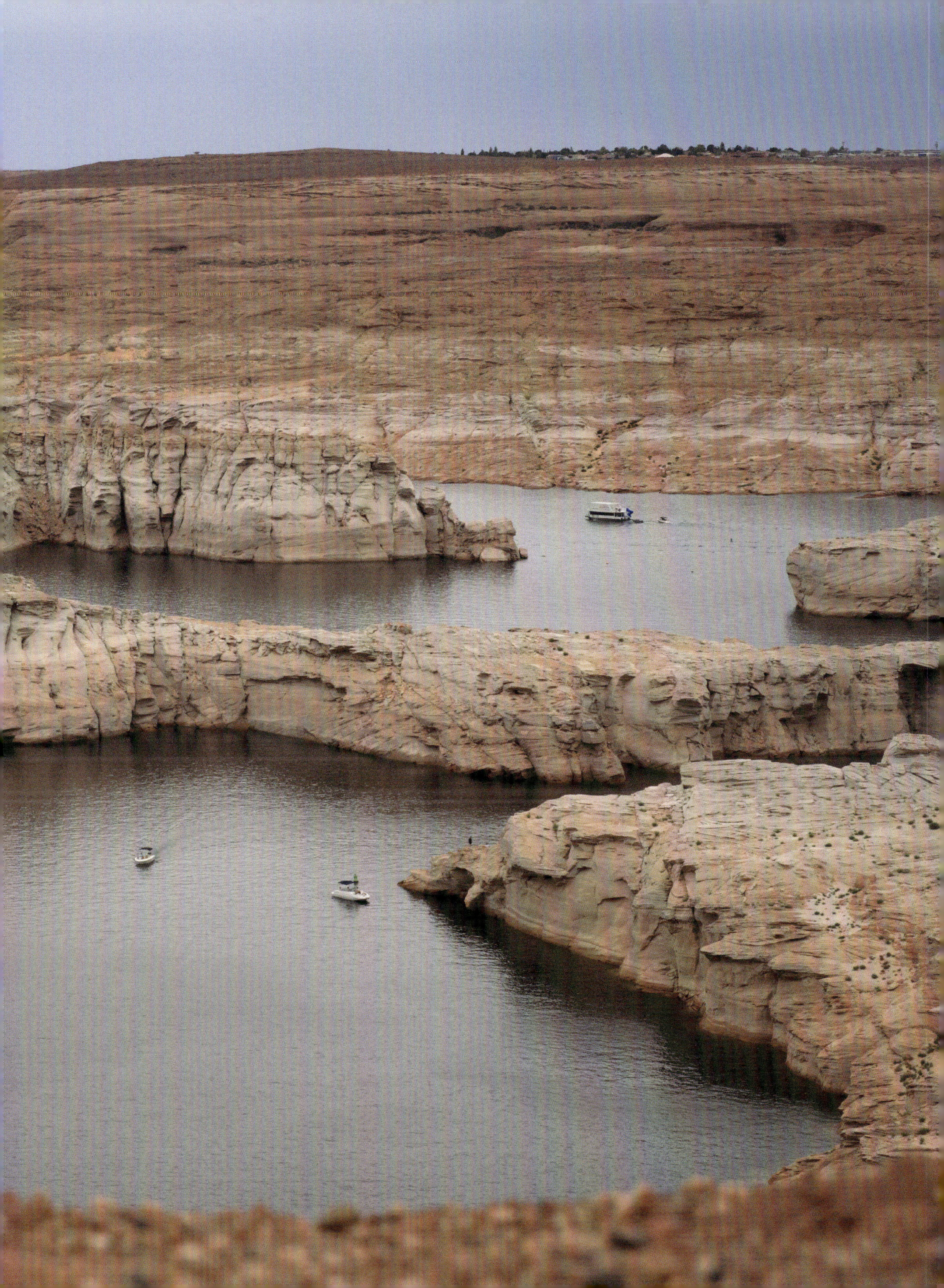

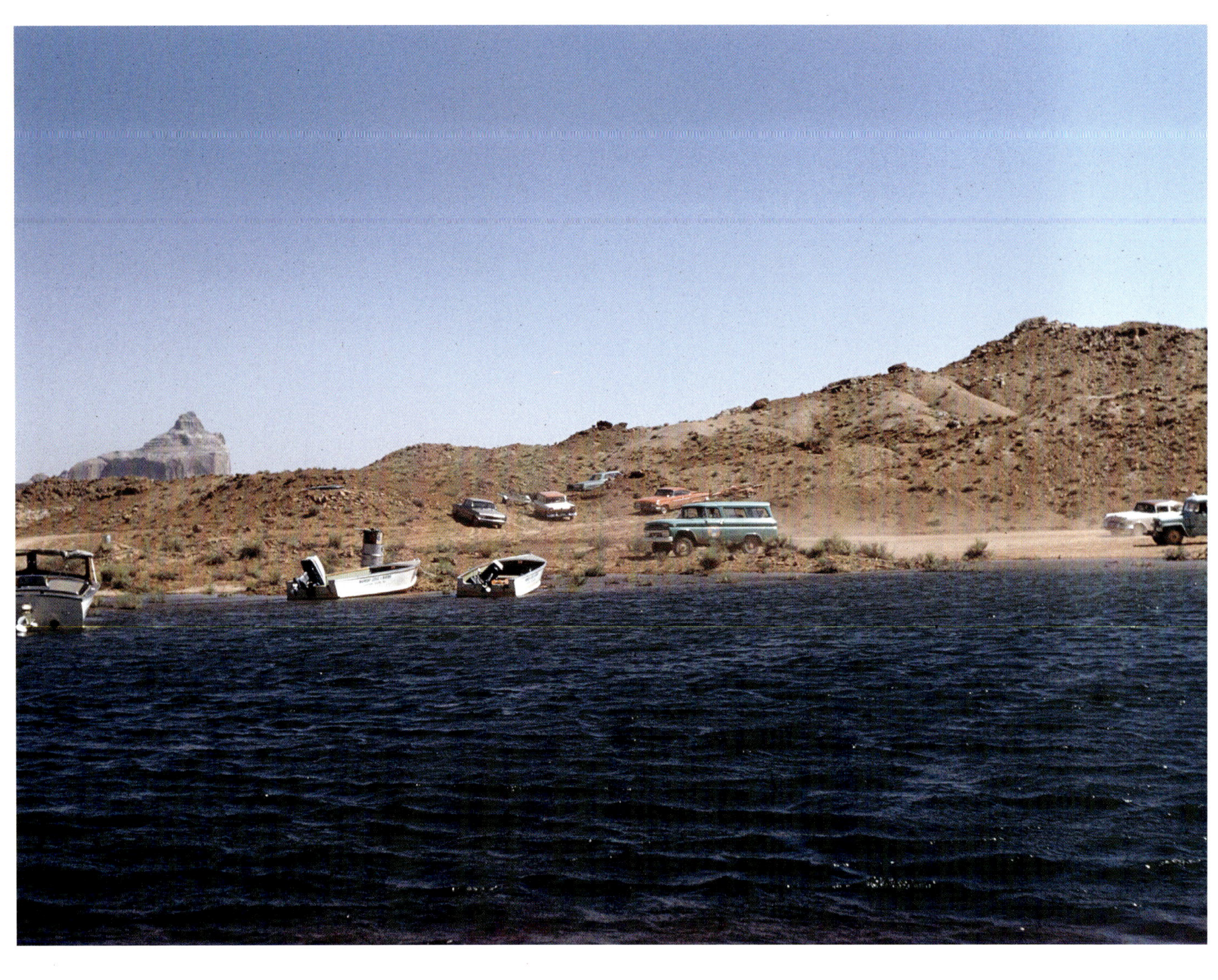

View of Lake Powell shore from lake,
ca. 1960s. Bass, William G., NAU.
PH.96.24.46.156. Northern Arizona
University. Cline Library.

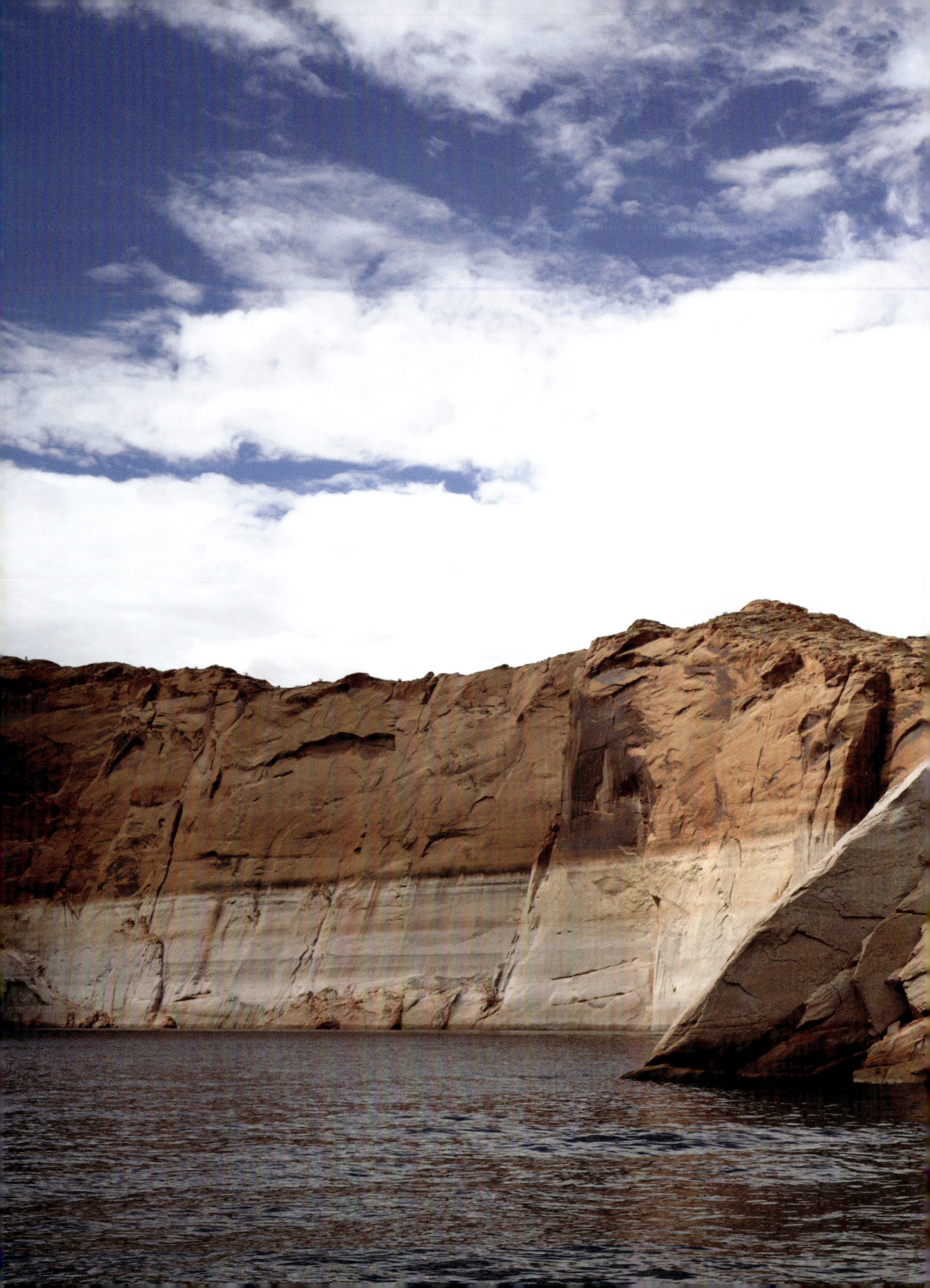

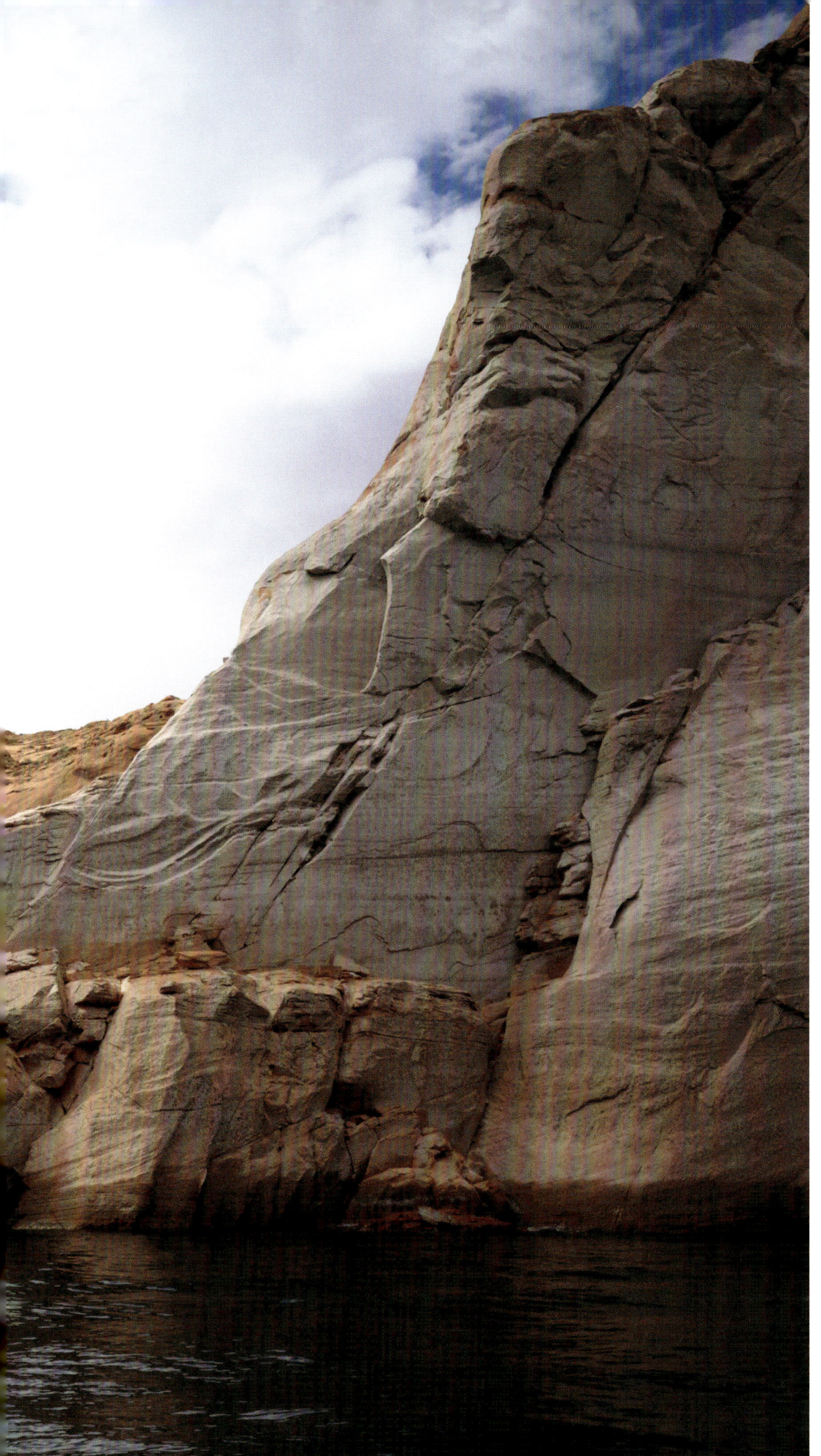

Tapestry walls and
bathtub ring on
Lake Powell.

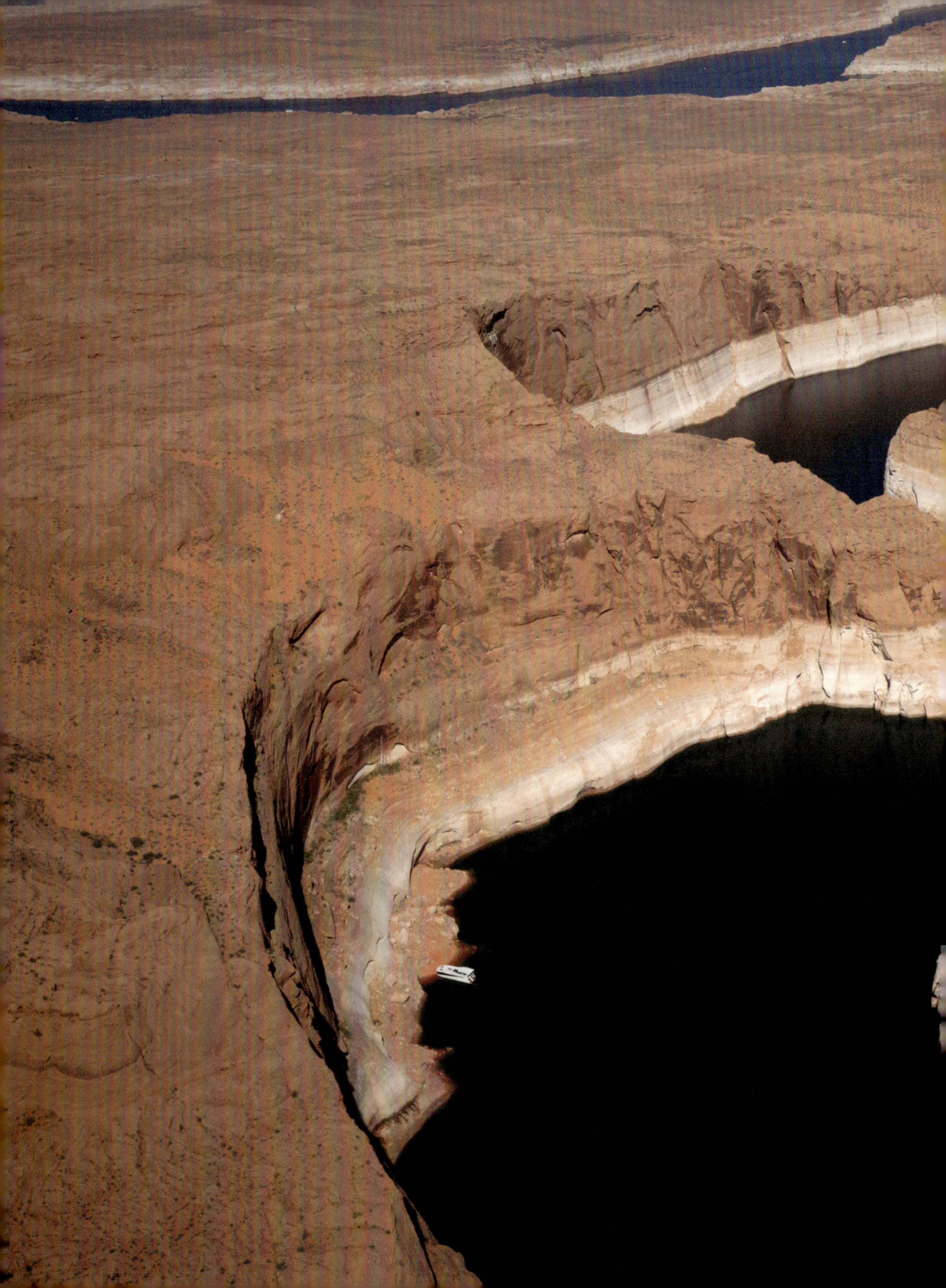

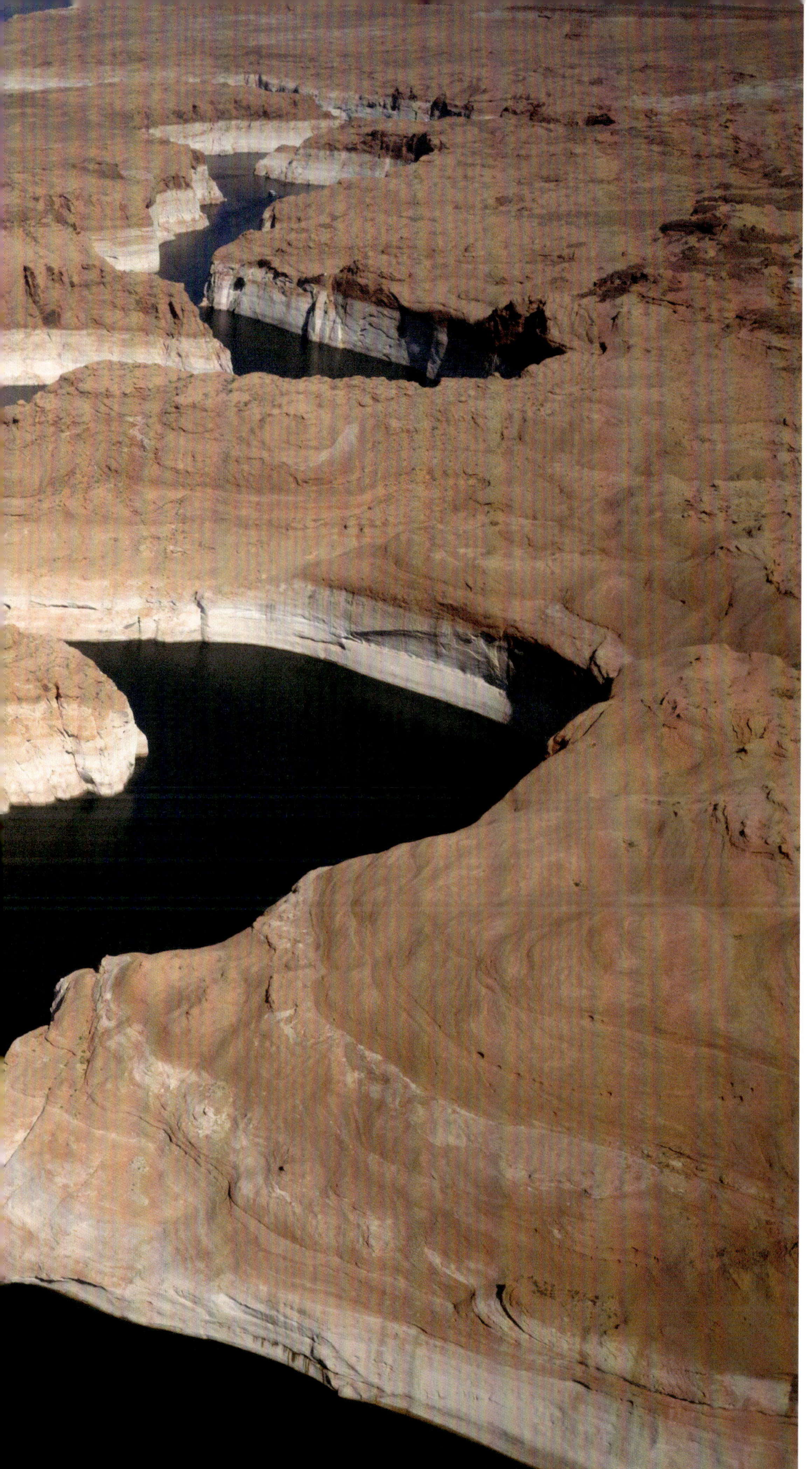

Aerial view of Lake
Powell with bathtub
ring.

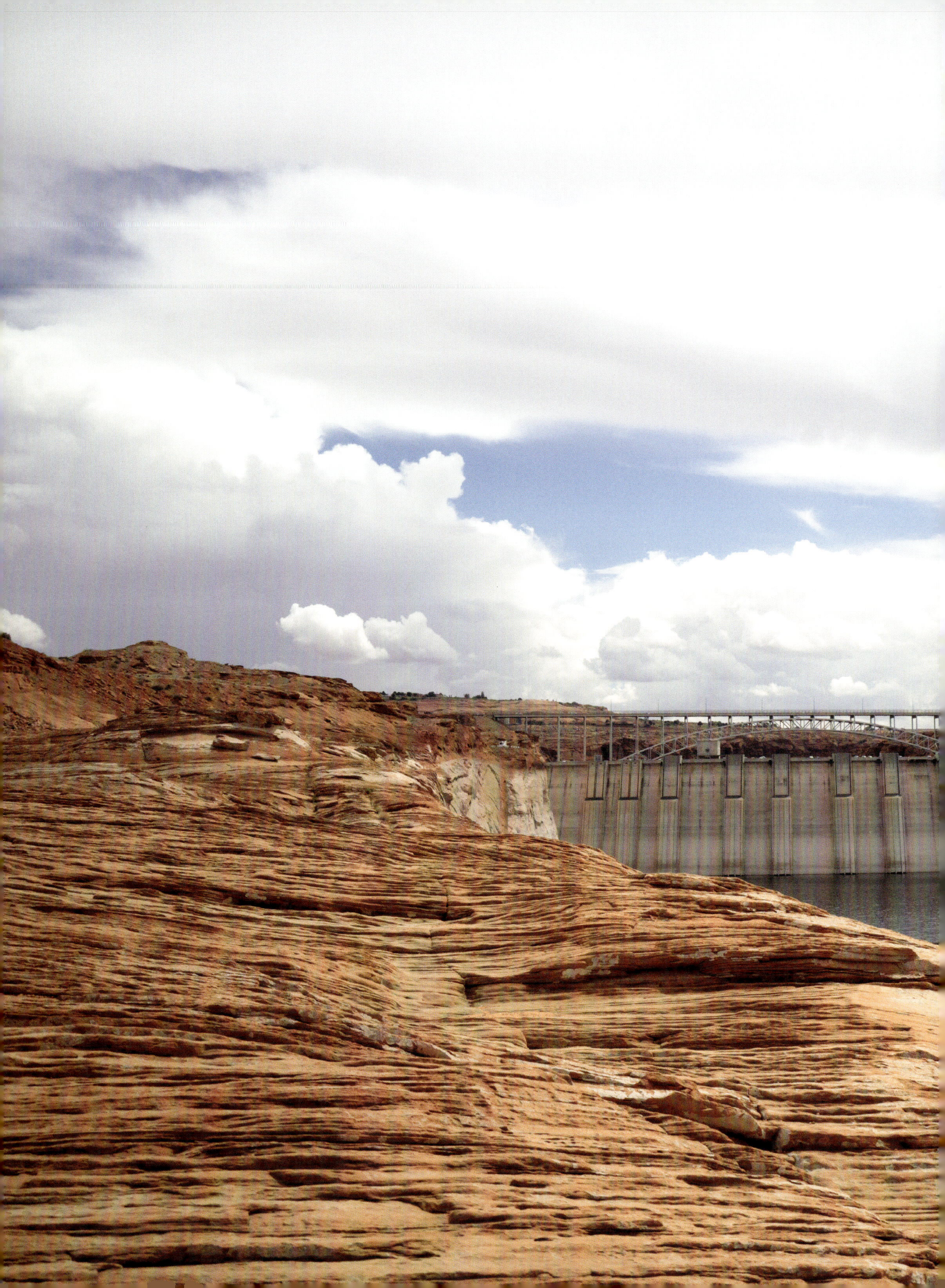

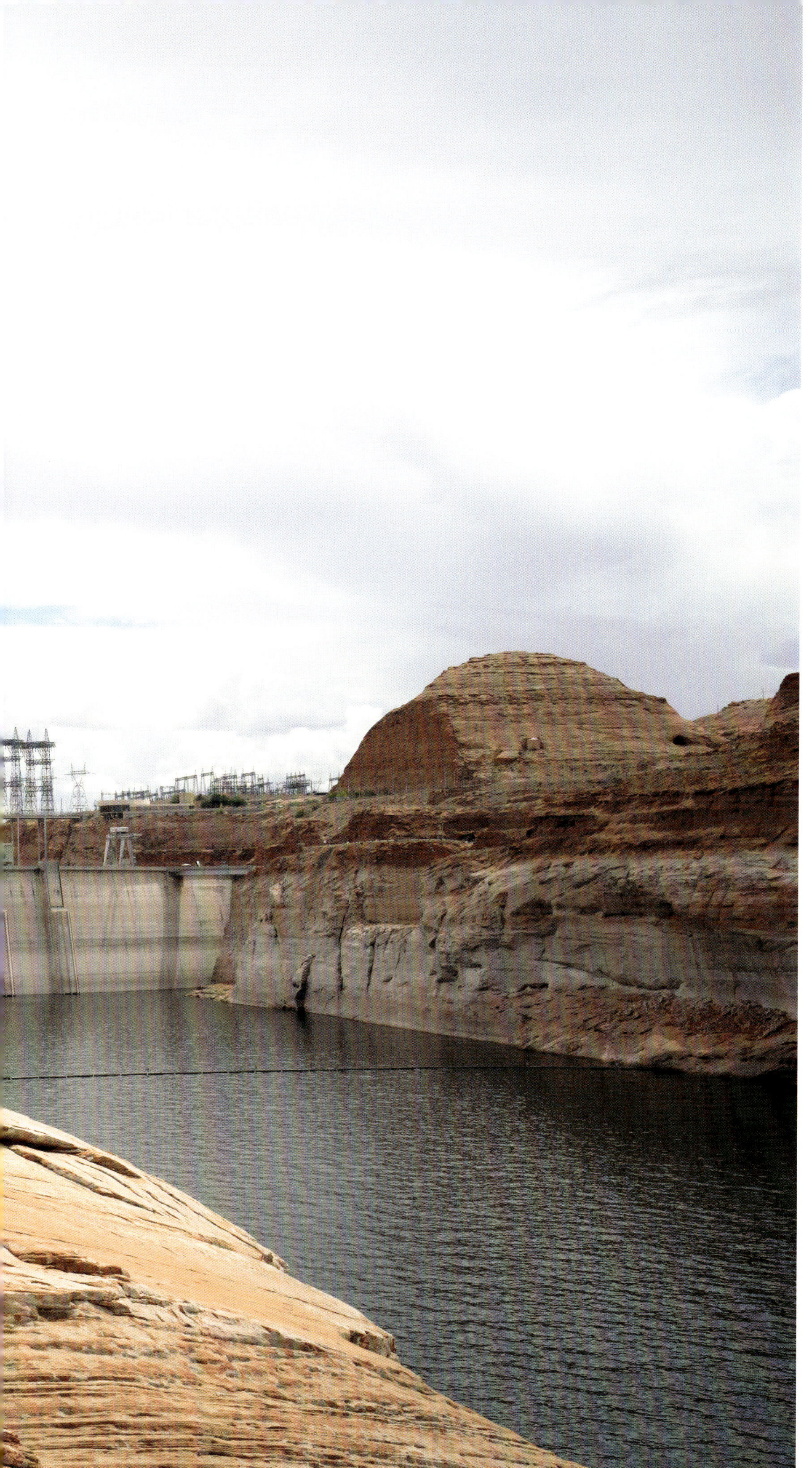

Internal penstocks
from the Chains.

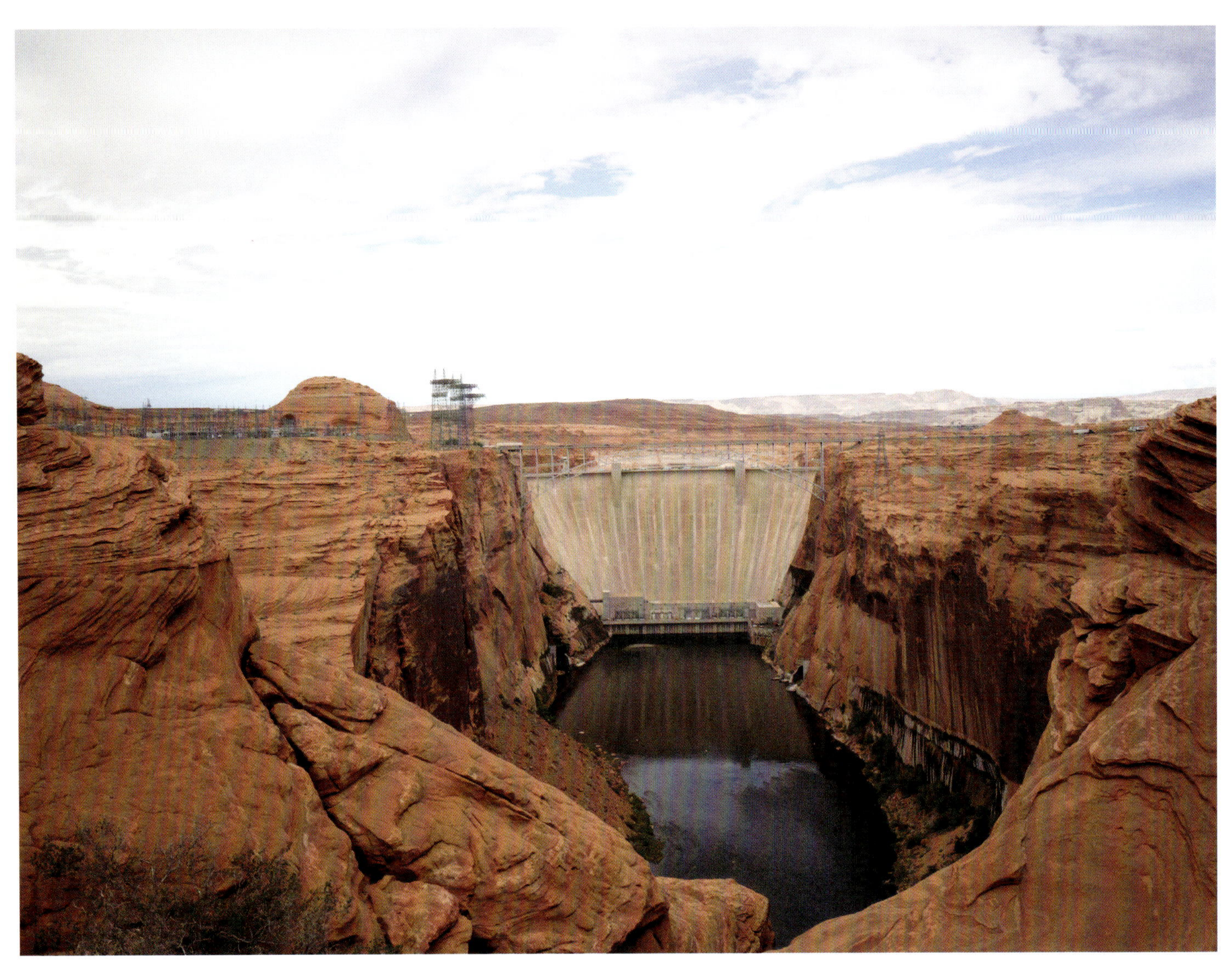

Glen Canyon Dam.

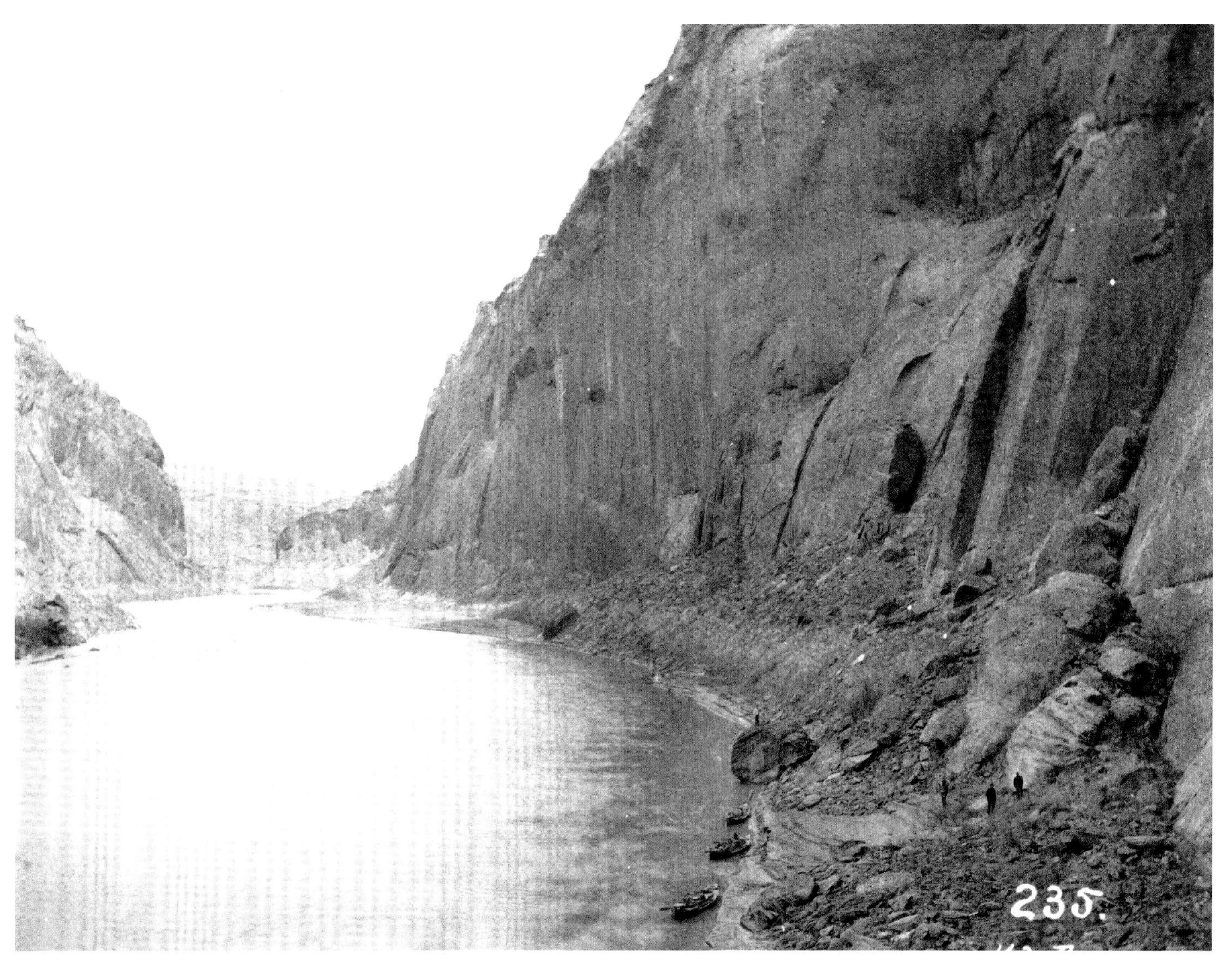

Historical view of Glen Canyon site
prior to dam. Franklin A. Nims, original
courtesy of the National Archives,
57-RS-235, public domain. 1889.

"Man has flung down a giant barrier directly in the path of the turbulent Colorado in Arizona. It has tamed the wild river—made it a servant to man's will.

Big Red has lost meaning as a name for the Colorado. The colossus called Glen Canyon is now storing and releasing blue water.

Glen Canyon Dam rises over 500 feet from the canyon floor. Its graceful bulk holds 5 million cubic yards of concrete. In the powerhouse at its toe, 475-ton generators spin quietly as they pour energy by the billions of watts into cross-country transmission lines. Behind it, 186-mile-long Lake Powell is filling.... Built of rock and cement and sweat and skill, Glen Canyon Dam stands as a monument to the talent of its builders—and to reaffirmation of the pioneering spirit that is America.

The manmade rock of the dam has become as one with the living rock of the canyon.

It will endure as long as time endures."

—from "Lake Powell: Jewel of the Colorado," US Department of the Interior and Bureau of Reclamation publication. US Printing office, 1965.

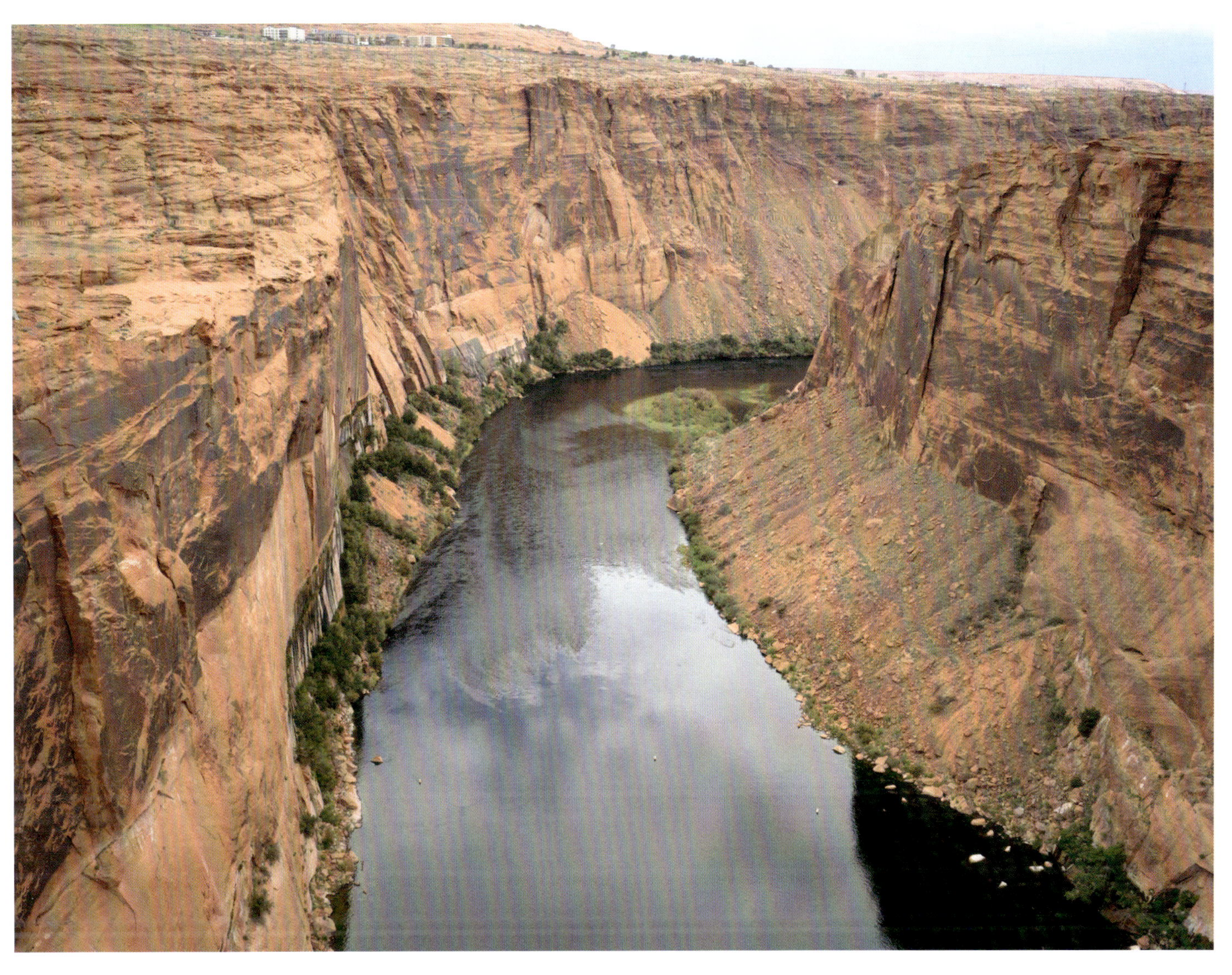

Released river
waters flowing from
Glen Canyon Dam.

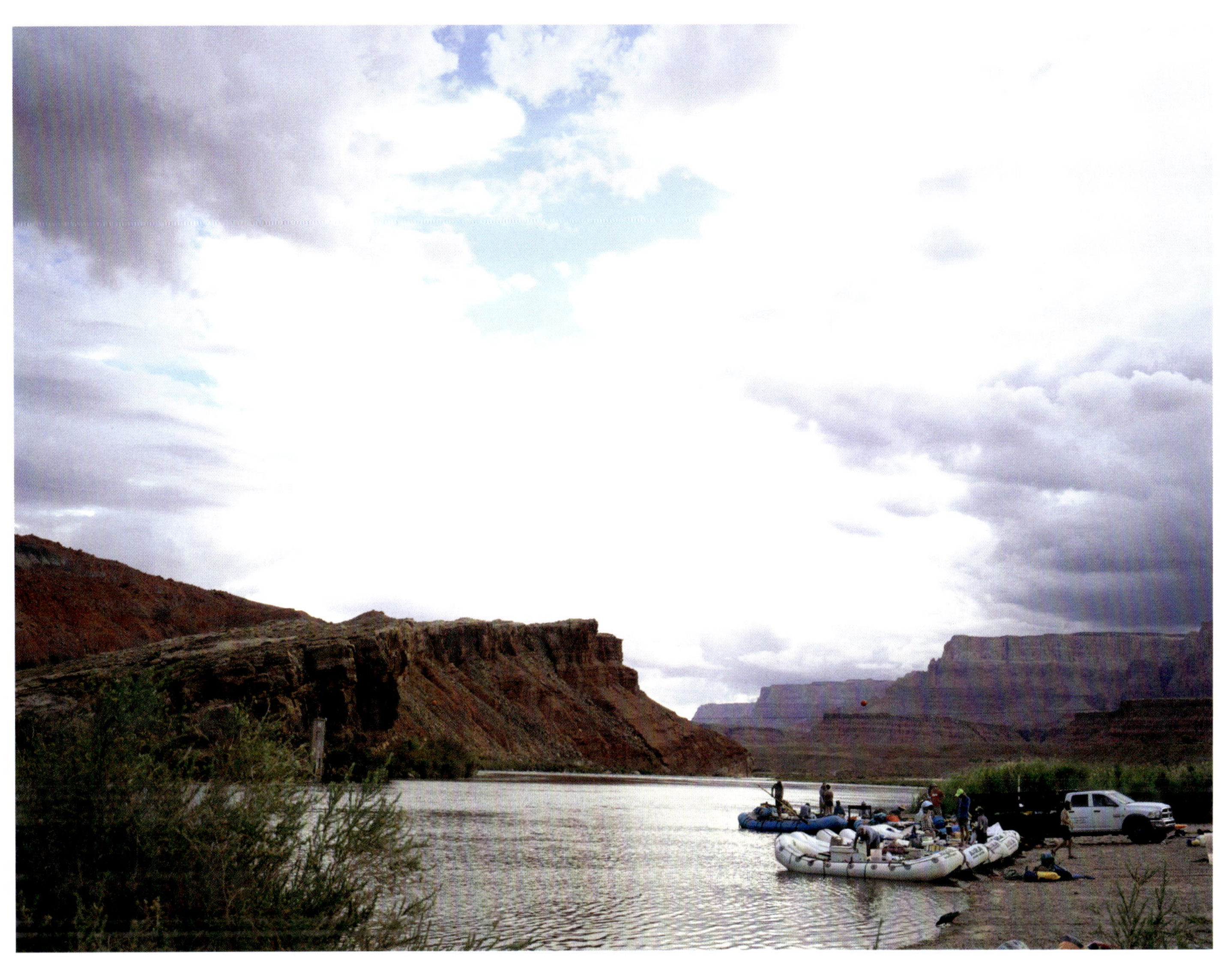

Launching into the
Colorado River at
Lee Ferry, Arizona.

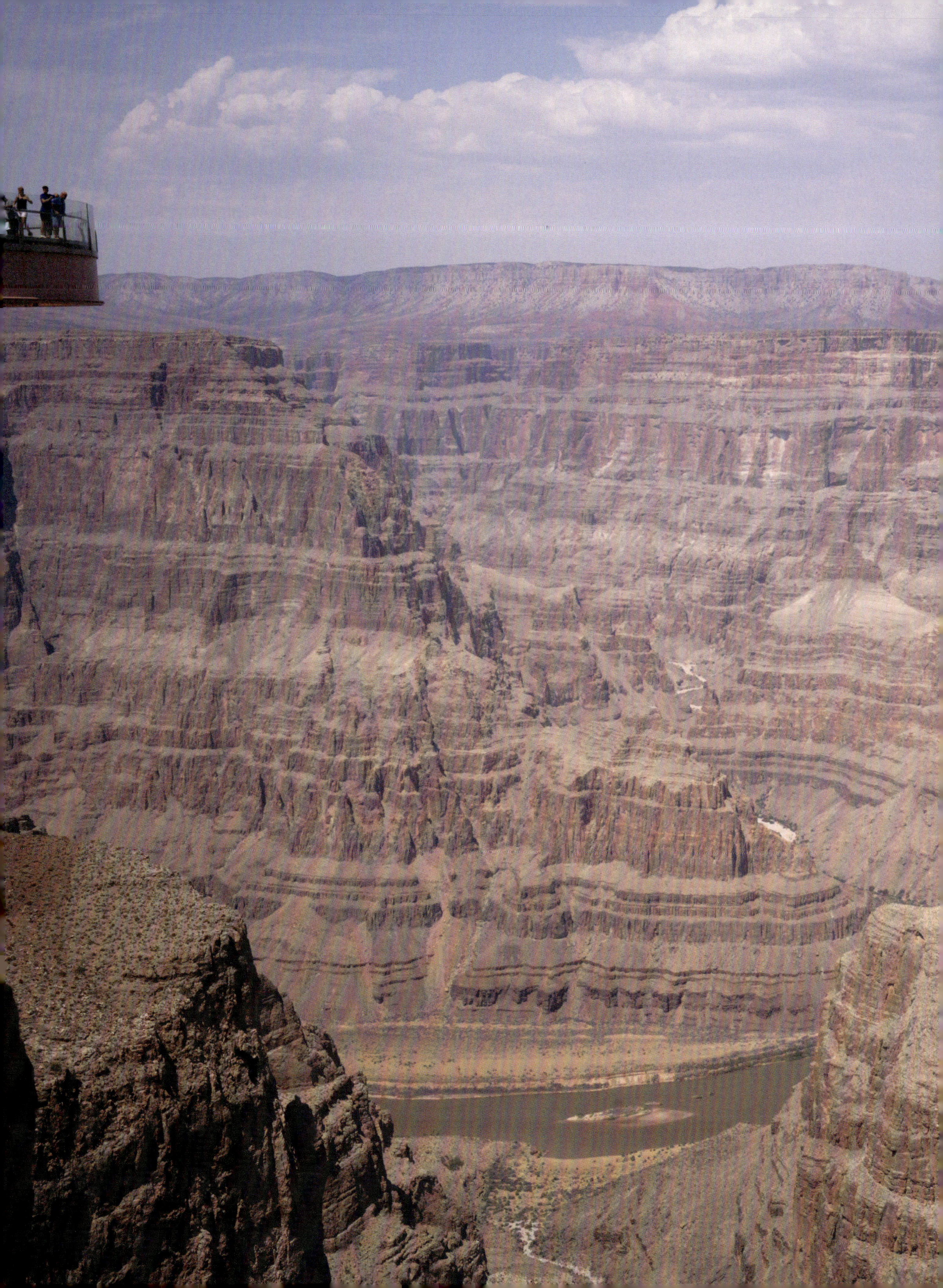

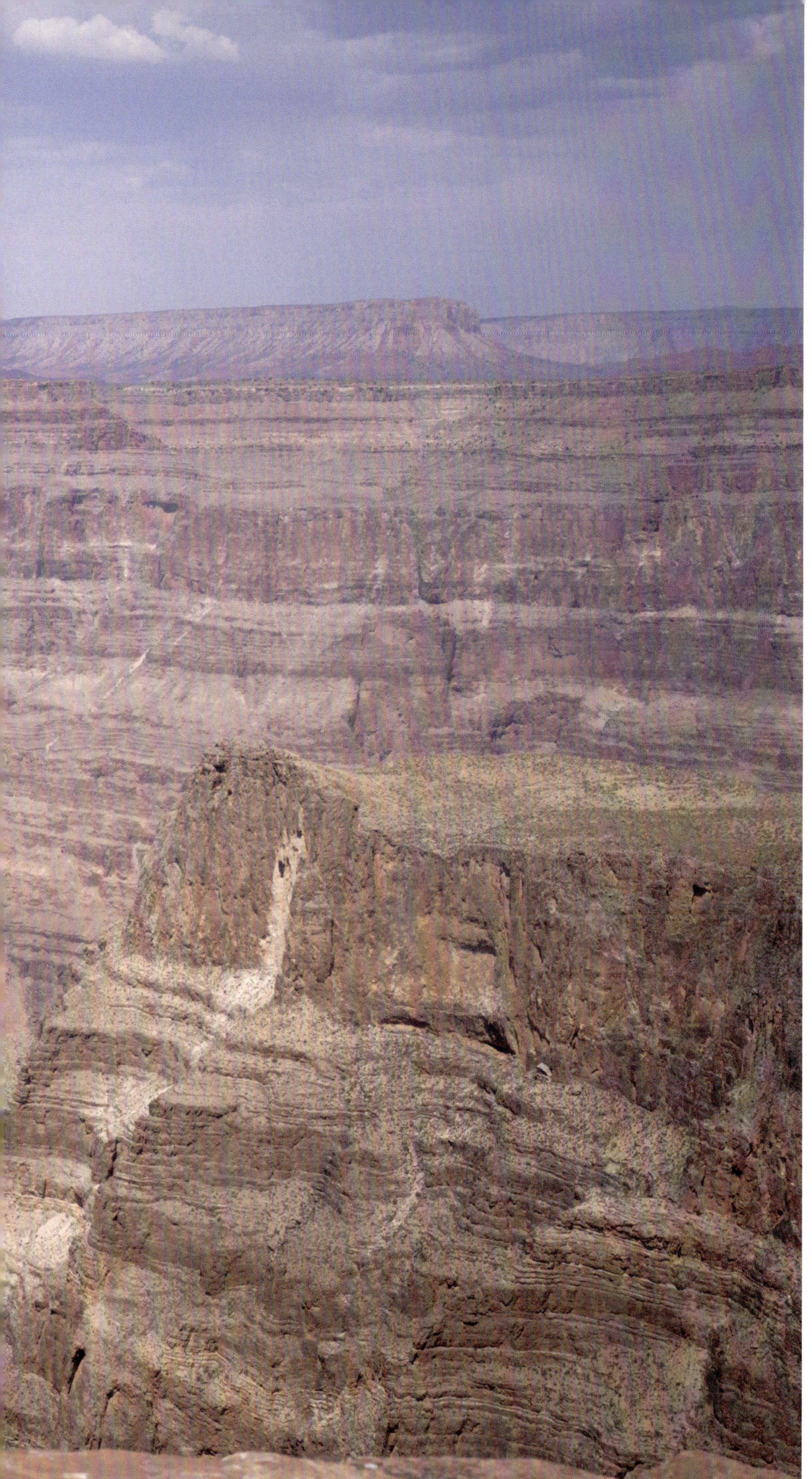

Skywalk at Grand
Canyon with
Colorado River
below, Arizona.

HOOVER DAM

In the early twentieth century, the Bureau of Reclamation devised plans for a massive dam on the Arizona-Nevada border to tame the Colorado River and provide water and hydroelectric power for the developing Southwest.

During this time, farmers sought to divert the Colorado River to new Southwestern communities via a series of canals. When the Colorado River broke through an attempted cut and diversion at Pilot Knob in 1905, the Salton Sea was born. The entire flow of the Colorado River entered the Salton Sink until 1907. The job of "controlling" the raging river then fell to the Bureau of Reclamation.

In 1922, Bureau director Arthur Powell Davis outlined a plan before Congress for a multipurpose dam in Black Canyon, located on the Arizona-Nevada border. Named the Boulder Canyon project, after the original proposed site, the dam would not only control flooding and irrigation, but would also generate and sell hydroelectric power to recoup its costs. Still, the proposed $165 million price tag concerned some lawmakers, while representatives of six of the seven states in the river drainage area—Colorado, Wyoming, Utah, New Mexico, Arizona, and Nevada—worried that the water would primarily go to California.

Then Secretary of Commerce Herbert Hoover brokered the 1922 Colorado River Compact to divide the water proportionally among the seven states, but the legal wrangling continued until outgoing President Calvin Coolidge authorized the Boulder Canyon Project in December 1928. In honor of the new president's contributions, Secretary of the Interior Ray L. Wilbur announced the structure would be called Hoover Dam, at a 1930 dedication ceremony, though the name didn't become official until 1947.

Colorado River water is impounded behind the massive Hoover Dam in Lake Mead. In 1935, the Bureau of Reclamation and the Soil Conservation Service mapped Lake Mead's topography to calculate the reservoir's storage capacity. This study resulted in an estimated capacity of over 31 maf of water at an elevation of 1,221.4 feet. Lake Mead provides Colorado River water to roughly 25 million people and farmlands.

Hoover Dam is owned by the US government and operated by the Bureau of Reclamation.

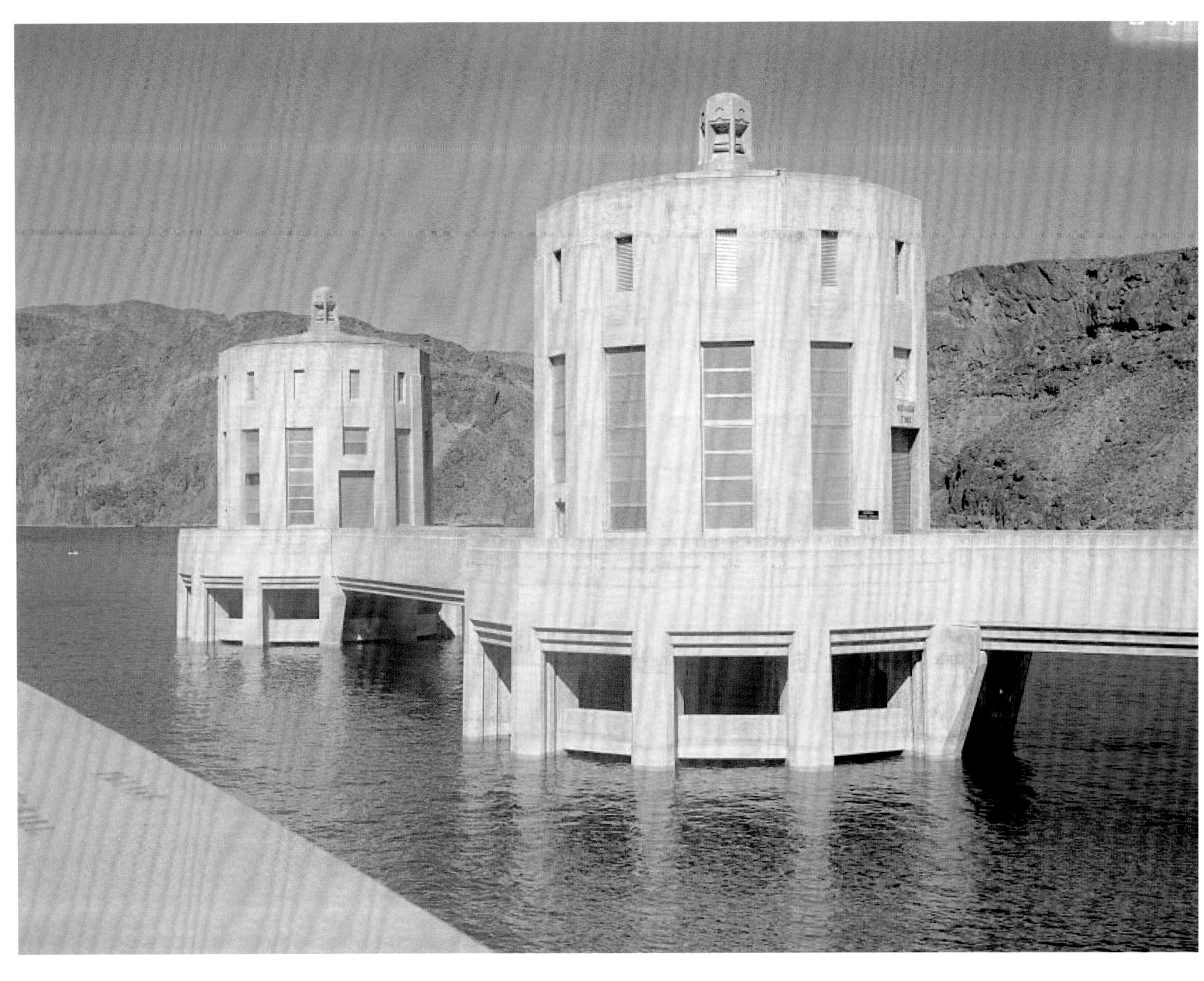

Historical image of
Penstocks at full pool,
circa 1987.

Historic American Engineering Record, Creator, Herbert Hoover, and Owner Bureau of Reclamation, photographer by Lowe, Jet. *Hoover Dam, Spanning Colorado River at Route 93, Boulder City, Clark County, NV.* trans by Larson, Katemitter Documentation Compiled After. Photograph. Retrieved from the Library of Congress.

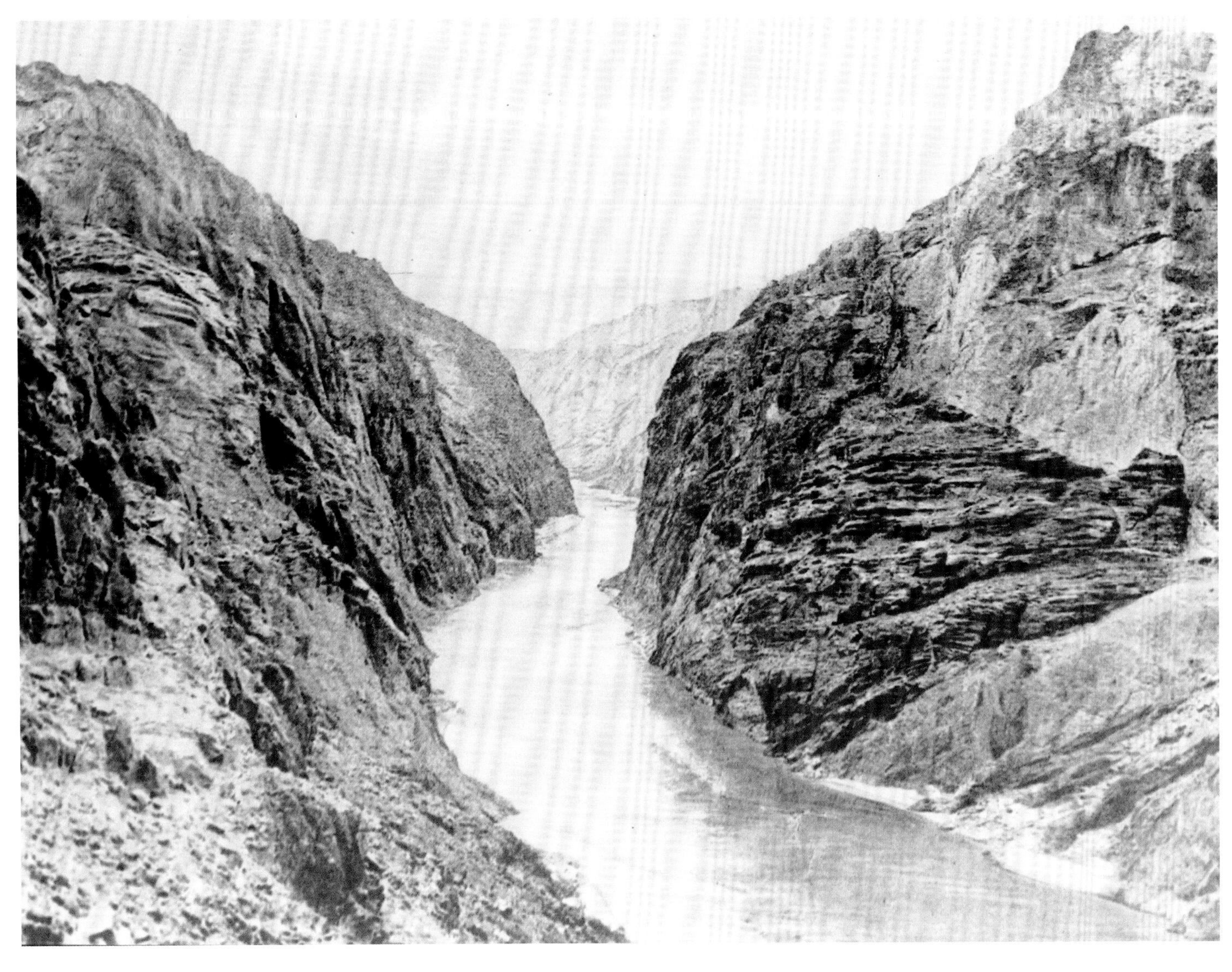

Historical image of
Hoover Dam site in
Black Canyon.

Ben D. Glaha, *Black Canyon prior to Boulder Dam construction, from an old print.* Library of Congress.

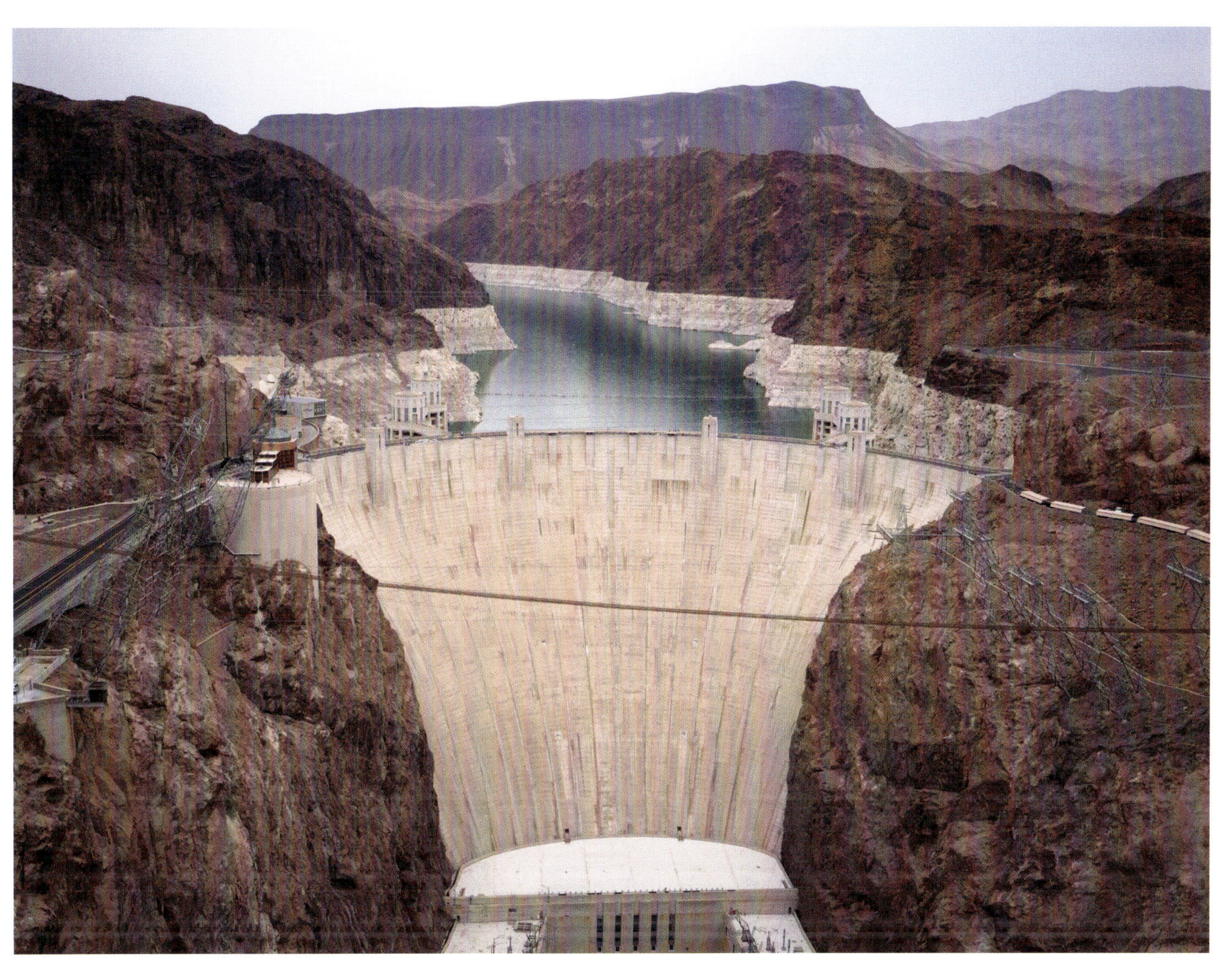

Hoover Dam,
Arizona and
Nevada.

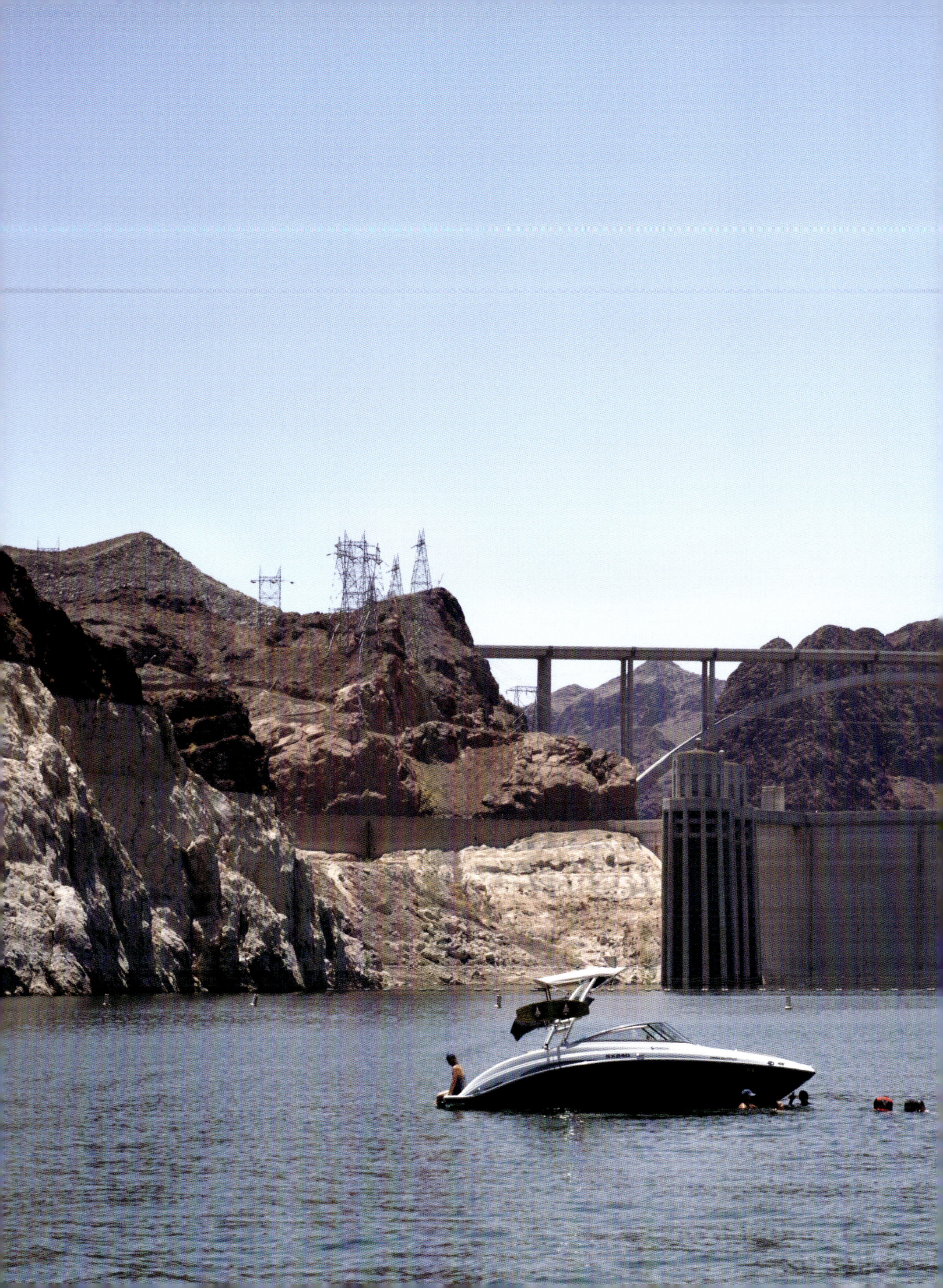

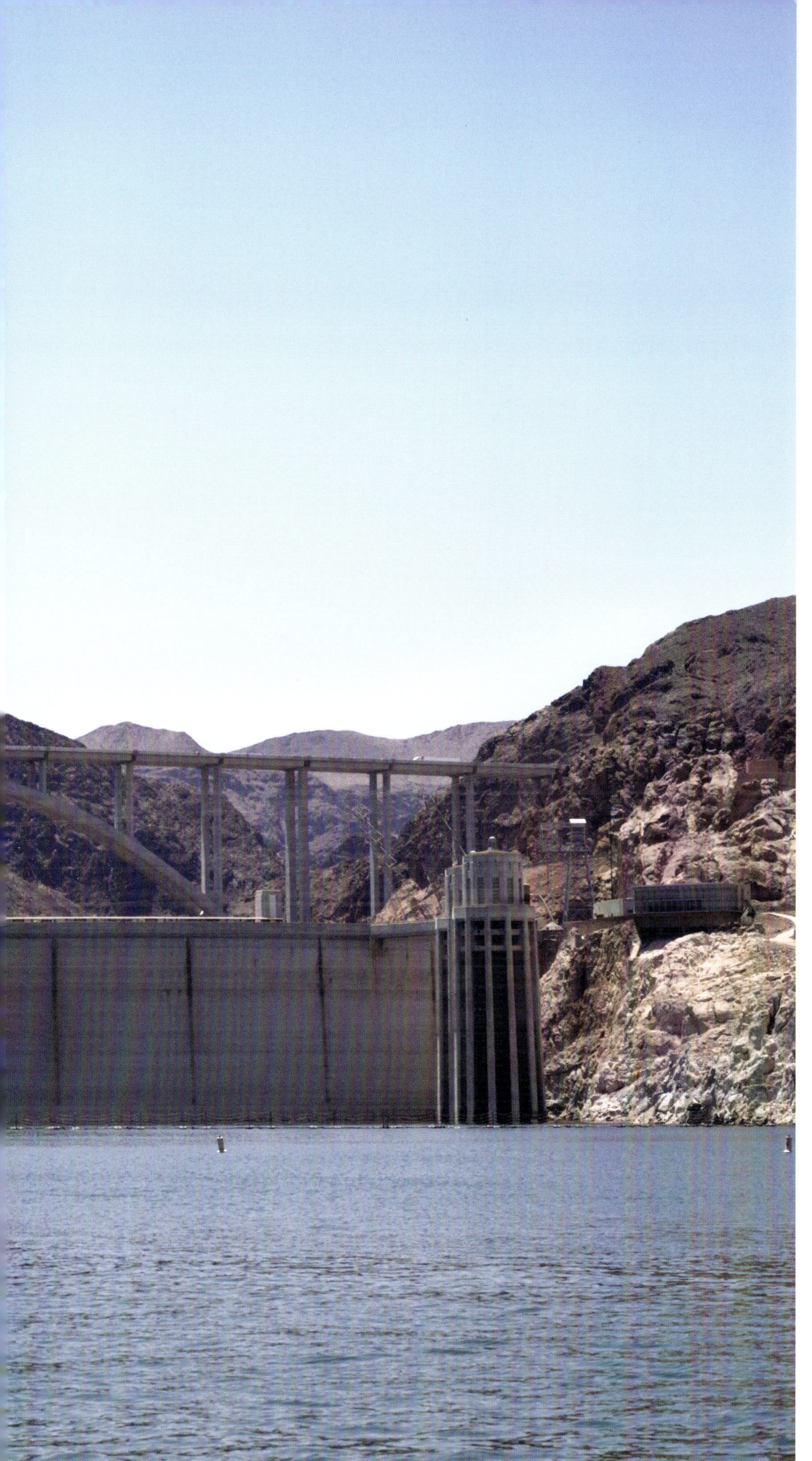

Behind Hoover Dam
on Lake Mead.

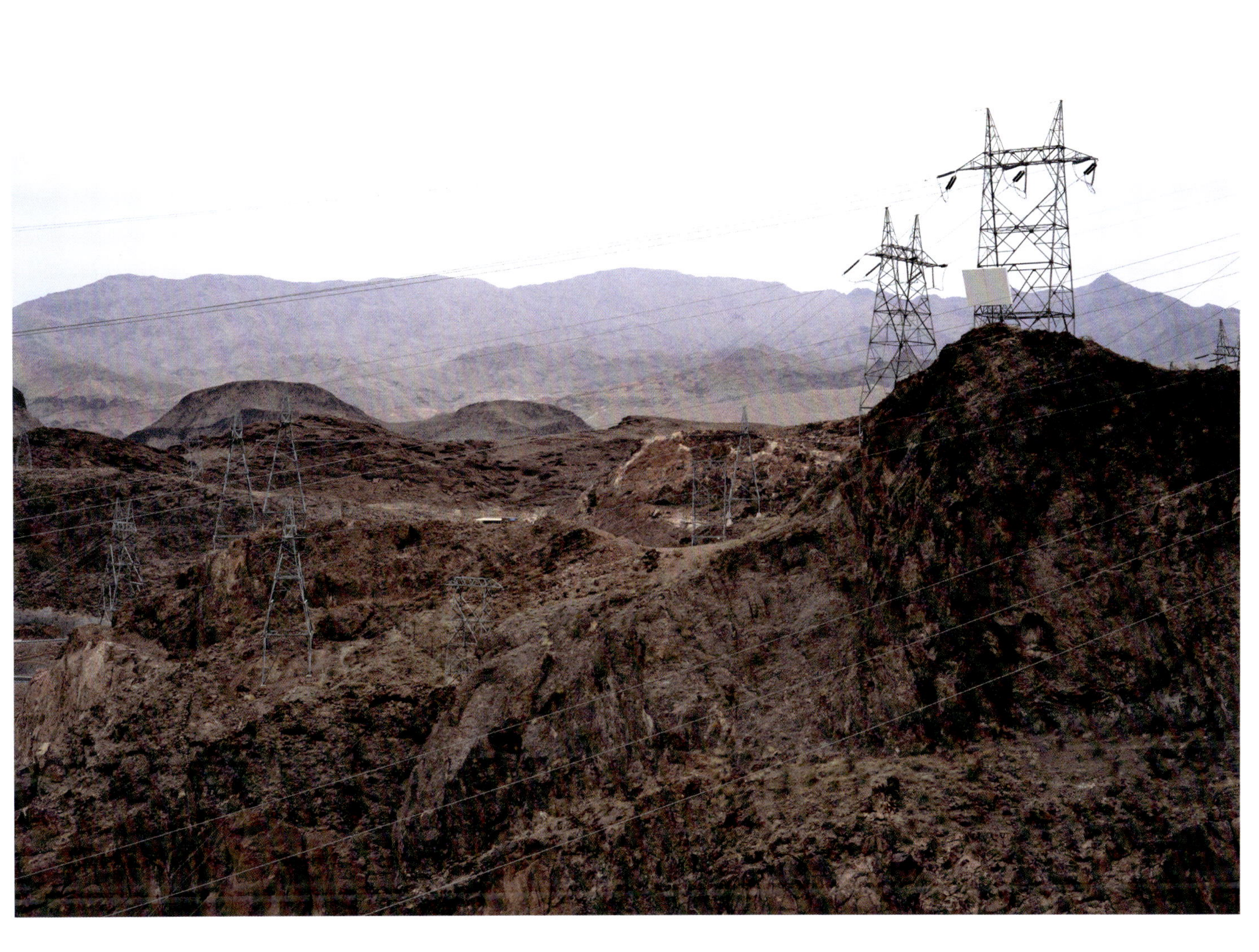

Transmission lines
at Hoover Dam.

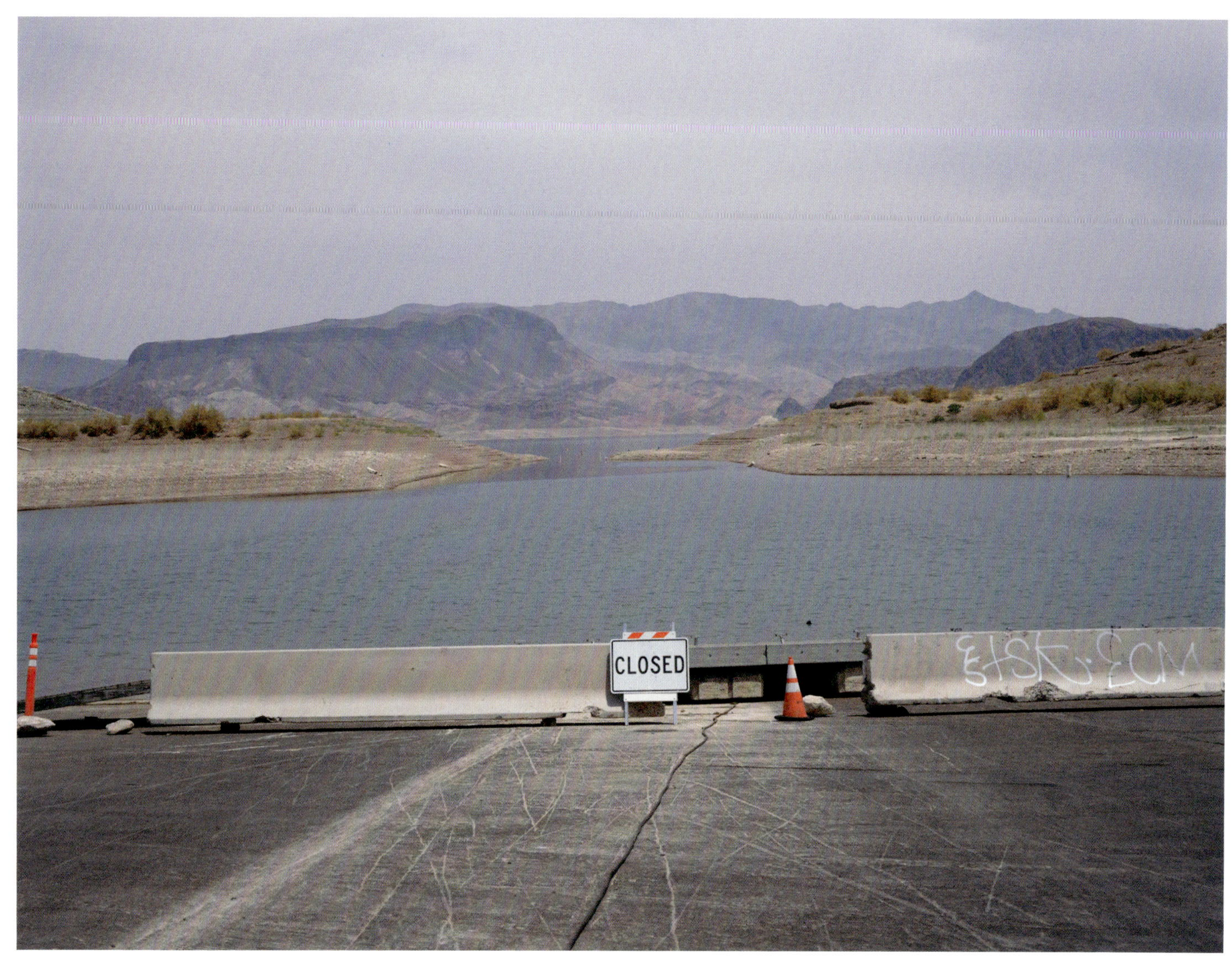

Closed Boulder
Harbor, 2021.

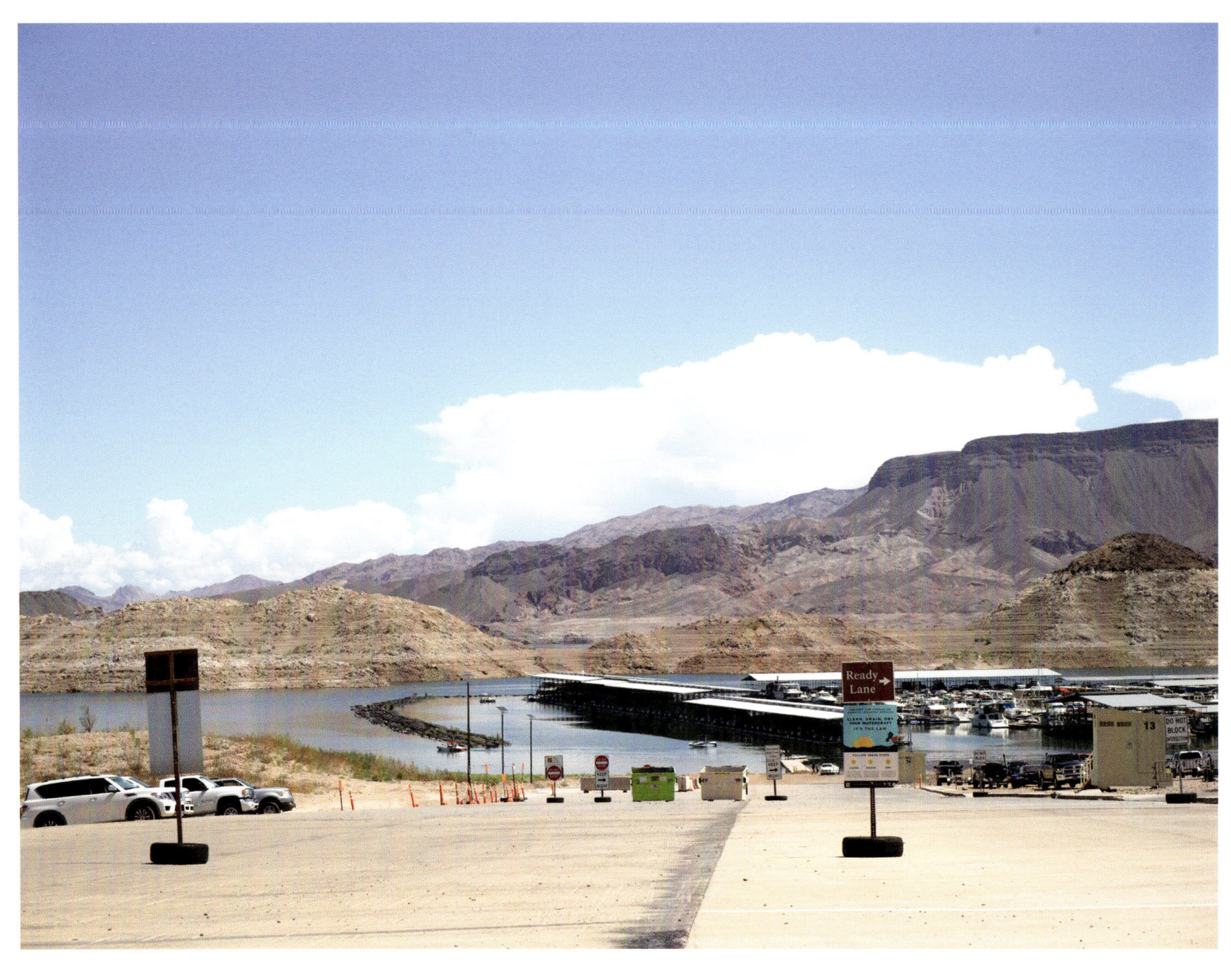

Hemmenway Harbor
boat launch at Lake
Mead, Nevada.

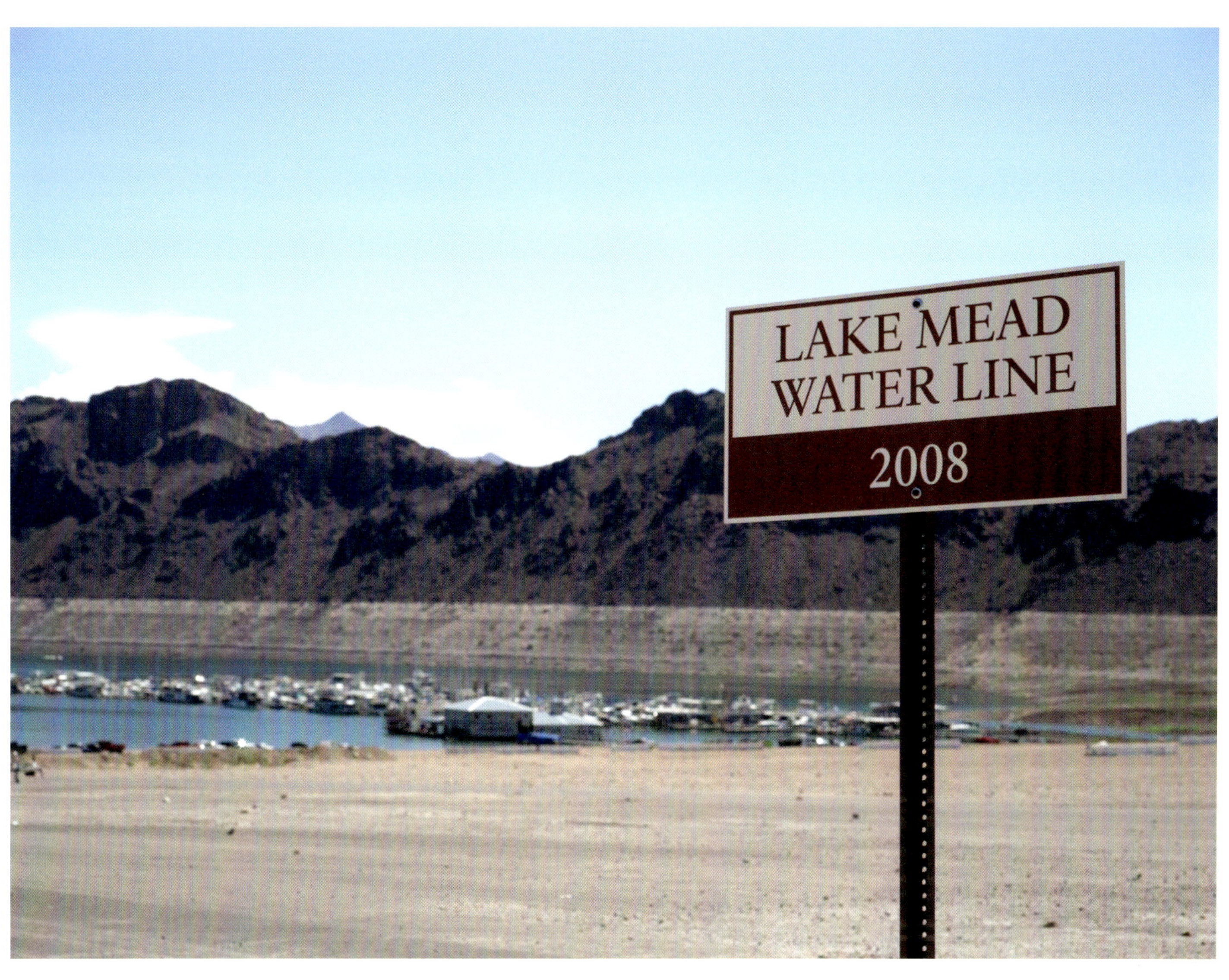

Previous water-level
sign at Lake Mead
Marina, Nevada.

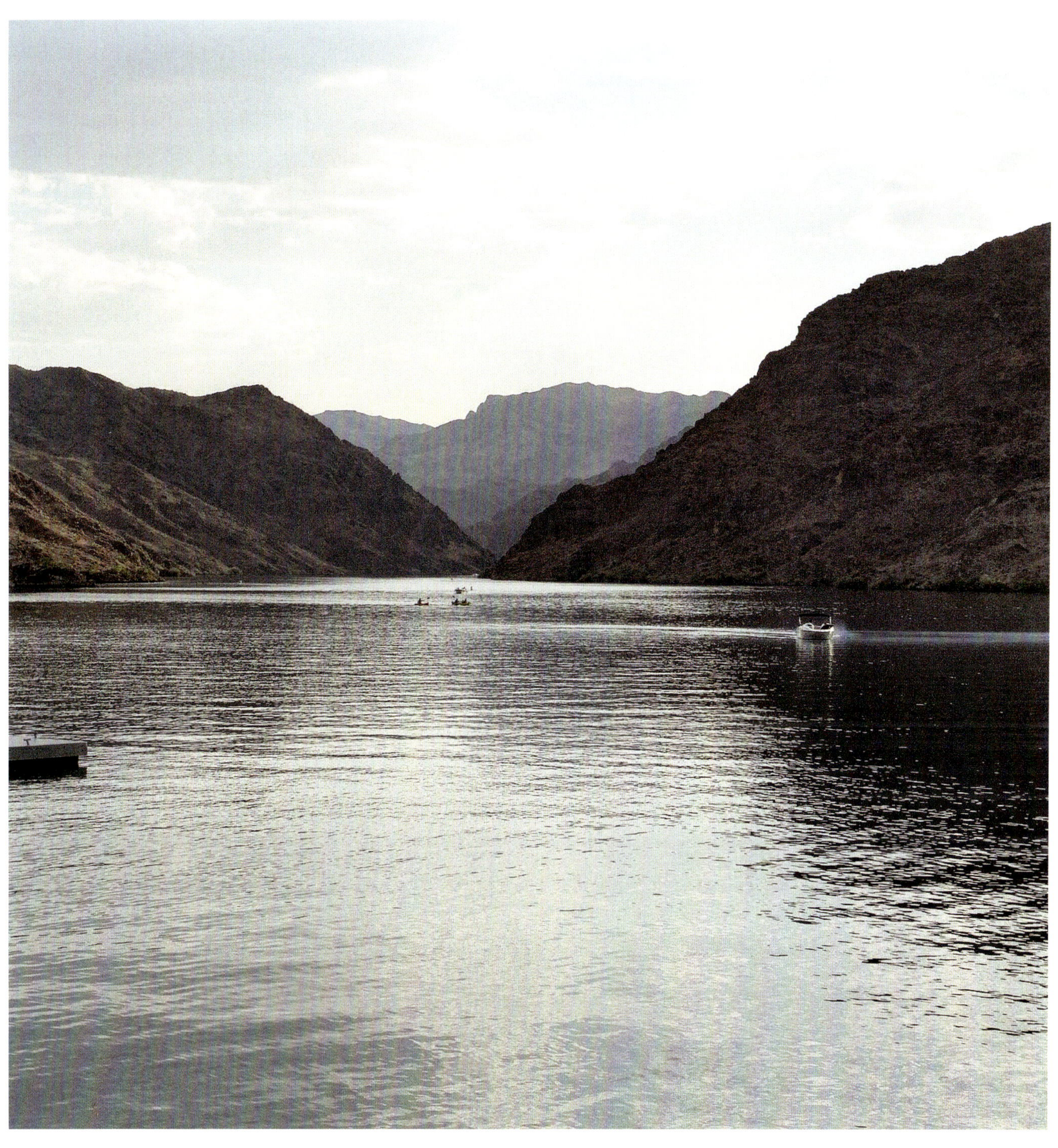

Colorado River after
release from Hoover
Dam.

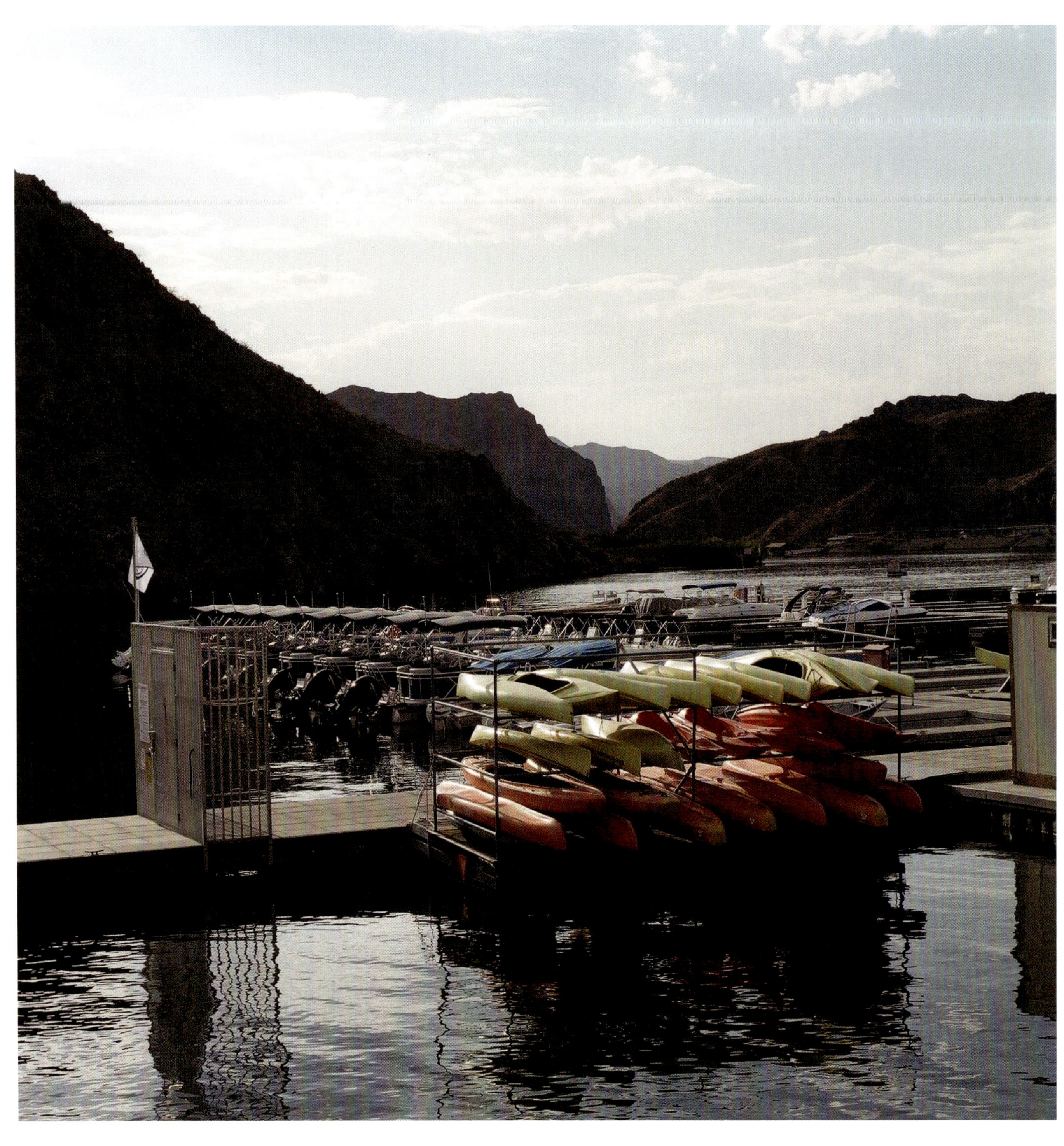

Colorado River after release
from Hoover Dam at Willow
Beach, Arizona.

"We know that, as an unregulated river, the Colorado added little of value to the region this dam serves. When in flood the river was a threatening torrent. In the dry months of the year it shrank to a trickling stream. For a generation the people of Imperial Valley had lived in the shadow of disaster from this river which provided their livelihood, and which is the foundation of their hopes for themselves and their children. Every spring they awaited with dread the coming of a flood, and at the end of nearly every summer they feared a shortage of water would destroy their crops.

The mighty waters of the Colorado were running unused to the sea. Today we translate them into a great national possession...."

—Franklin D. Roosevelt, from "Address at the Dedication of Boulder Dam" by Gerhard Peters and John T. Woolley, The American Presidency Project.

DAVIS DAM

Davis Dam spans the Colorado River in Pyramid Canyon sixty-seven miles downstream from Hoover Dam and eighty-eight miles upstream from Parker Dam, in Nevada.

Davis was authorized in 1941, but work was halted after the War Production Board revoked its priority rating, which was needed to procure the materials necessary for construction. Work resumed in 1946, with completion in 1953.

The primary purpose of Davis Dam, and the Colorado River waters impounded behind it in Lake Mohave, is to reregulate Hoover Dam releases to meet downstream needs, including the annual delivery of 1.5 maf of water to Mexico. This requirement complies with a 1944 water treaty. Lake Mohave has a capacity of 1,818,300 acre-feet. Davis Dam's power plant generates roughly 1 to 2 billion kilowatt-hours annually.

Davis is operated by the Bureau of Reclamation.

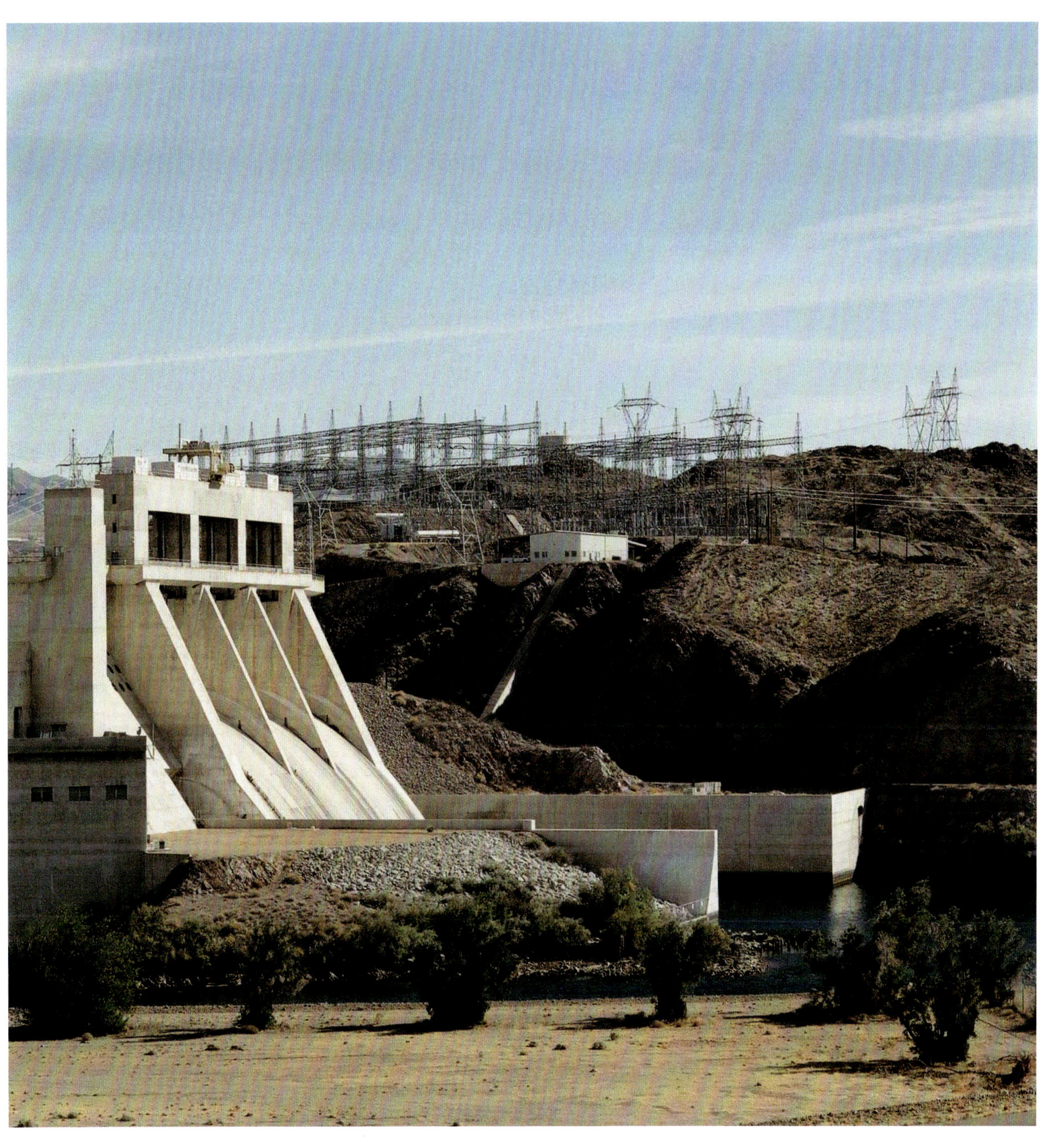

Davis Dam, Arizona
and Nevada.

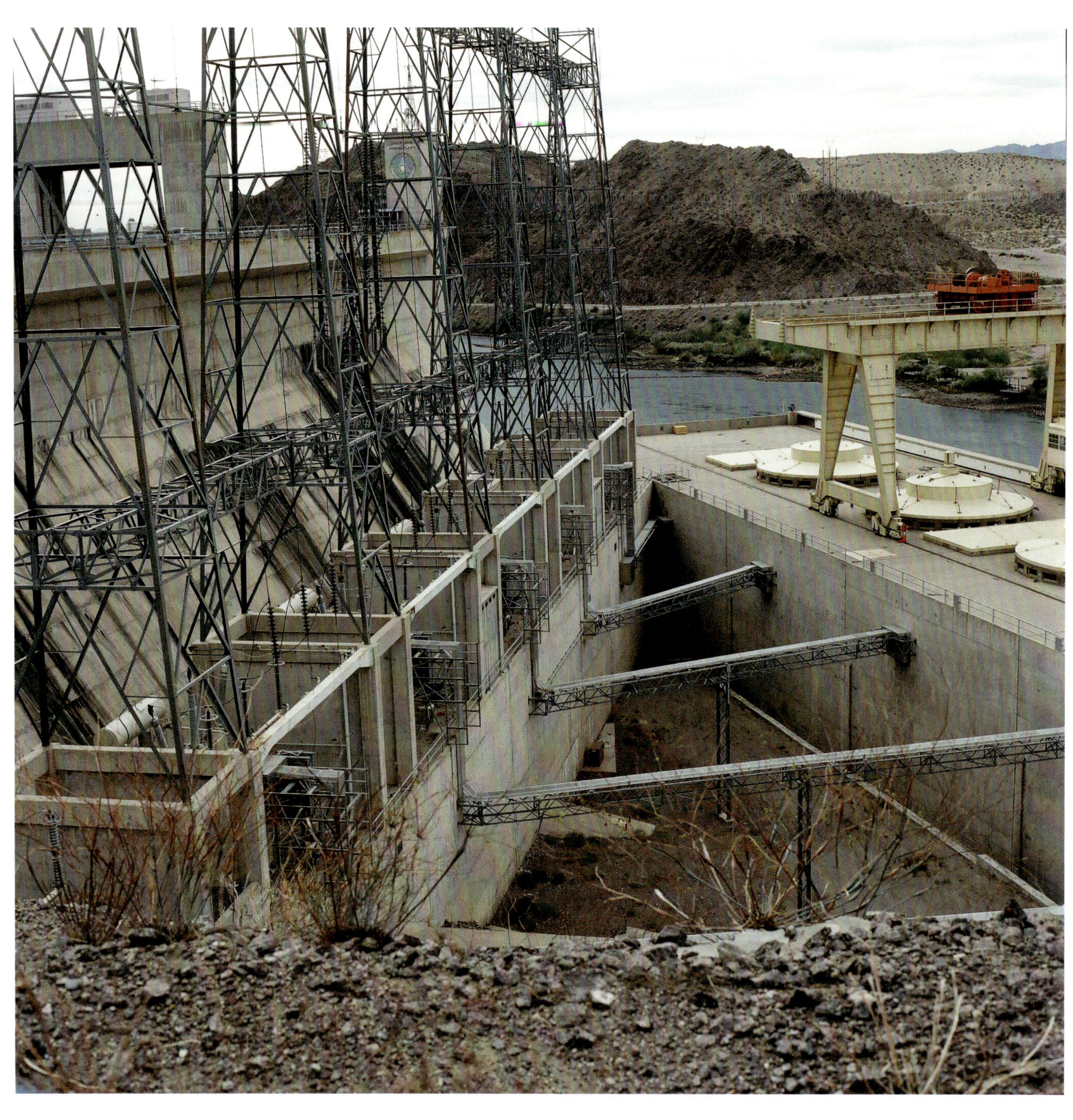

Davis Dam and
transmission lines.

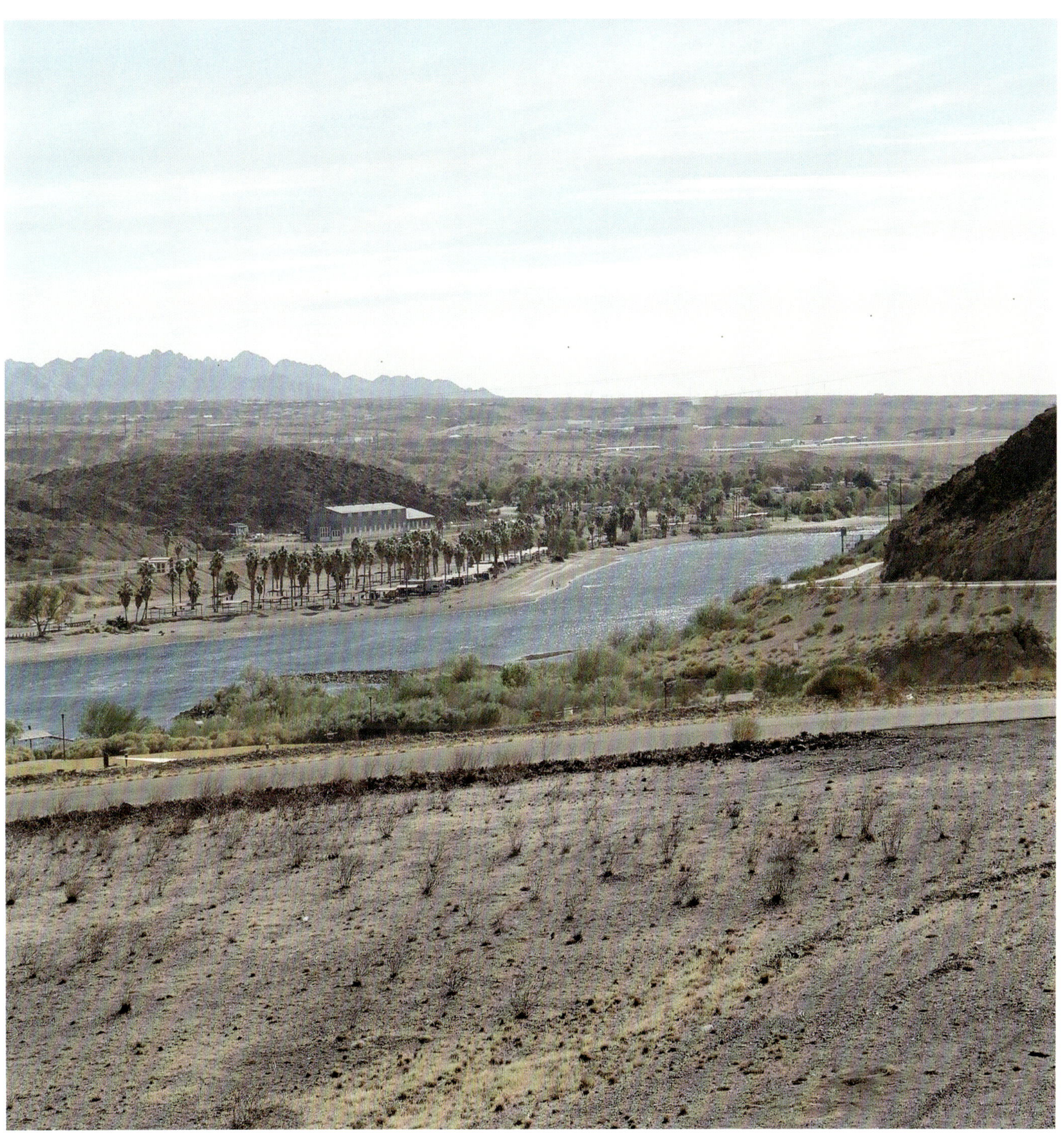

The river after Davis
Dam, Nevada.

PARKER DAM

Parker Dam is a concrete arch structure commonly referred to as the "deepest dam in the world." Seventy-three percent of the dam's structural height of 320 feet is below the original riverbed; only about eighty-five feet of the dam's structural height is visible. Water control is provided by five fifty-square-foot gates. Parker Dam is operated in coordination with Hoover and Davis Dams by the Bureau of Reclamation.

Colorado River waters are impounded by Parker Dam at Lake Havasu. The reservoir backs up behind the dam for forty-five miles and covers more than 20,400 acres. The reservoir's total capacity is 646,200 acre-feet. The purpose of the dam is to pump water into the Colorado River Aqueduct (California) and Central Arizona Project.

The Colorado River Aqueduct can deliver 1 billion gallons of Colorado River water daily to Southern California. The Central Arizona Project can divert an average of 1.5 maf, or 489 billion gallons yearly to users in central and southern Arizona.

Roughly half of the power generated by Parker Dam is reserved by the Metropolitan Water District of Southern California to pump water along the Colorado River Aqueduct.

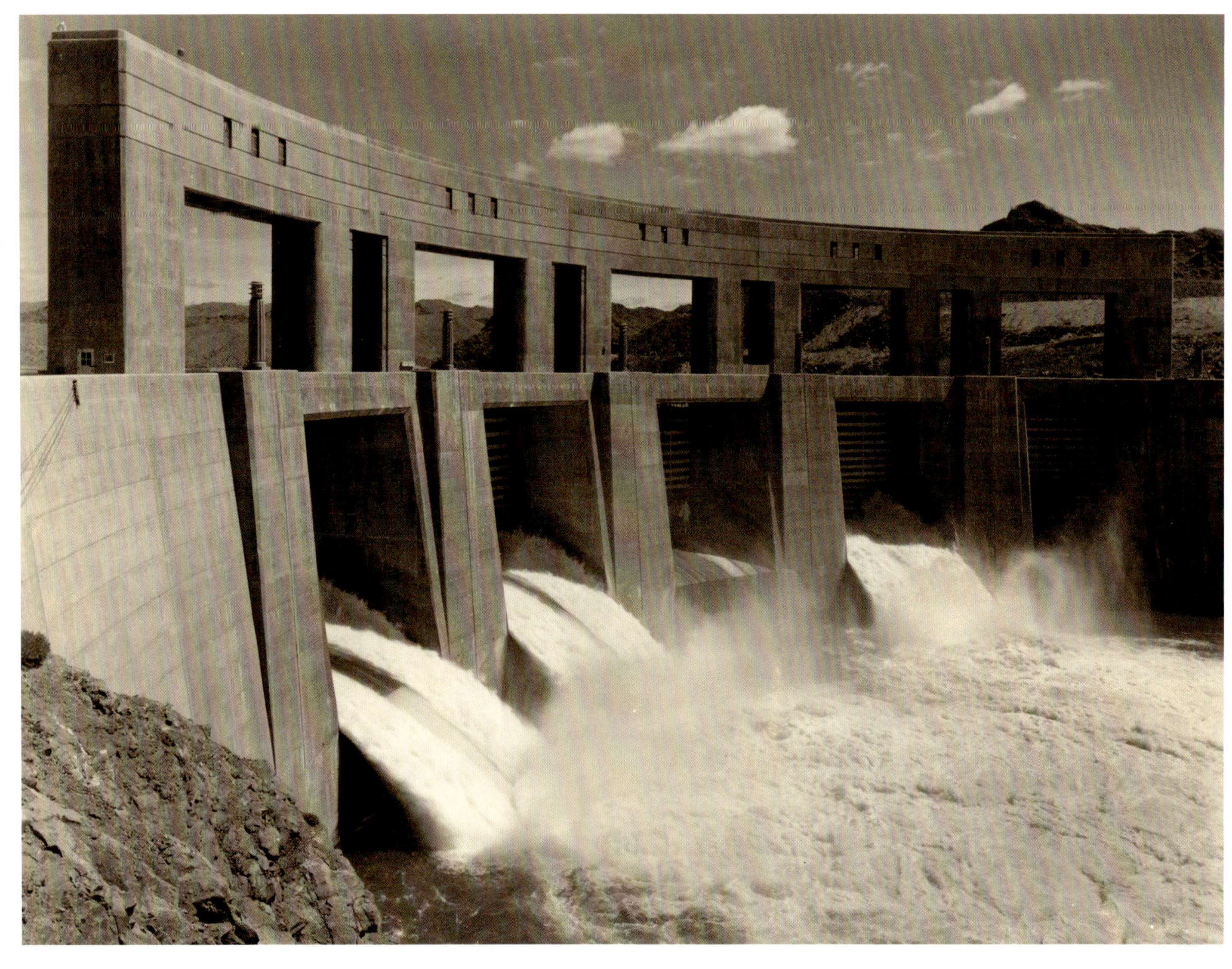

Historical image of
Parker Dam.

Parker Dam power project, Ariz. and Calif. View of Parker Dam from the California side.
June. Photograph. Retrieved from the Library of Congress.

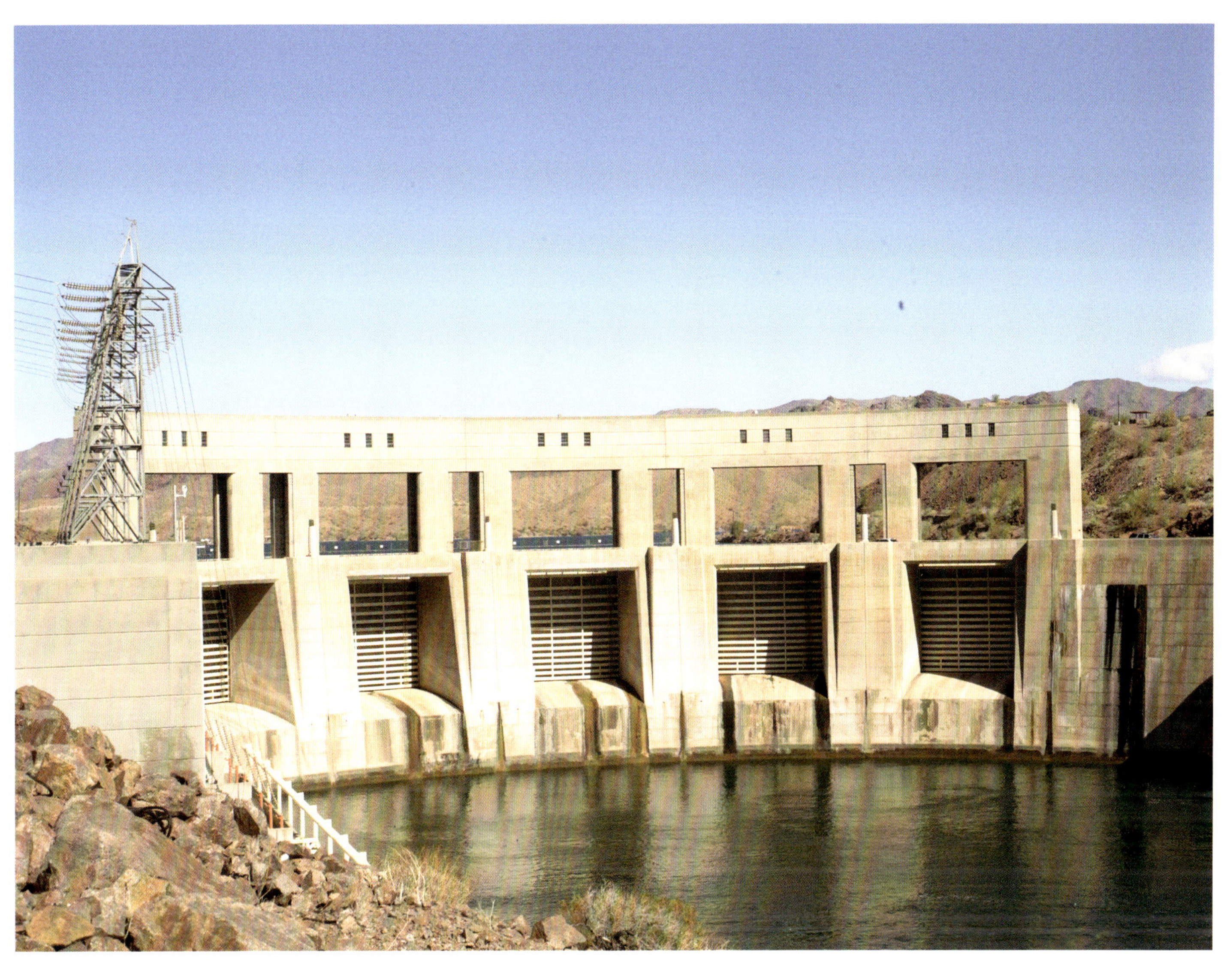

Parker Dam.

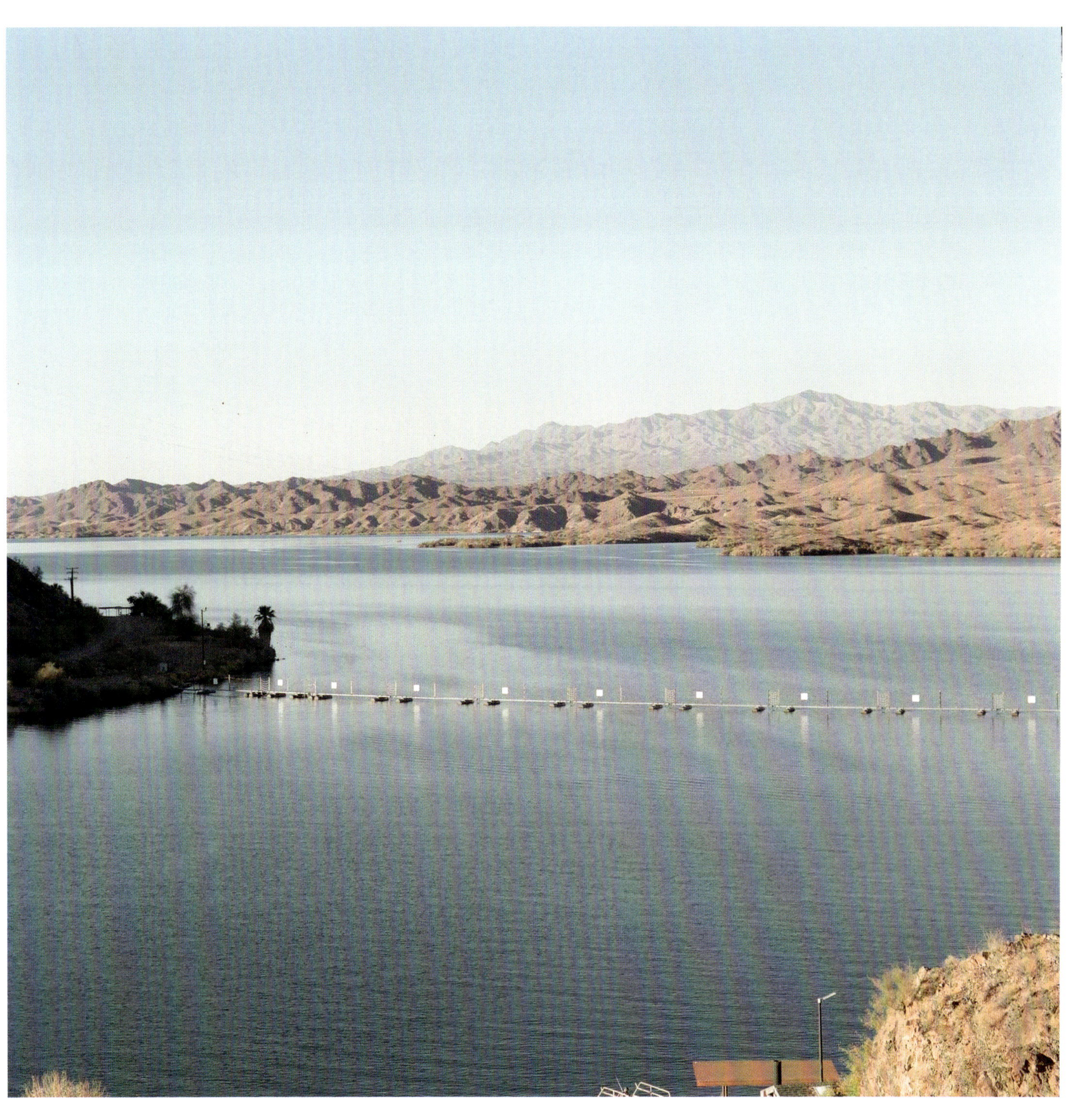

Lake Havasu
behind Parker Dam.

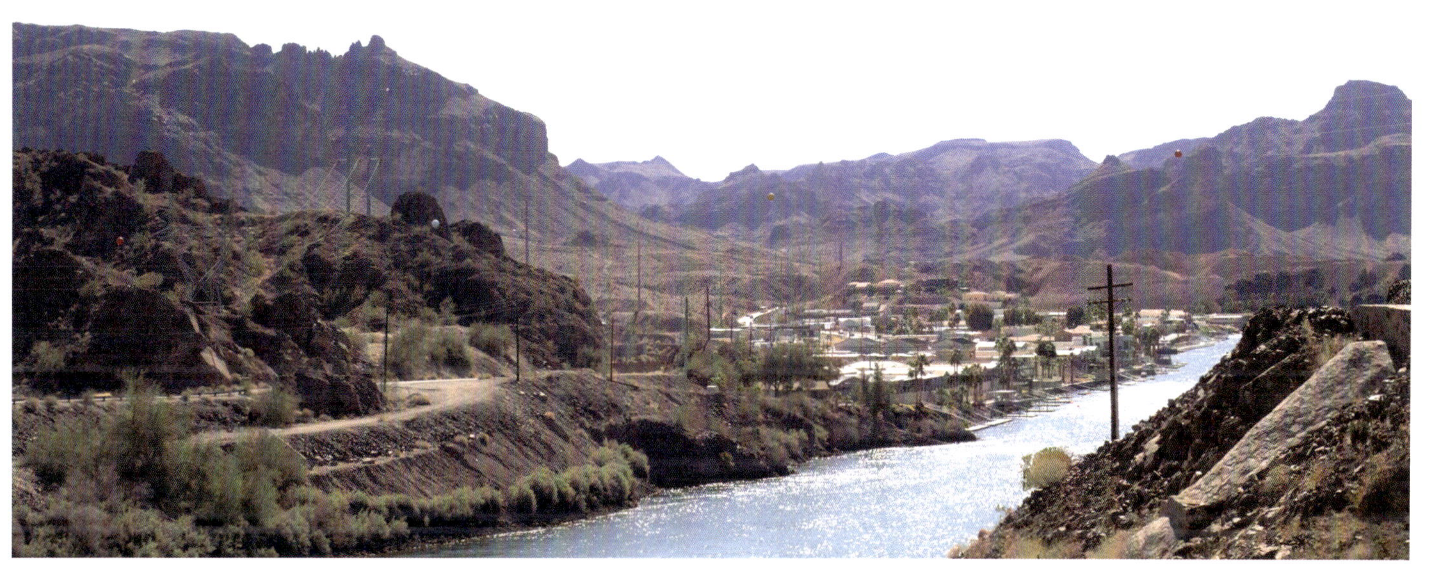

Parker Dam release
toward Laughlin,
Nevada.

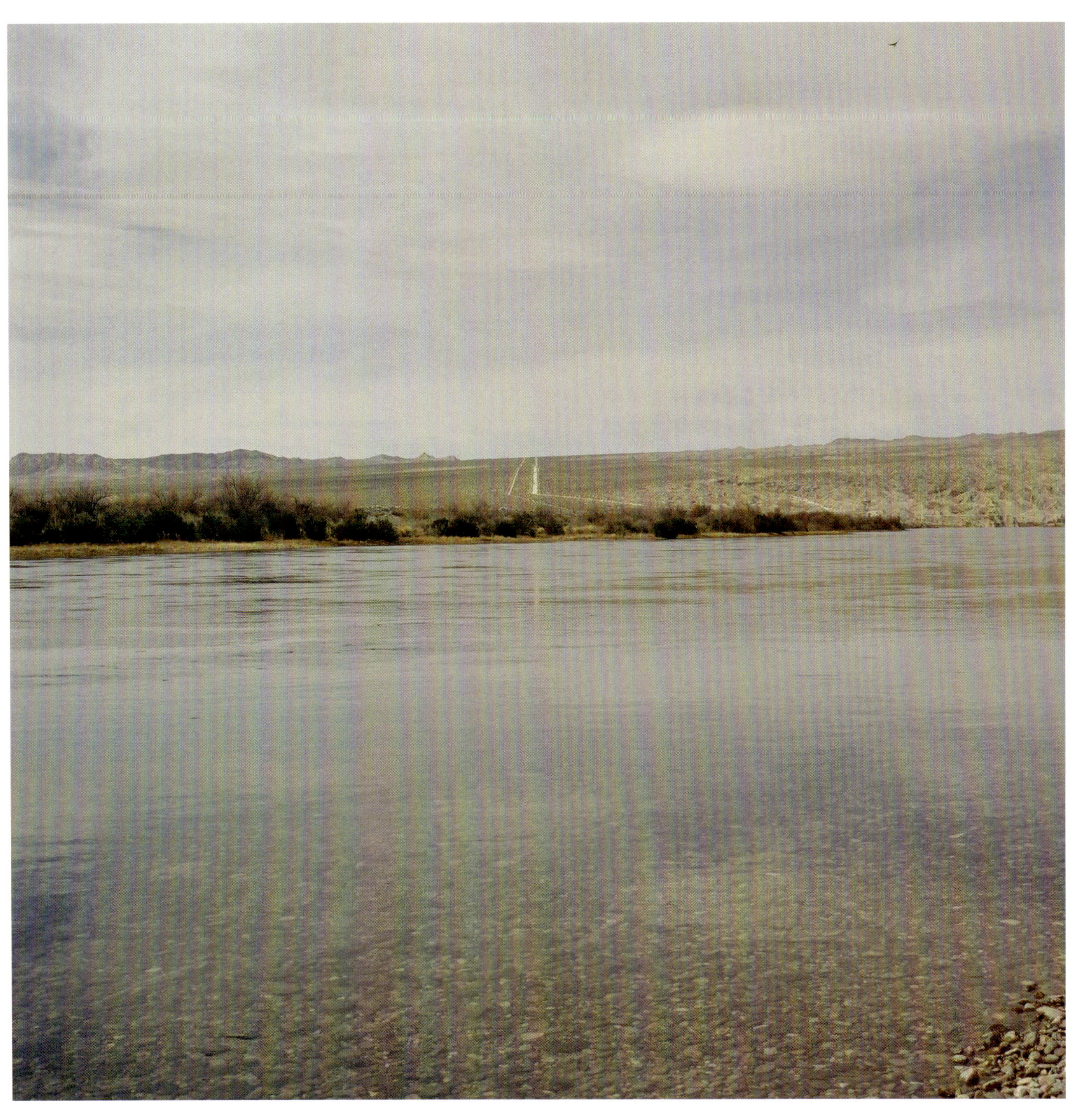

Colorado River
at Bullhead City,
Arizona.

HEADGATE ROCK DAM

Headgate Rock Dam was completed in 1941 and is operated by the Bureau of Indian Affairs. Lake Moovalya is created by this dam, providing irrigation water to Colorado River Indian Reservation farms sufficient to irrigate approximately 100,000 acres of land.

Headgate Rock Dam's power plant generates 76,651.9 mWh (megawatt-hours) per year.

On an annual basis, the water levels at Lake Moovalya are "drawn down" for maintenance on the canals operated by the Colorado River Indian Tribes. Releases from Parker Dam and flows below Headgate Rock Dam vary as necessary to meet downstream water-delivery requirements. The Bureau of Reclamation advises all river users that fluctuating river flows may conceal or create natural hazards, such as moving sandbars, gravel bars, unstable riverbanks, floating or submerged debris, or other unfamiliar obstacles. Caution is advised when on the river between Davis Dam and the Mexican border at San Luis, Arizona.

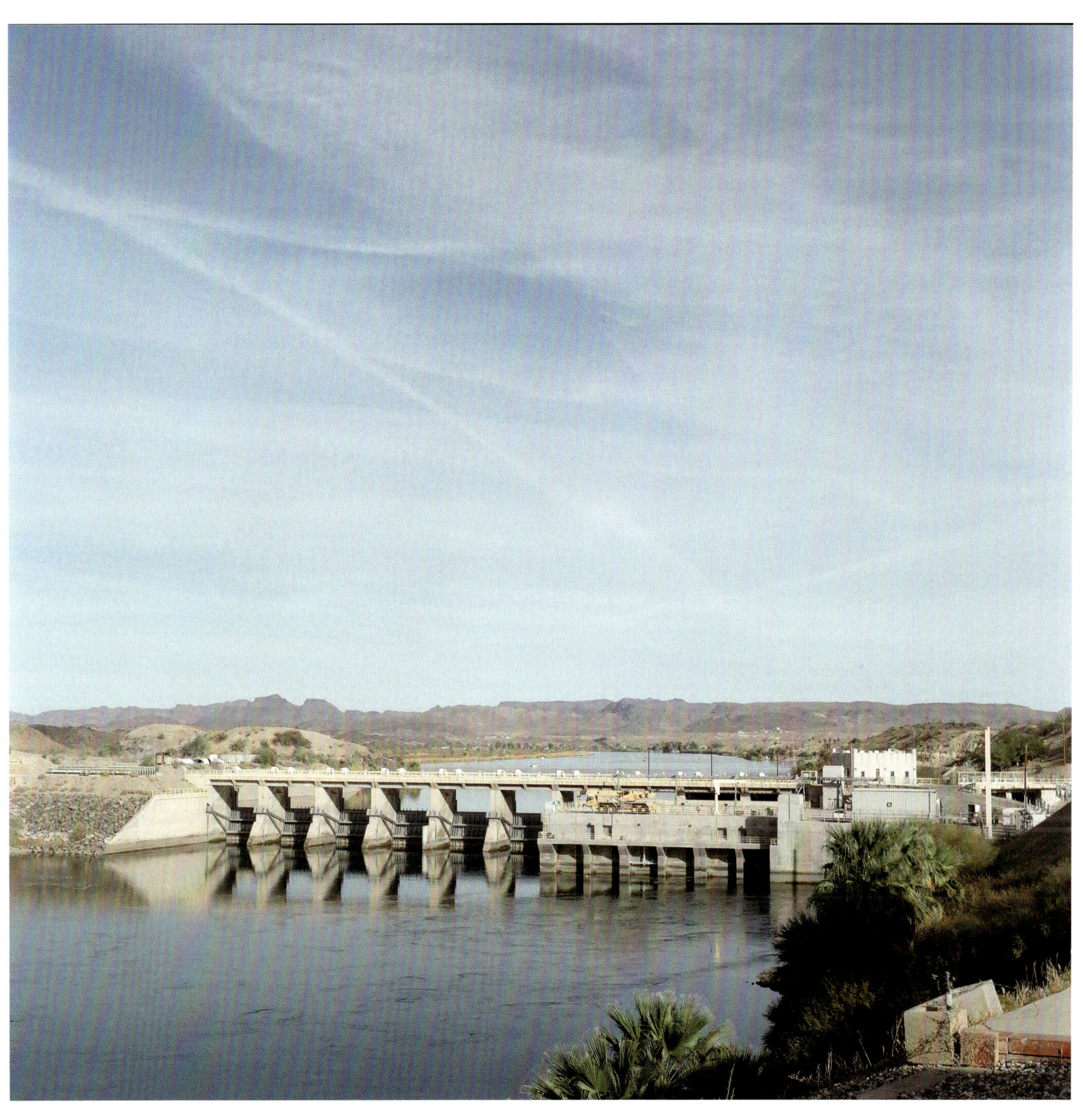

Headgate Rock
Dam, Arizona.

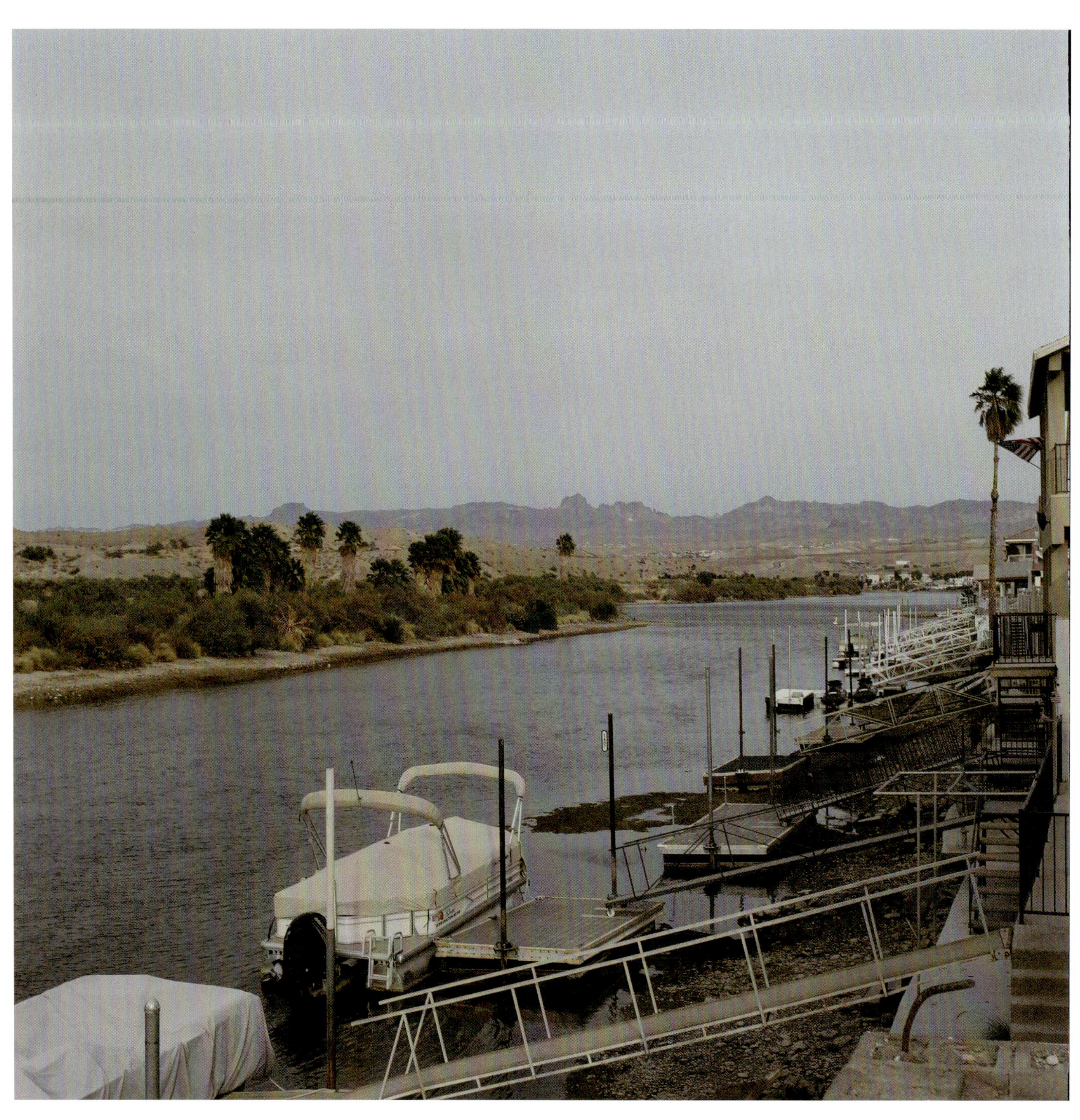

After release from
Headgate Rock
Dam.

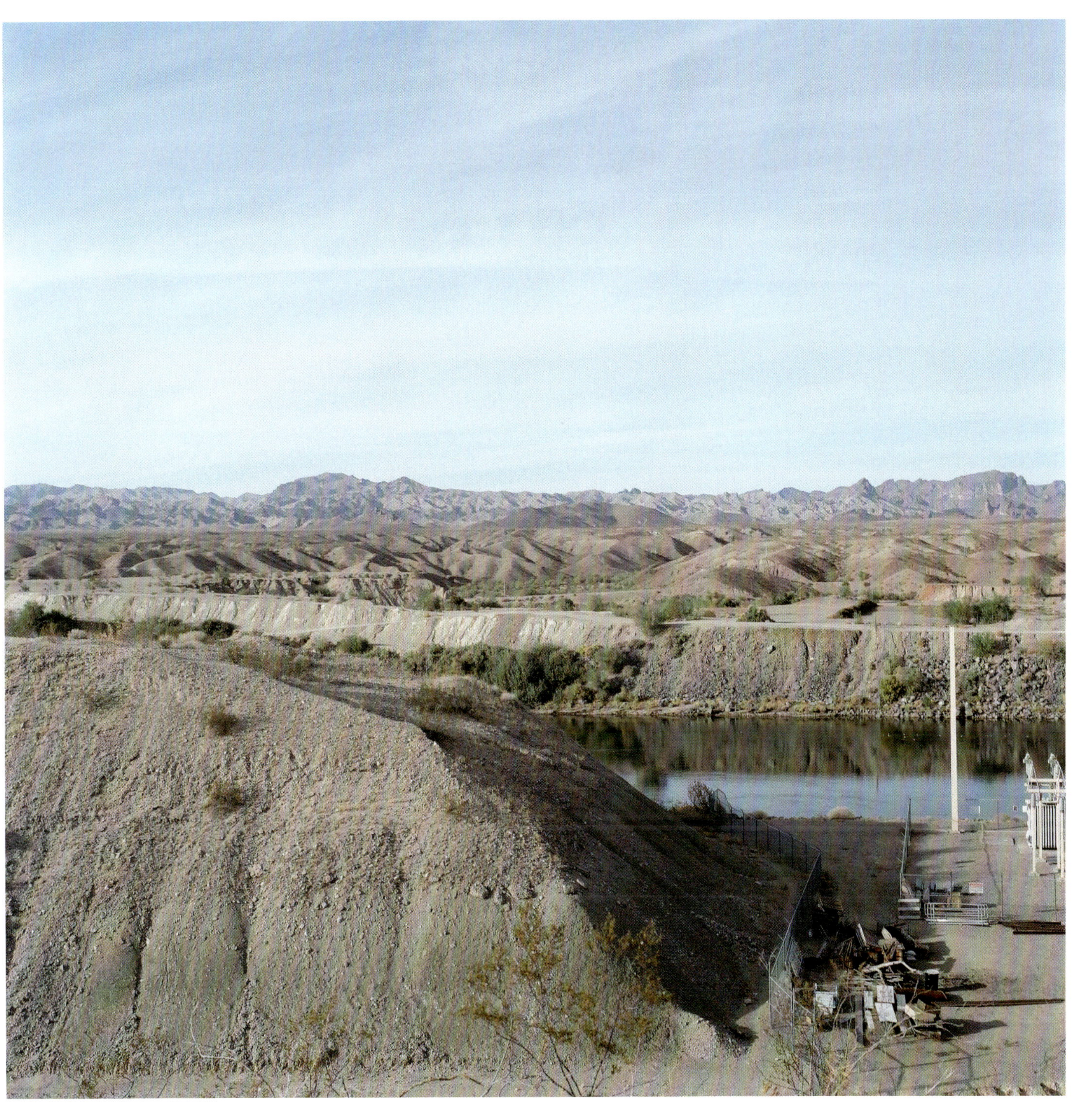

Downstream of
Headgate Rock
Dam.

PALO VERDE DIVERSION DAM

The Palo Verde Diversion Dam spans the Colorado River in La Paz County, Arizona, and Riverside County, California, approximately nine miles northeast of Blythe. The dam is earthen and rockfill, built solely to divert water into irrigation canals serving the Palo Verde Irrigation District. The dam raises the water level of the river, which is necessary because the upstream Hoover and Davis dams blocked sediment, causing significant degradation of the riverbed that ultimately hampered water diversion.

The dam diverts about 1,800 cubic feet of water per second to irrigate 121,000 acres of the Palo Verde Valley and mesa lands on the west side of the Colorado River in California. Water is delivered via a thirty-mile-long levee system and twenty-one-mile-long drain.

Construction of the dam, which began in 1956 and ended in 1958, was authorized by the Bureau of Reclamation. Operational control and maintenance of the dam and diversion works was turned over to the Palo Verde Irrigation District in 1957, with operation and maintenance of the levees and drain transferred to the Bureau of Indian Affairs in 1958.

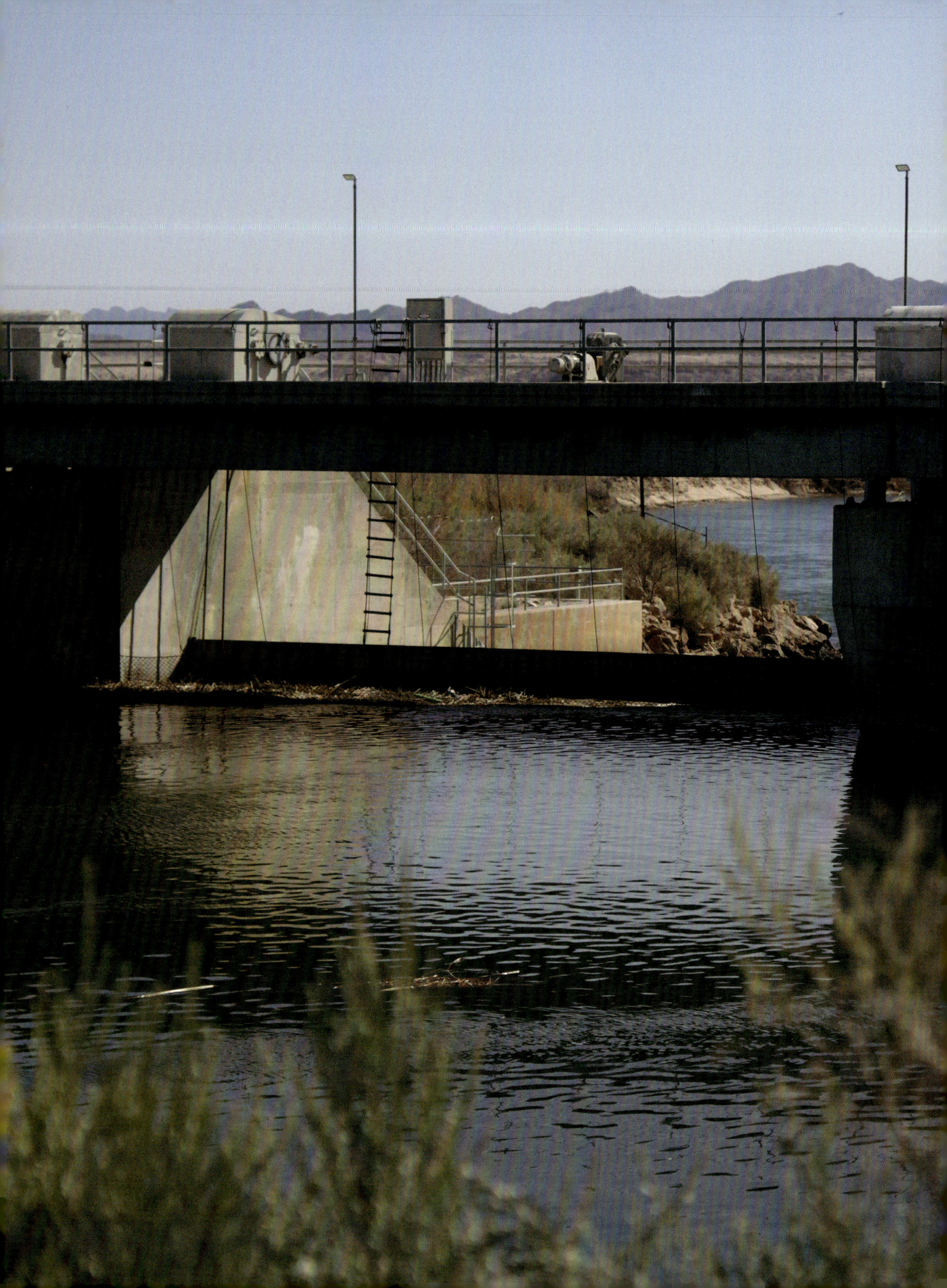

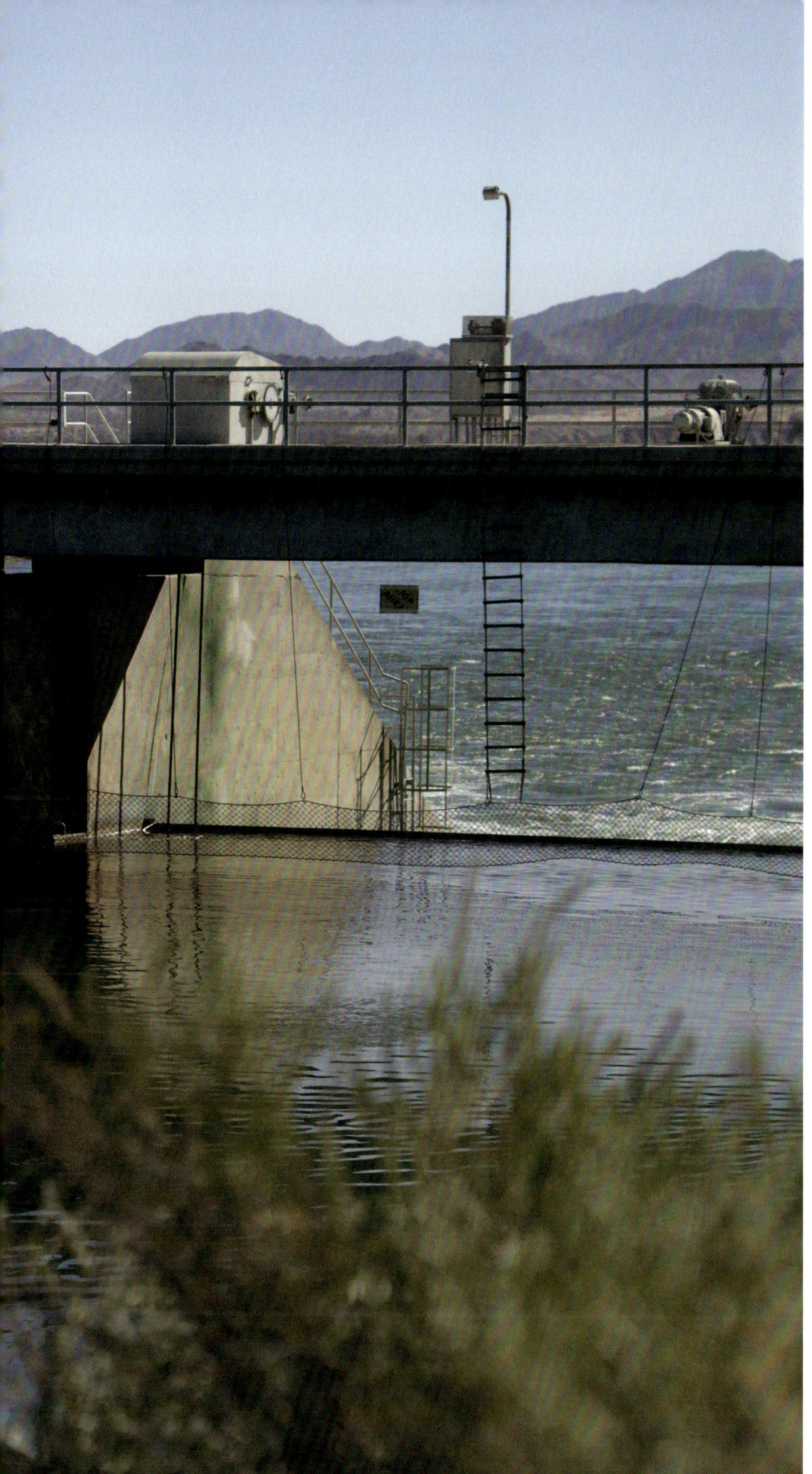

Palo Verde
Diversion Dam,
California and
Arizona.

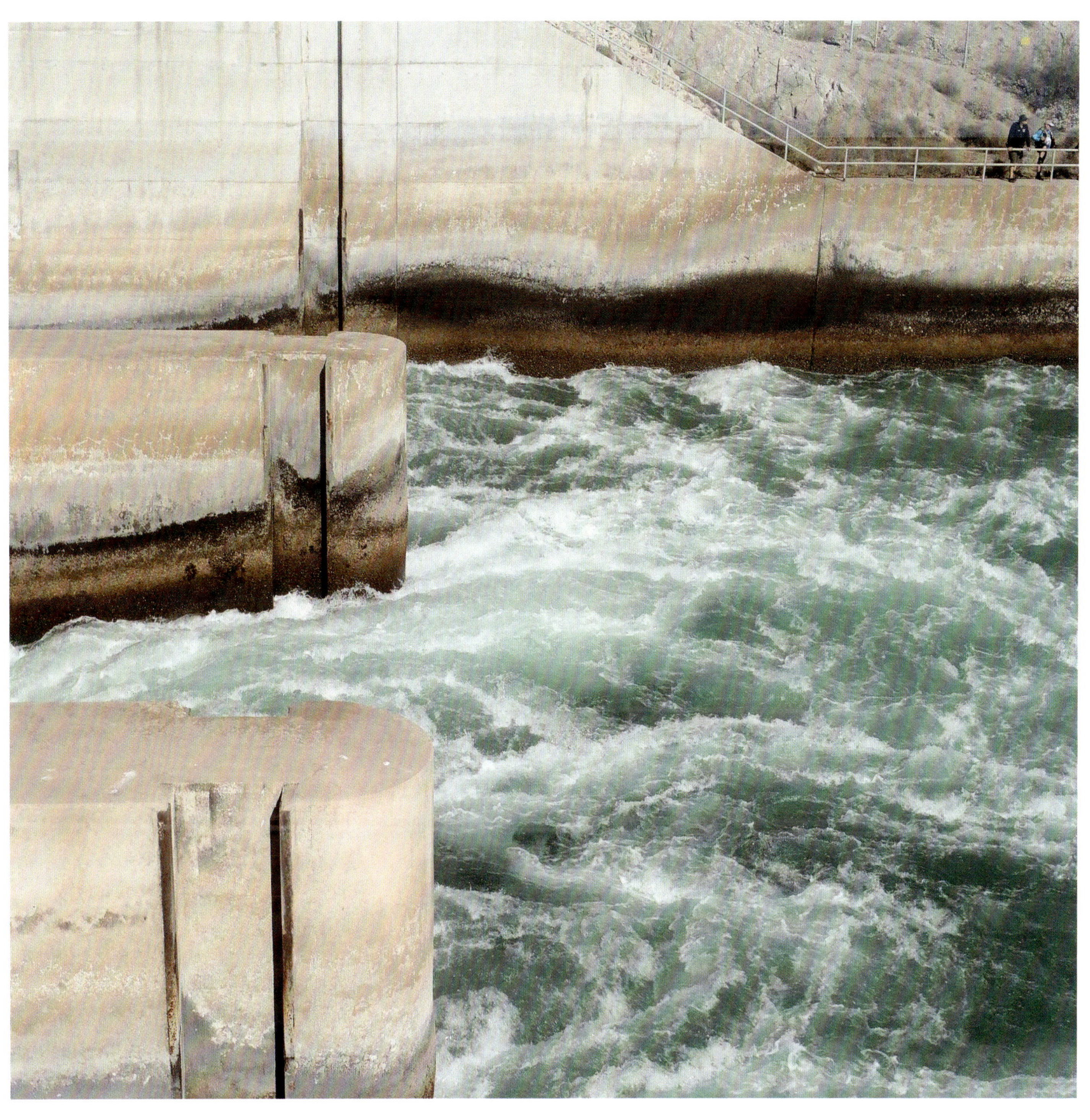

Flow through Palo
Verde Diversion
Dam.

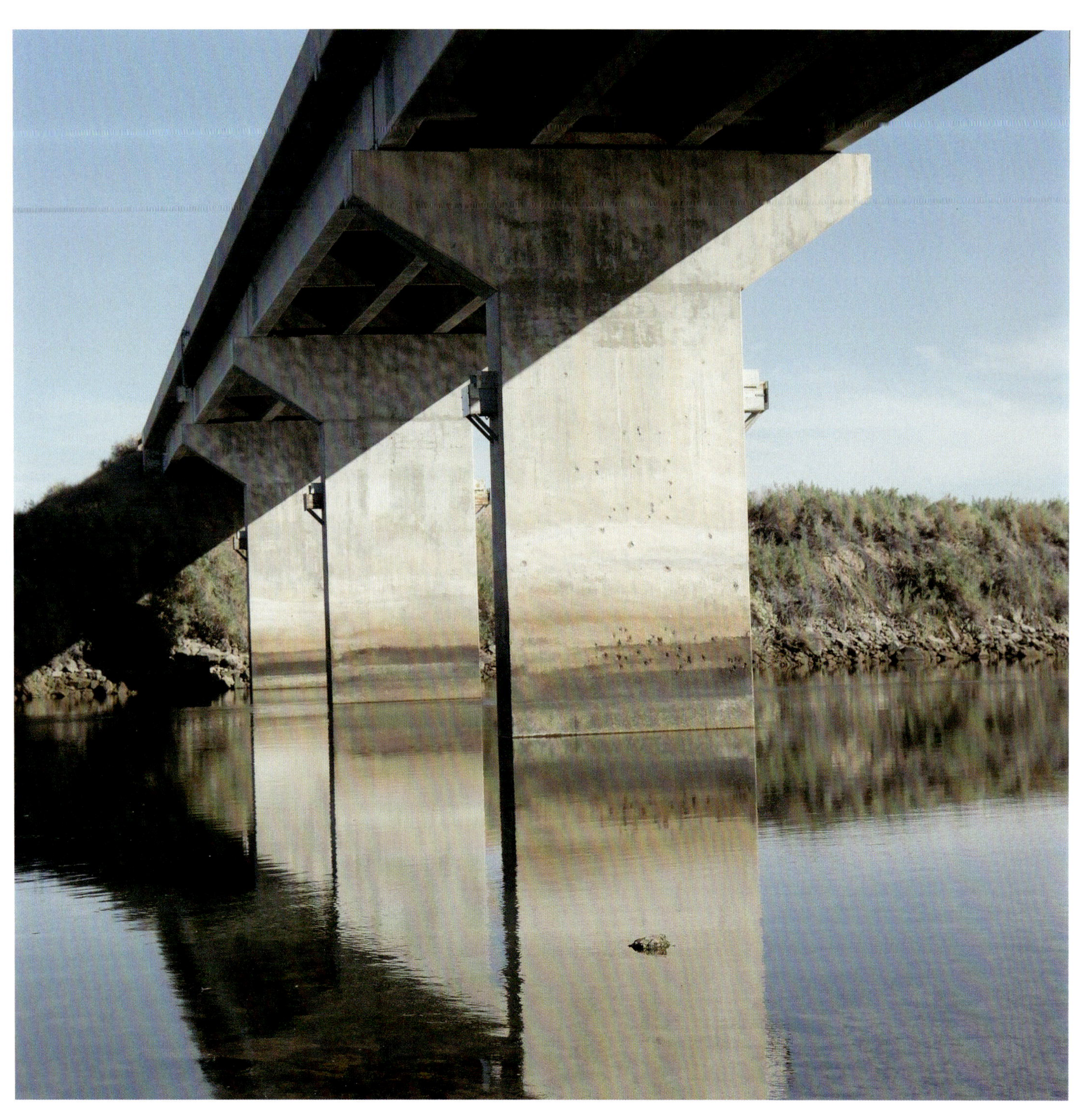

Colorado River
downstream of
Palo Verde after
diversion.

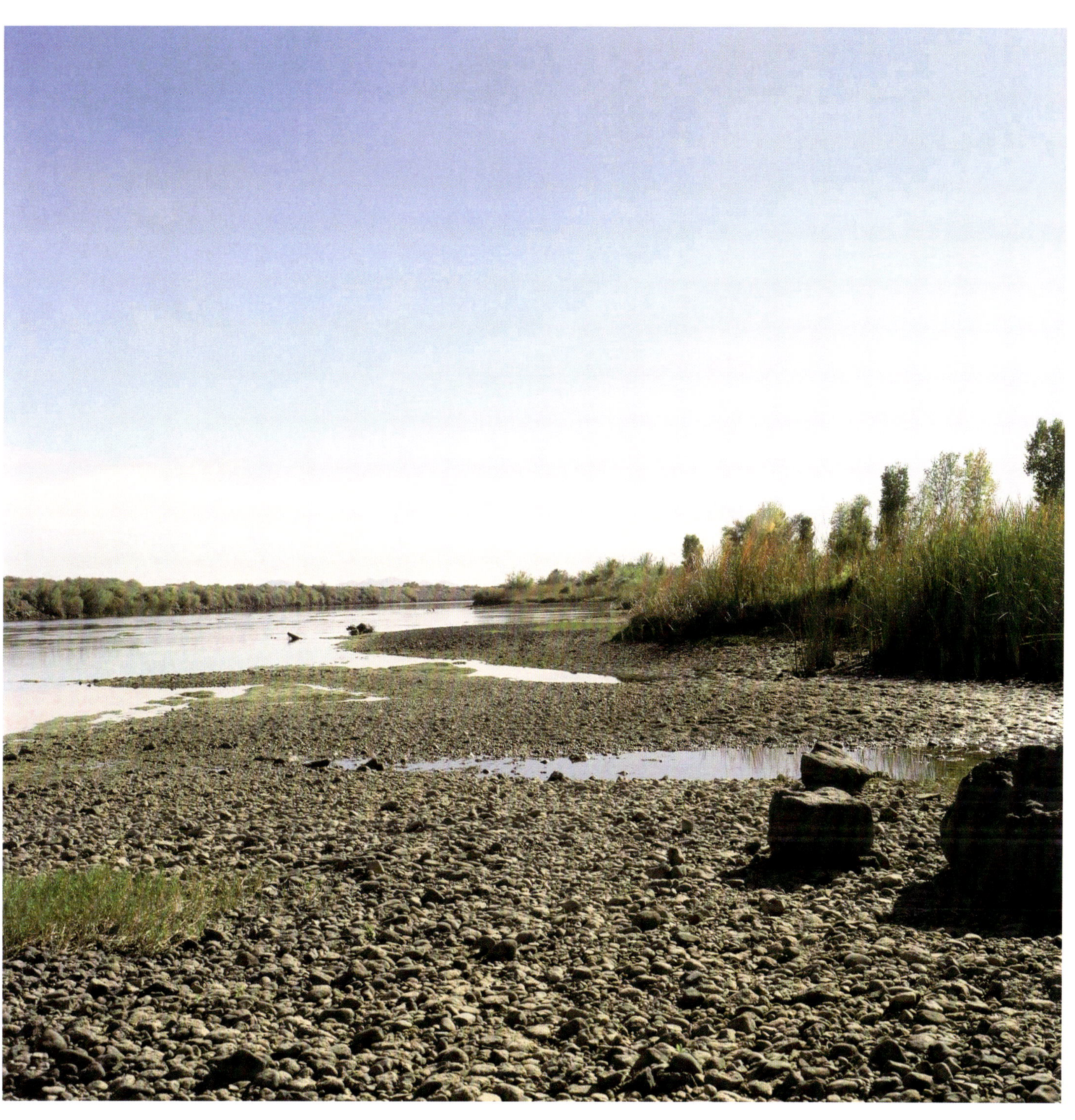

The river
downstream of
Palo Verde after
diversion.

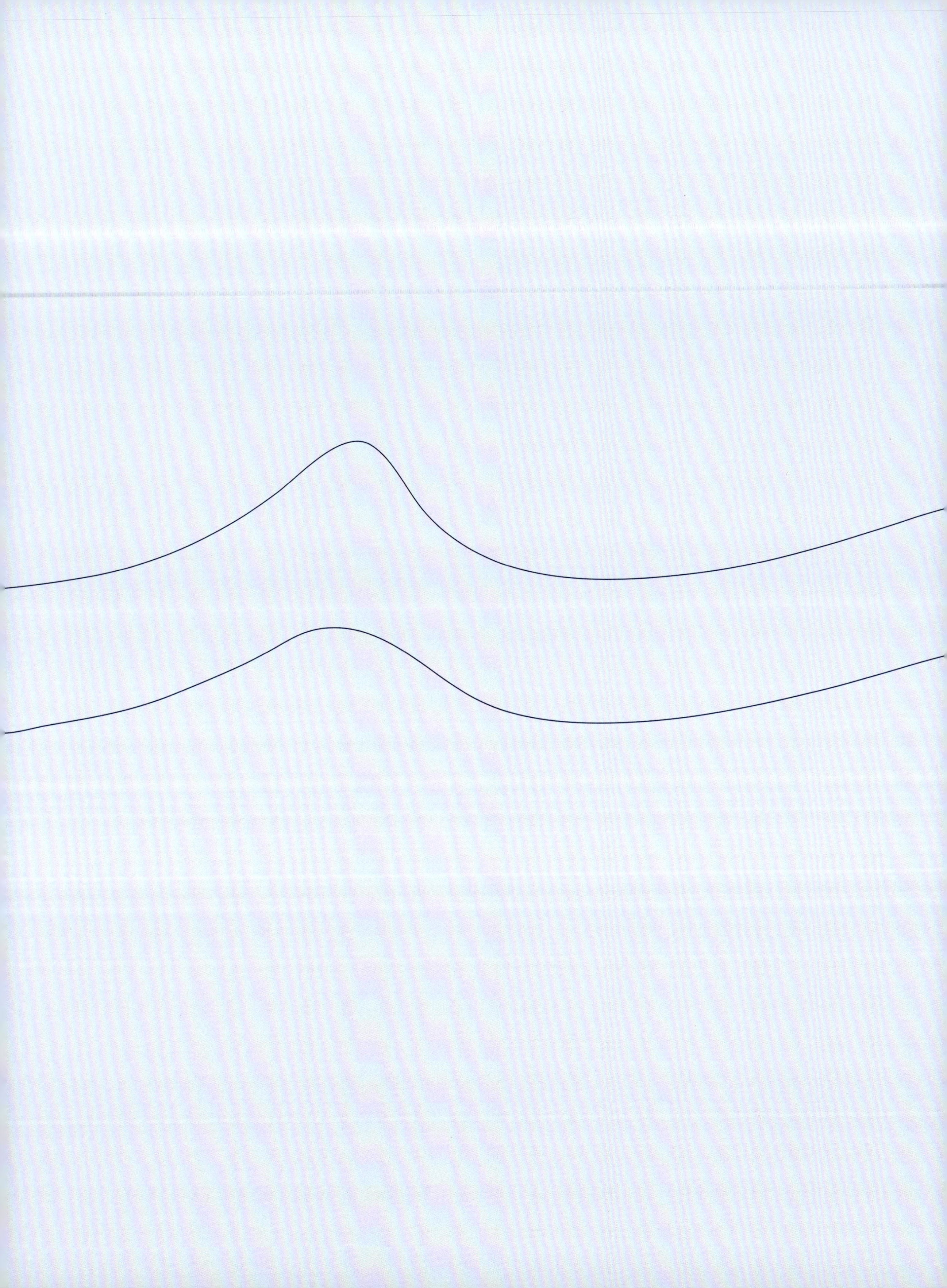

IMPERIAL DIVERSION DAM

The Imperial Diversion Dam and Desilting Works straddles the Colorado River on the California-Arizona border, eighteen miles northeast of Yuma, Arizona. The purpose of the dam is to raise the water surface twenty-five feet and provide controlled gravity flow of water into the All-American and Gila Gravity Main Canals, serving southeastern California, Arizona, and Mexico. The Imperial Diversion Dam has the capacity to divert 15,555 cfs to the All-American Canal, and 2,200 cfs to the Gila Canal.

The desilting works remove most of the sediment carried by the Colorado River to prevent clogging of the canals and subsequent extensive maintenance. Removed sediment is returned to the river by means of six sludge-return pipes that are deposited into the California Sluiceway.

Imperial Reservoir, impounded by the dam, has little storage capacity. Because it was shallow, the original storage space filled with silt and sand. The reservoir now consists of a shallow lake with channels to the All-American Canal and Gila Headworks.

Construction of the Imperial Diversion Dam and desilting works began in 1935 and was completed in 1938 under the authorization of the Boulder Canyon Project Act of 1928.

The dam is currently operated by the Imperial Irrigation District.

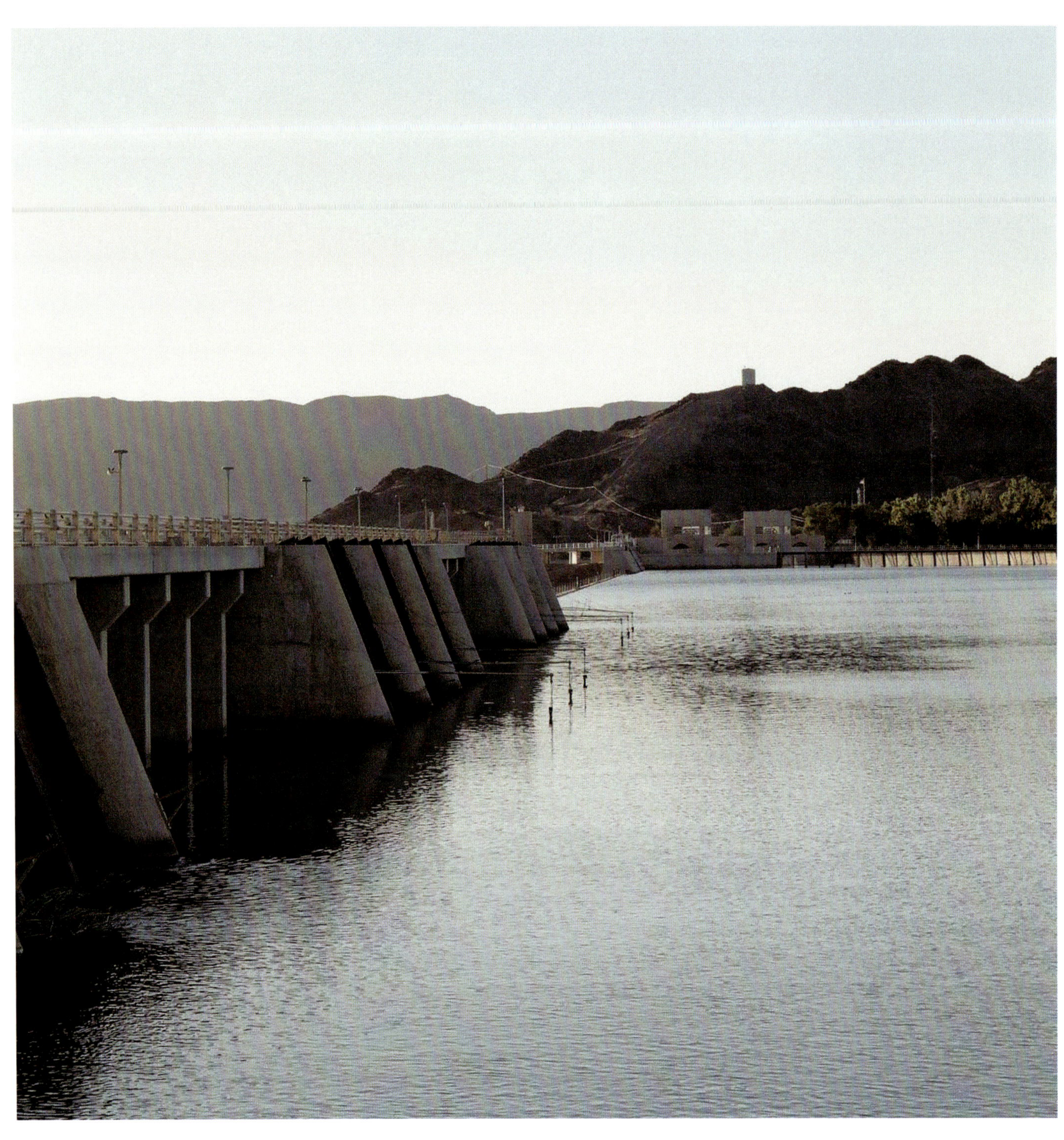

Imperial Dam,
California and
Arizona.

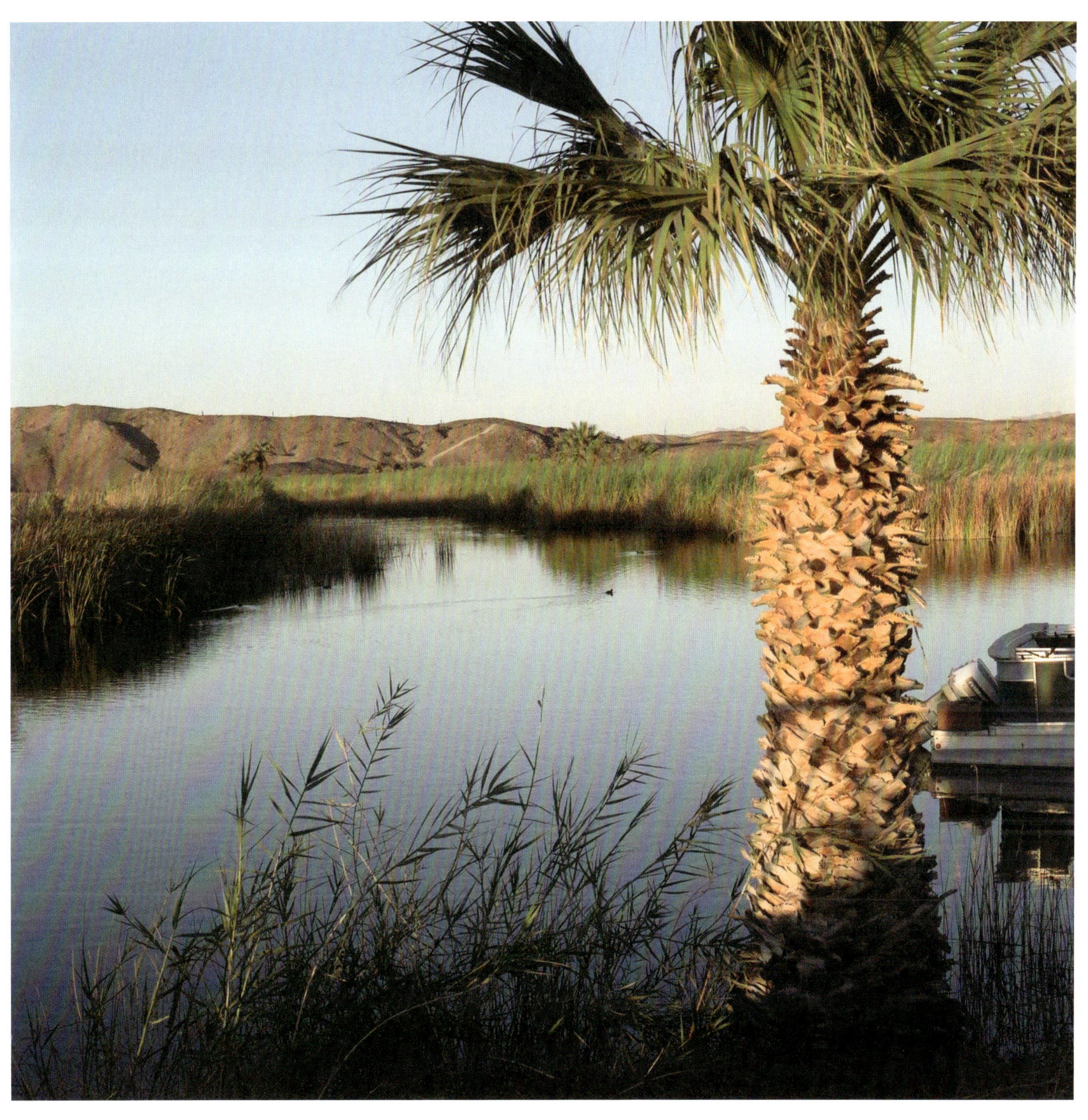

Impounded
Colorado River
behind Imperial
Dam.

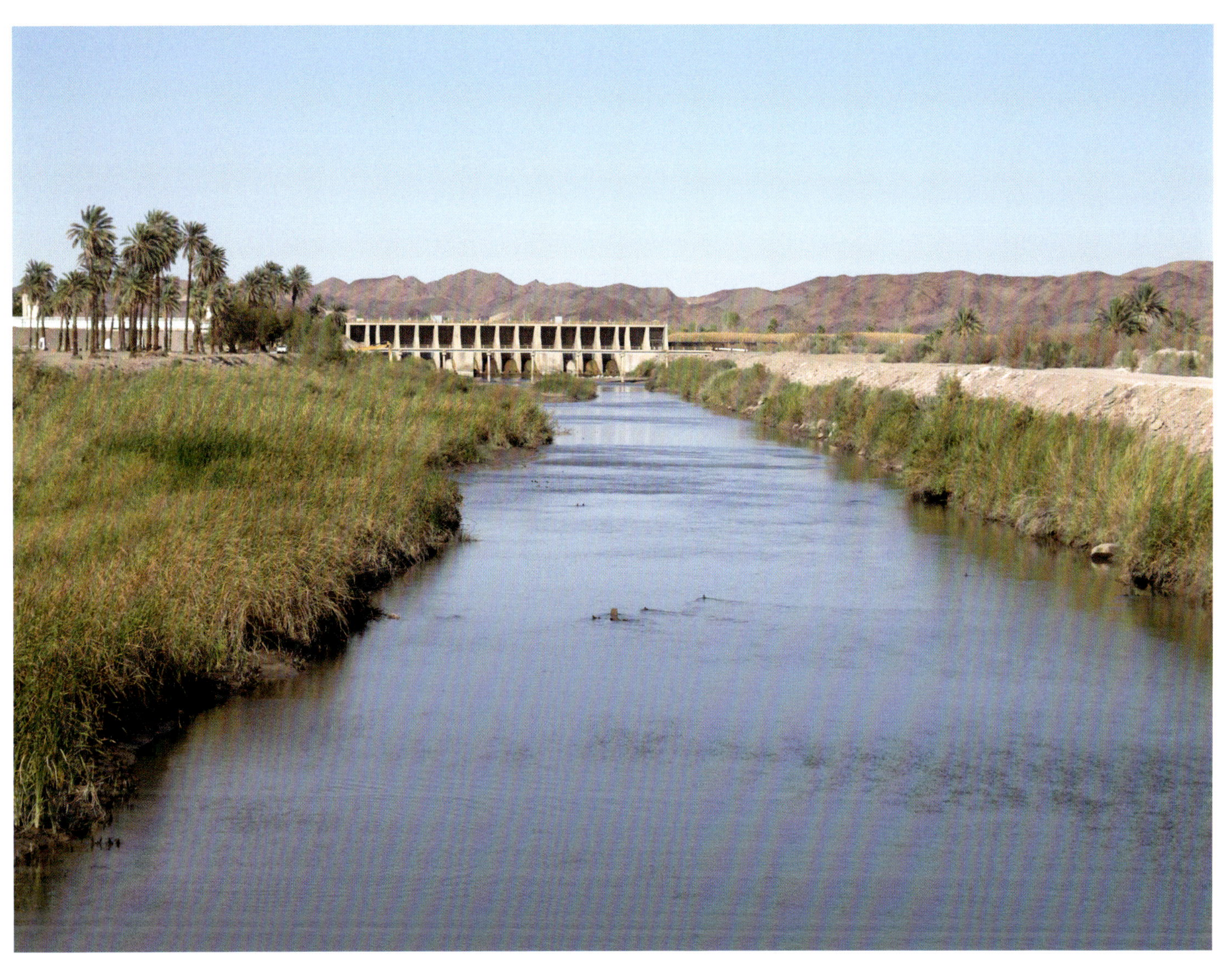

Colorado River
release from
Imperial Dam.

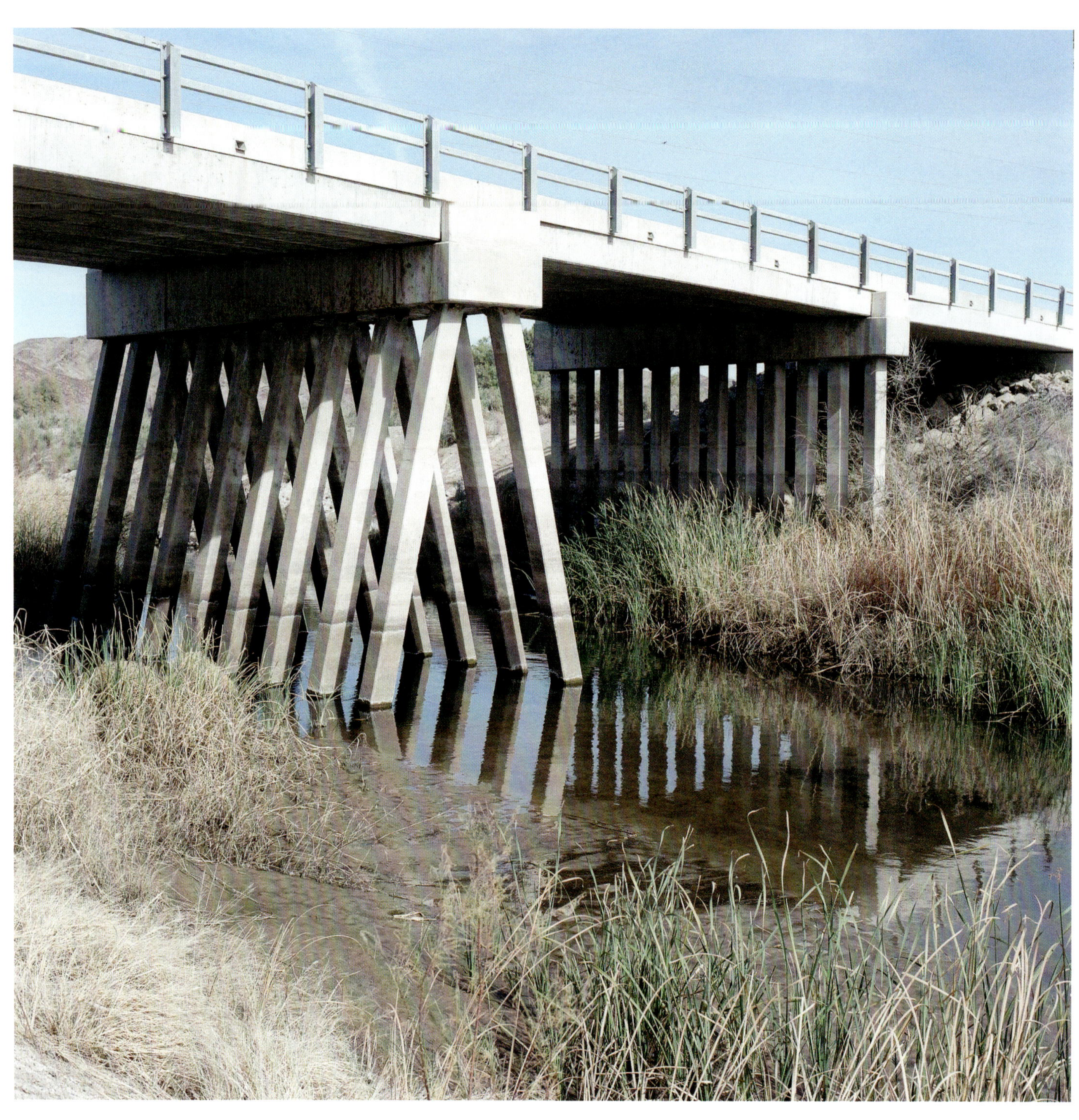

The river release from
Imperial on way to
Laguna Dam.

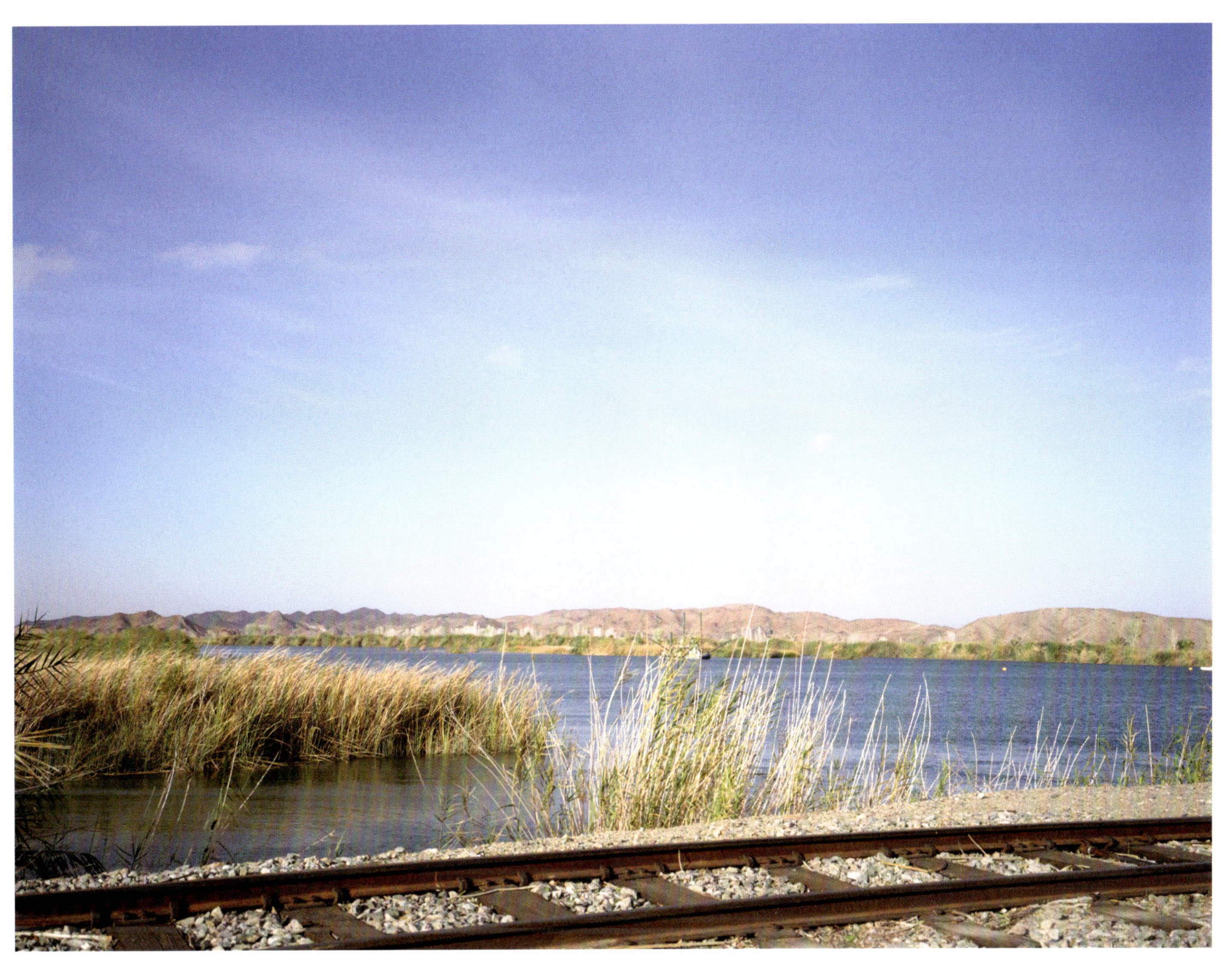

Imperial Reservoir
behind Imperial
Dam.

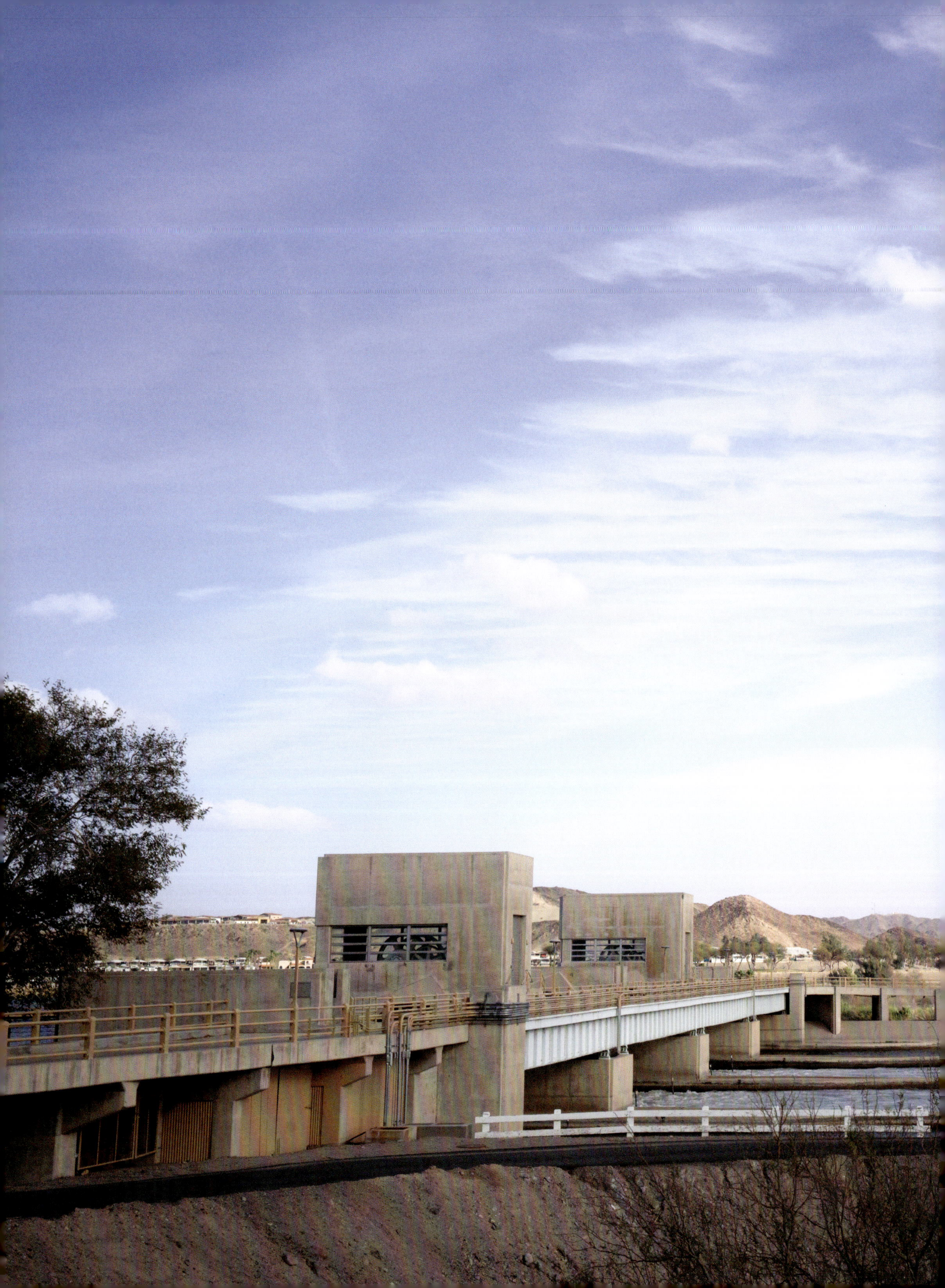

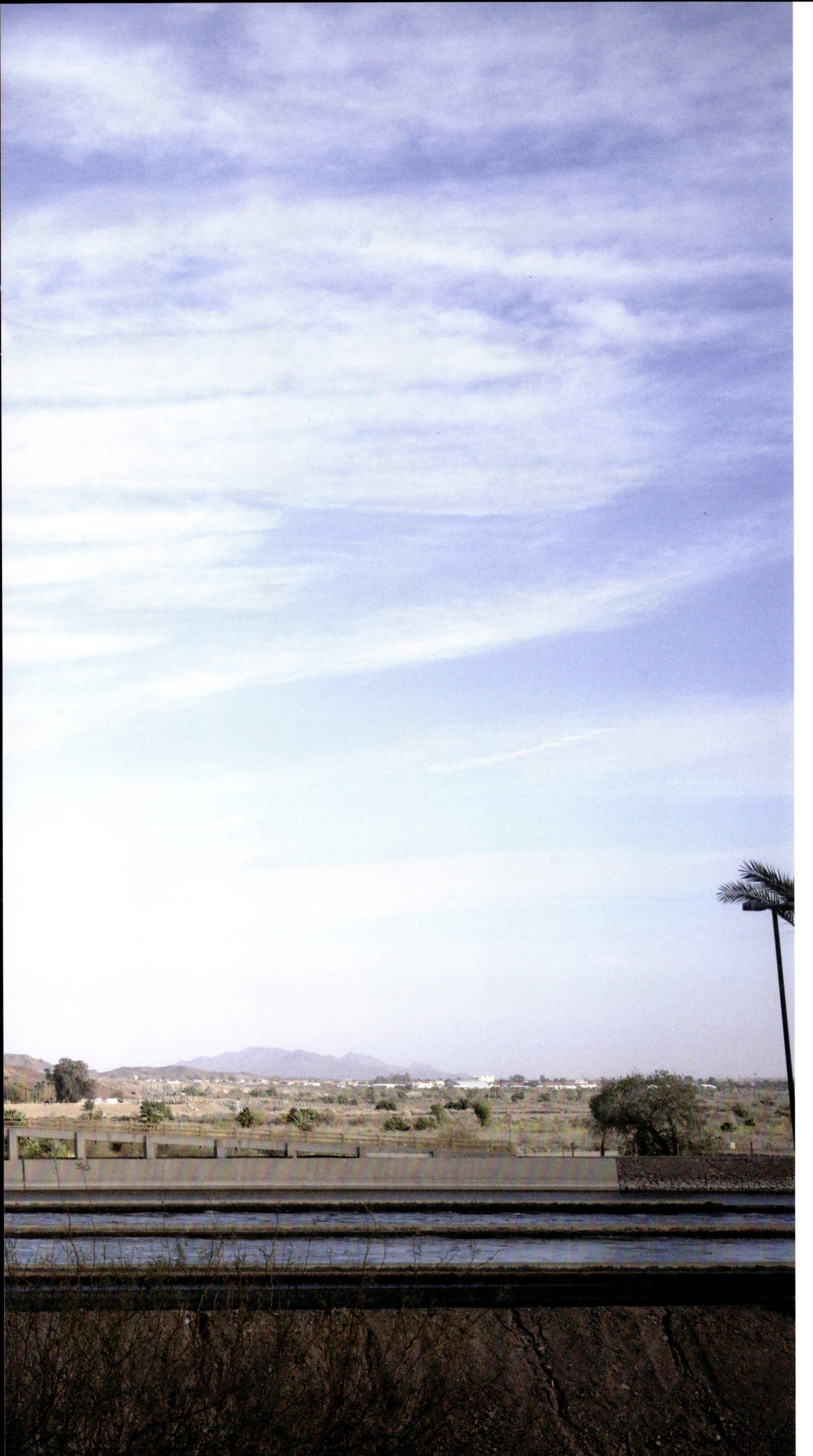

Imperial Dam Silt
Works.

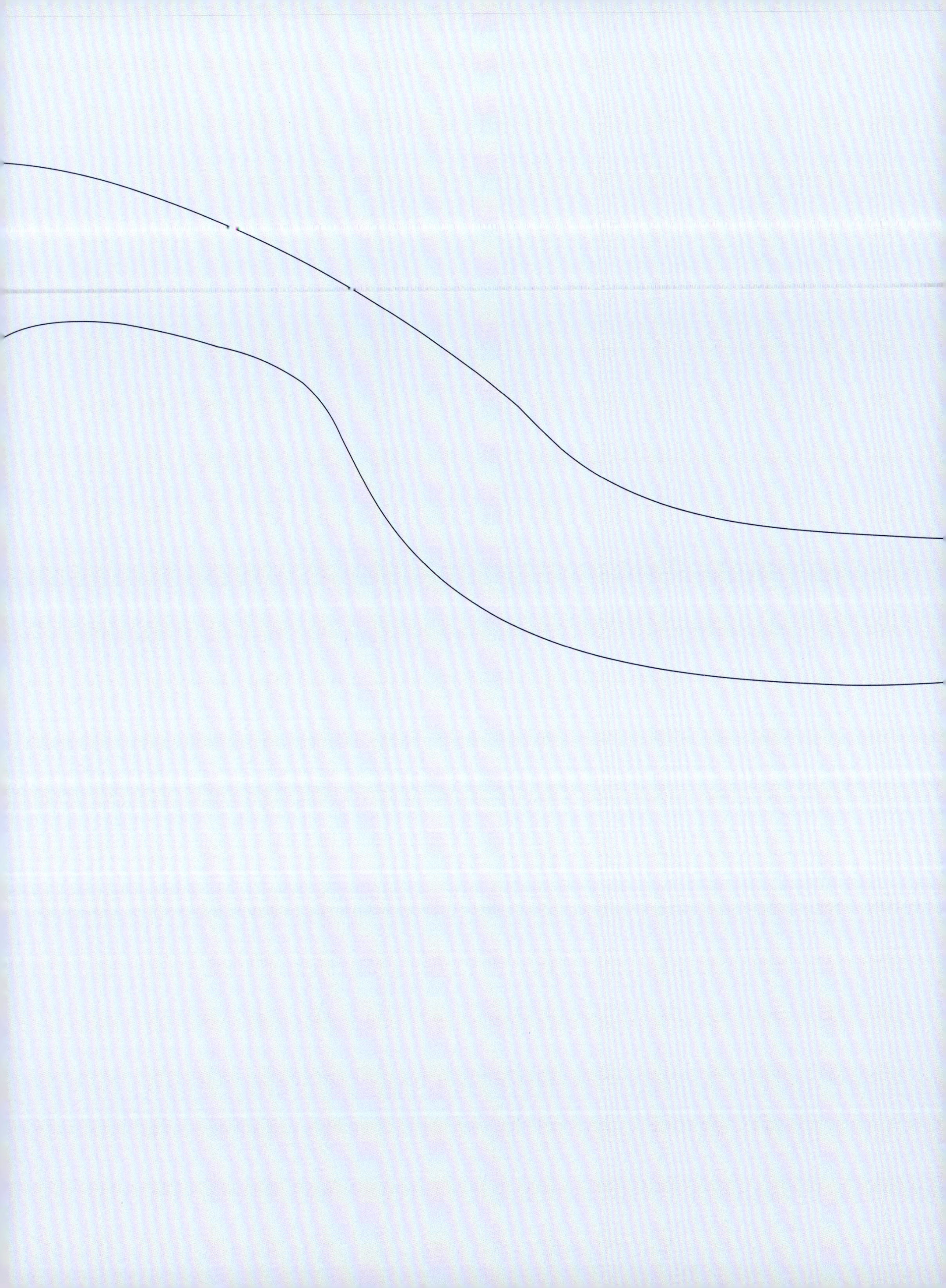

SENATOR WASH DAM

Senator Wash Dam and Reservoir, an off-stream pumping facility, is located about eighteen miles northeast of Yuma, Arizona, on the California side of the Colorado River two miles upstream from Imperial Dam and at the river end of Senator Wash. The purpose of this strategic off-stream retention reservoir is to improve water scheduling of the Colorado River. This is accomplished by storing part of the river flow upstream of Imperial Dam when it is not needed, and releasing it to the river for downstream use when needed.

The facility pumps water to storage when surplus is available and generates power as it's released back to the river to meet unforeseen demands. This facility was designed for use only in case of emergencies and is supplied normally by regulation of releases at Parker Dam.

Senator Wash Reservoir has a capacity of 14,000 acre-feet, but generally is kept at only 50% full to allow fill or draw as the river flow dictates. Due to seepage issues of the dam's levees, water elevation was restricted to 240 feet above sea level, which was an 11-foot decrease.

Senator Wash Dam is operated by the Imperial Irrigation District.

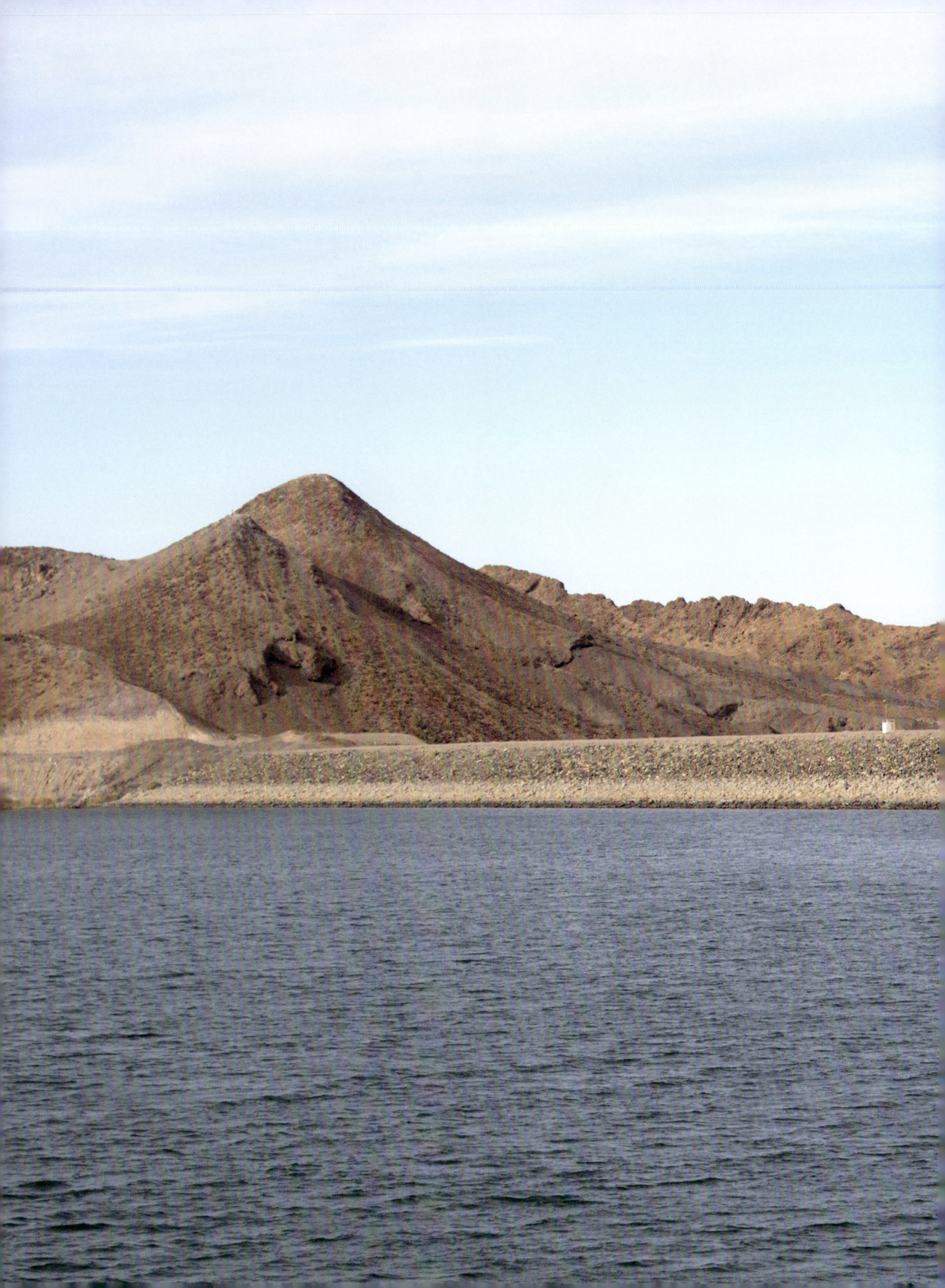

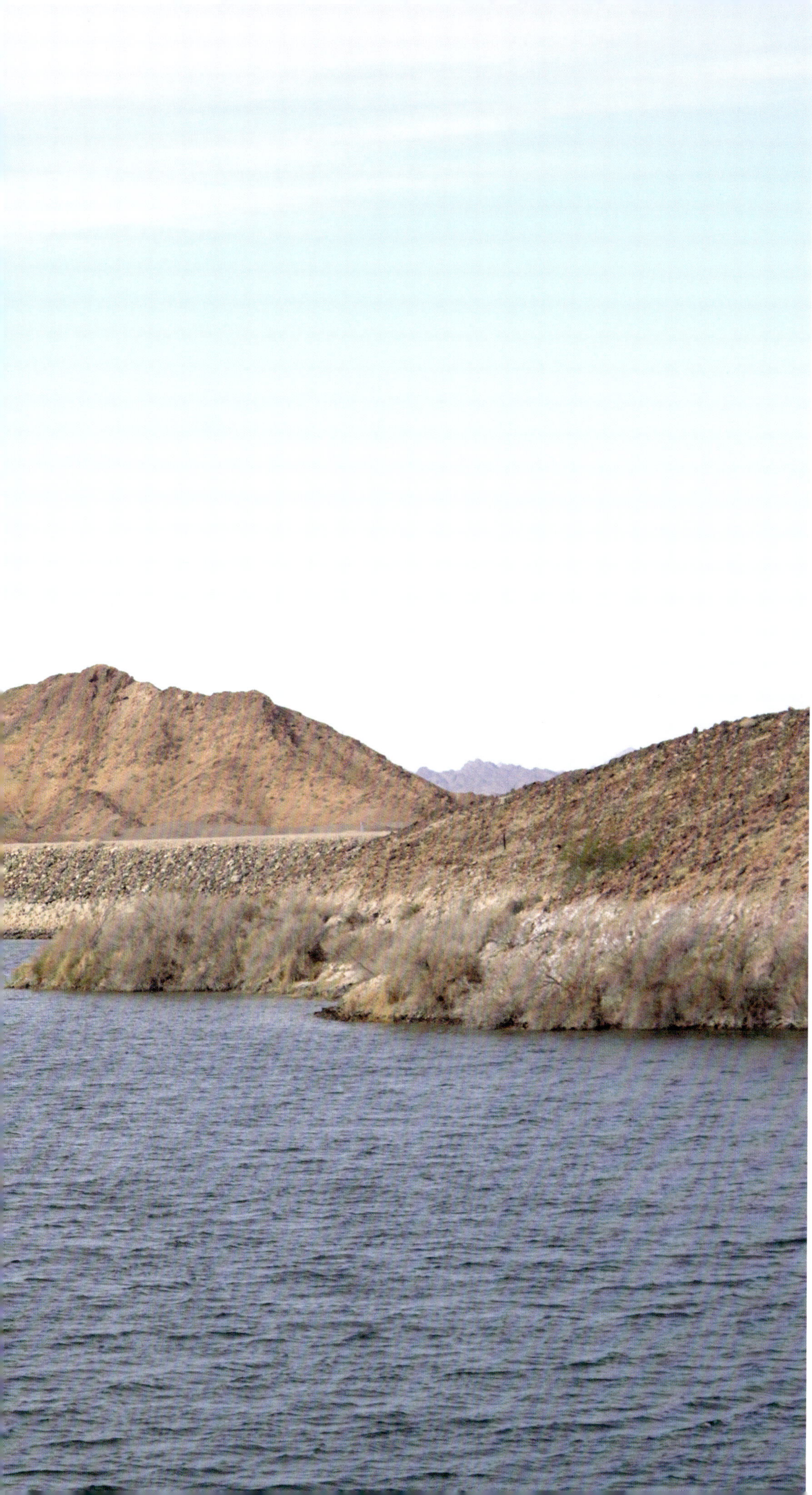

Senator Wash Dam,
California.

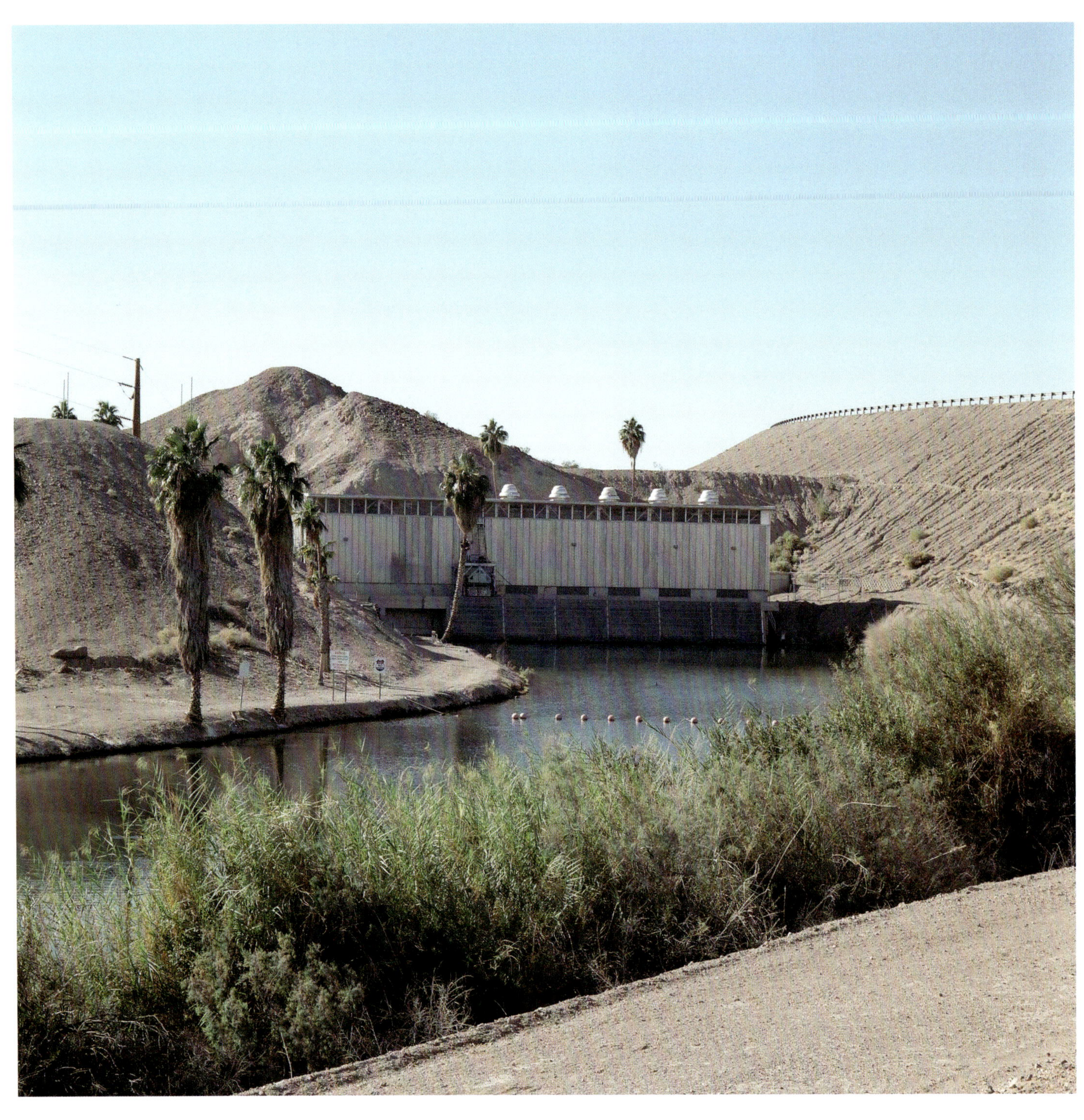

Senator Wash Dam
to reservoir.

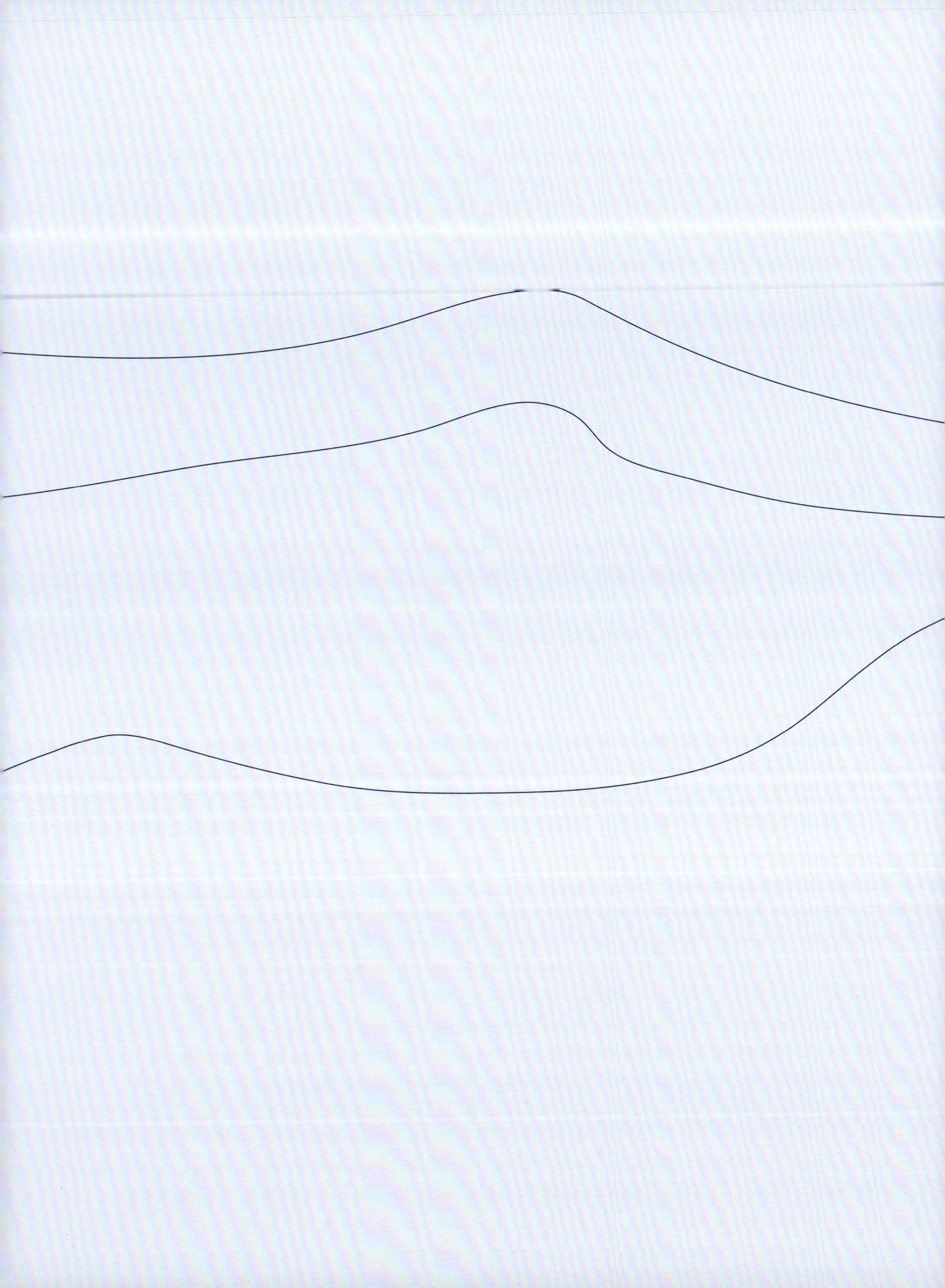

LAGUNA DIVERSION DAM

Work on the Laguna Dam began on July 19, 1905, making Laguna the oldest dam in the Colorado River dam system.

Laguna Diversion Dam, an original feature of the Yuma Project, is located on the Colorado River thirteen miles northeast of Yuma, Arizona, and about five miles downstream from Imperial Dam. Its original purpose was to divert Colorado River water to the Yuma Project area.

Since 1948, irrigation water for the project has been diverted at Imperial Dam. Laguna Dam now serves as a regulating structure for sluicing flows and for downstream toe protection for Imperial Dam.

Laguna Diversion Dam is operated by the Imperial Irrigation District.

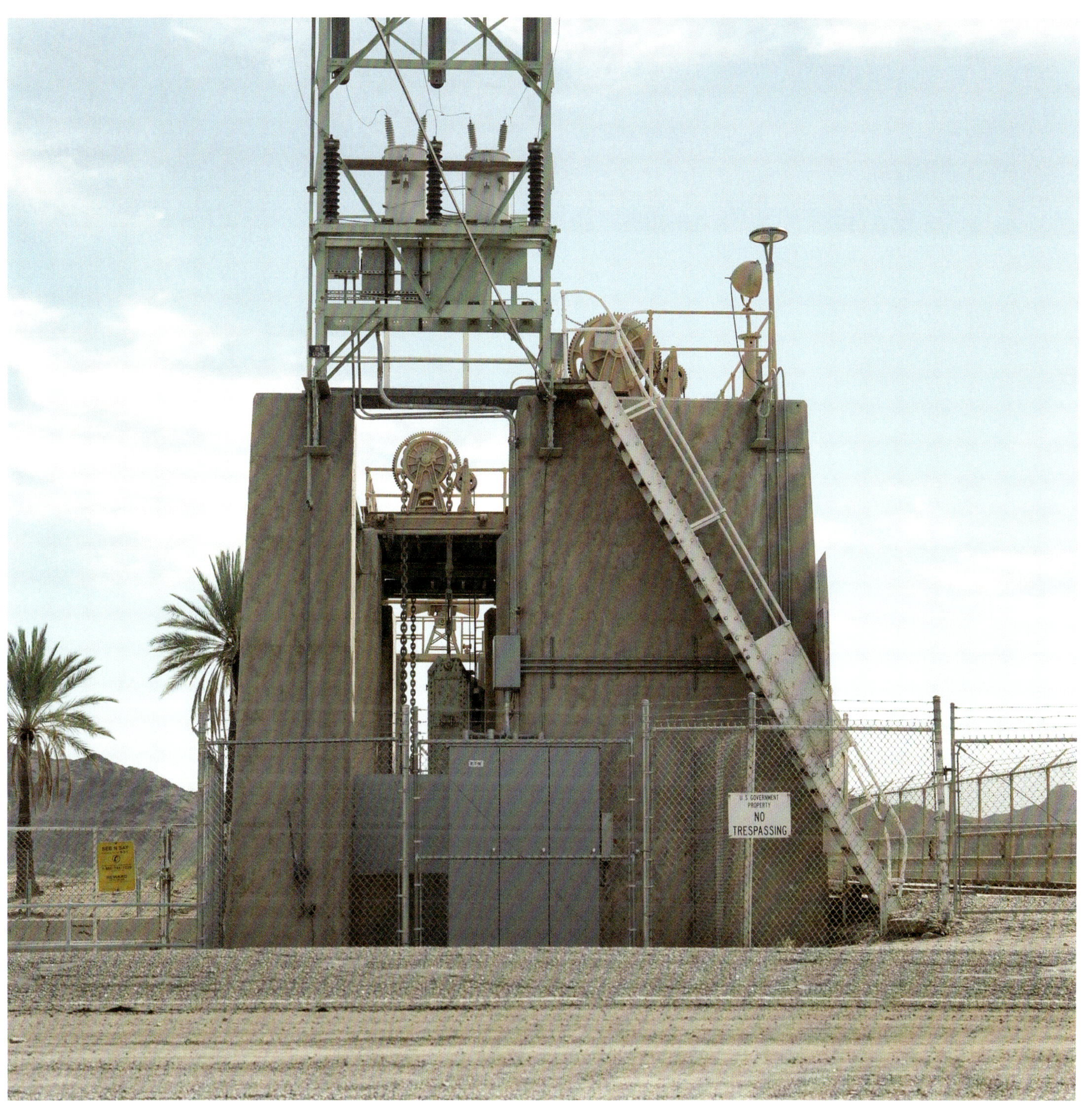

Laguna Diversion
Dam, California and
Arizona.

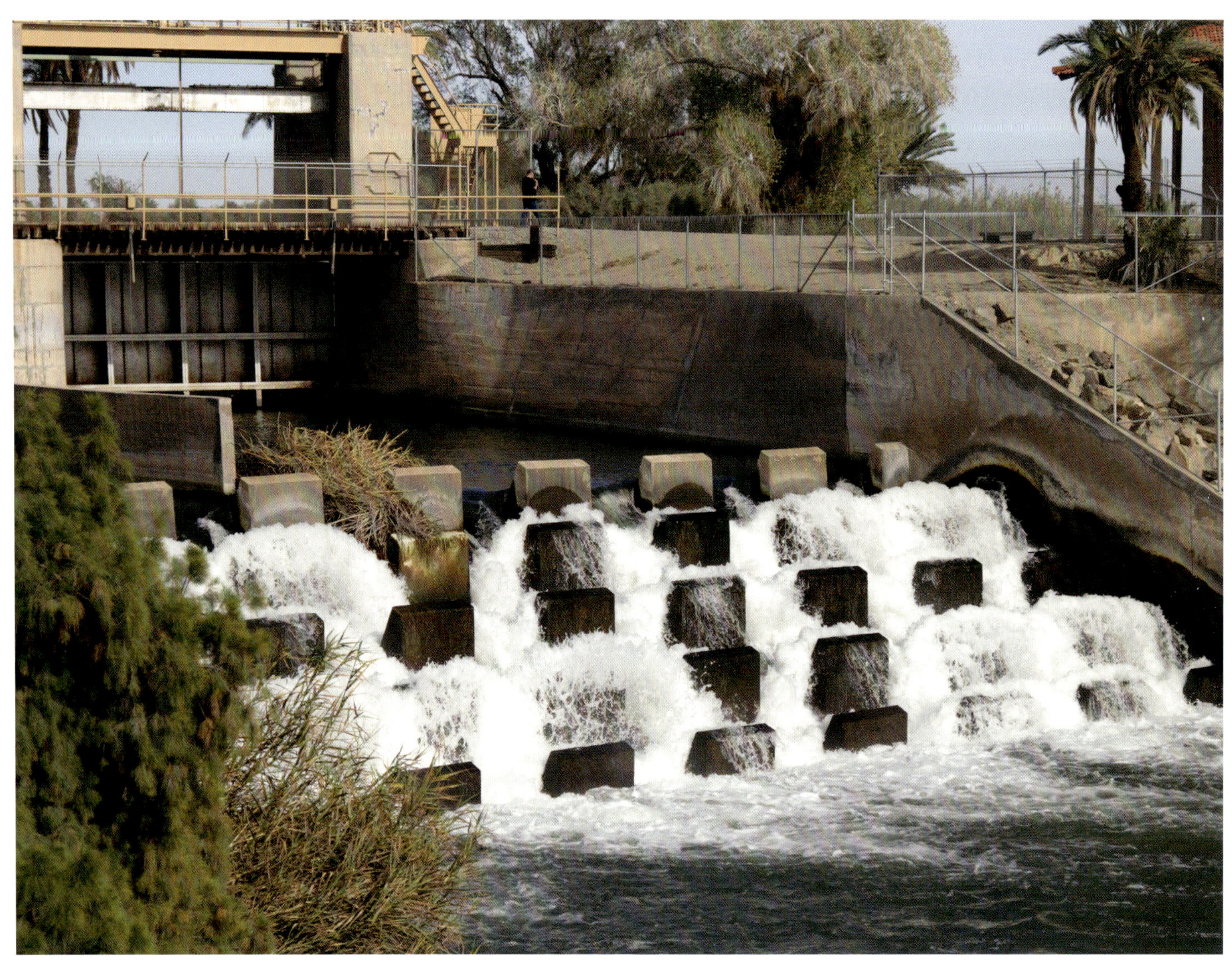

Laguna Dam
release.

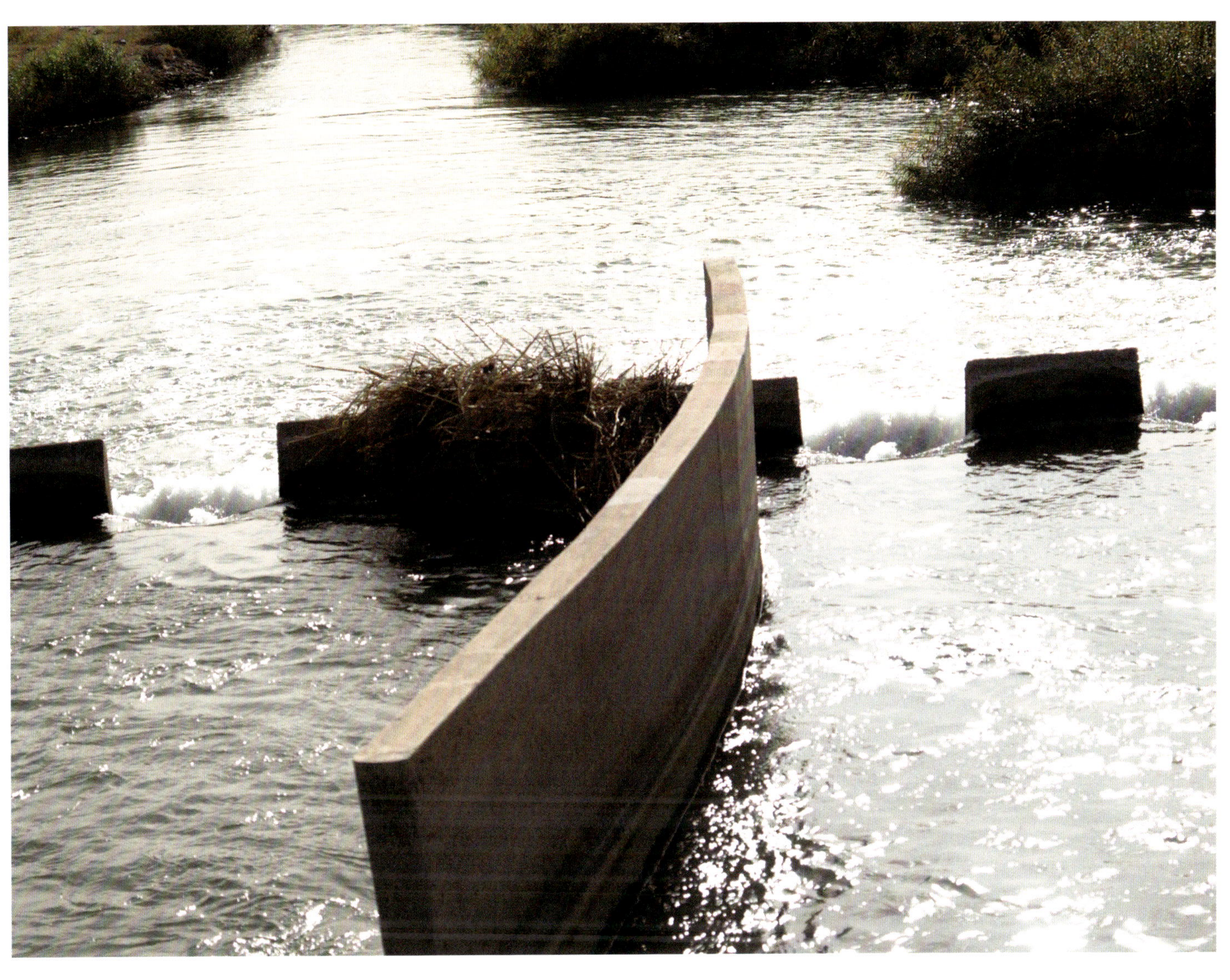

The river flowing
through Laguna
Dam.

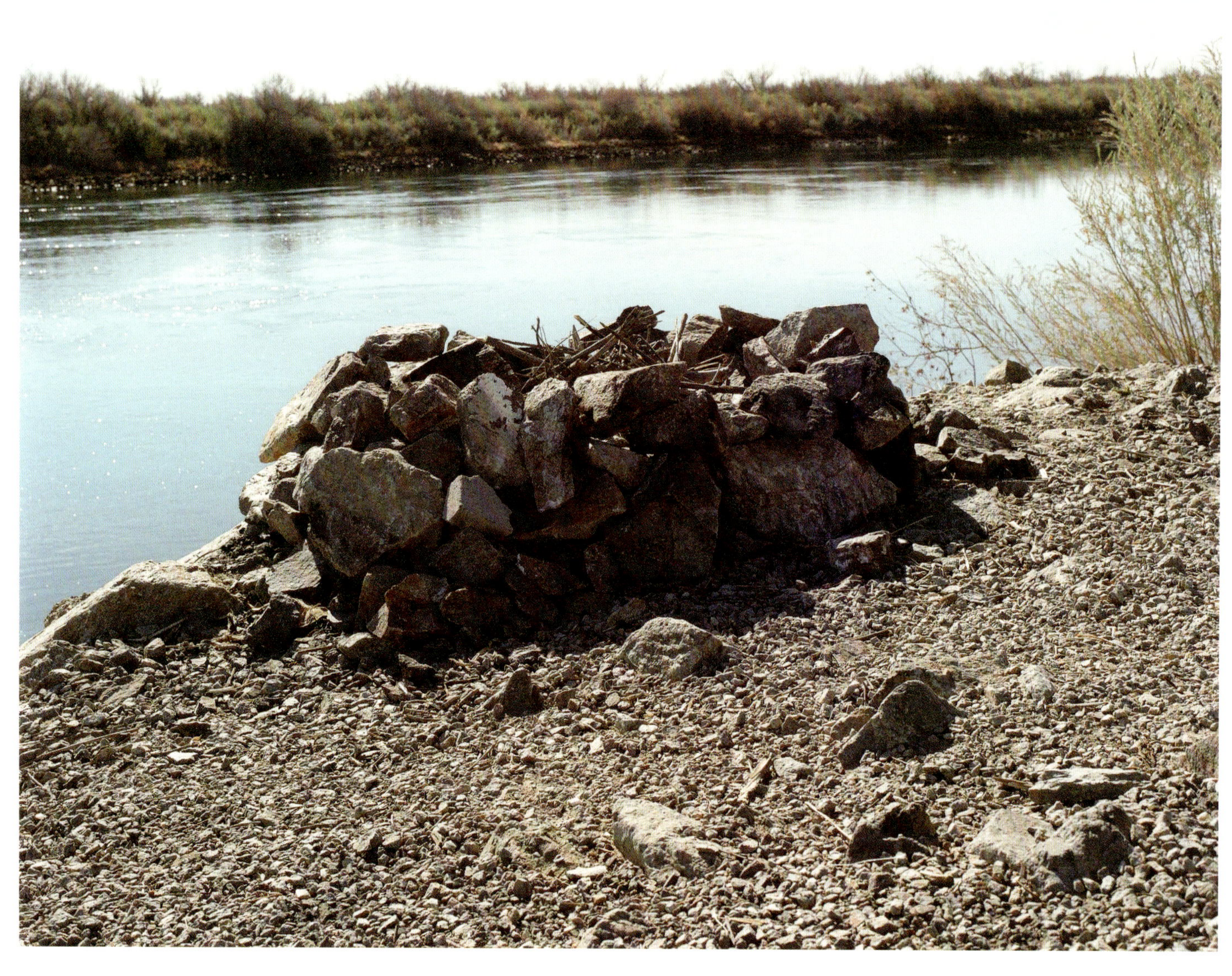

Camper fire pit near
Yuma, Arizona, after
Laguna Dam.

MORELOS DIVERSION DAM

After the 1944 US-Mexico Treaty, the Morelos Dam was built in 1950 across the Colorado River to deliver the agreed-upon 1.5 maf of Colorado River water per year. It is located about one mile below the junction of the California border and the Colorado River between the town of Los Algodones, Baja California, in northwestern Mexico and Yuma County, Arizona.

The eastern half of the dam lies inside US territory, but Mexico is responsible for all maintenance. The dam allows Mexico to divert its allotted water from the Colorado River to highly developed crop lands in the Mexicali Valley.

The Morelos Dam is the final dam on the main stem of the Colorado River. It is run by the International Boundary and Water Commission (IBWC).

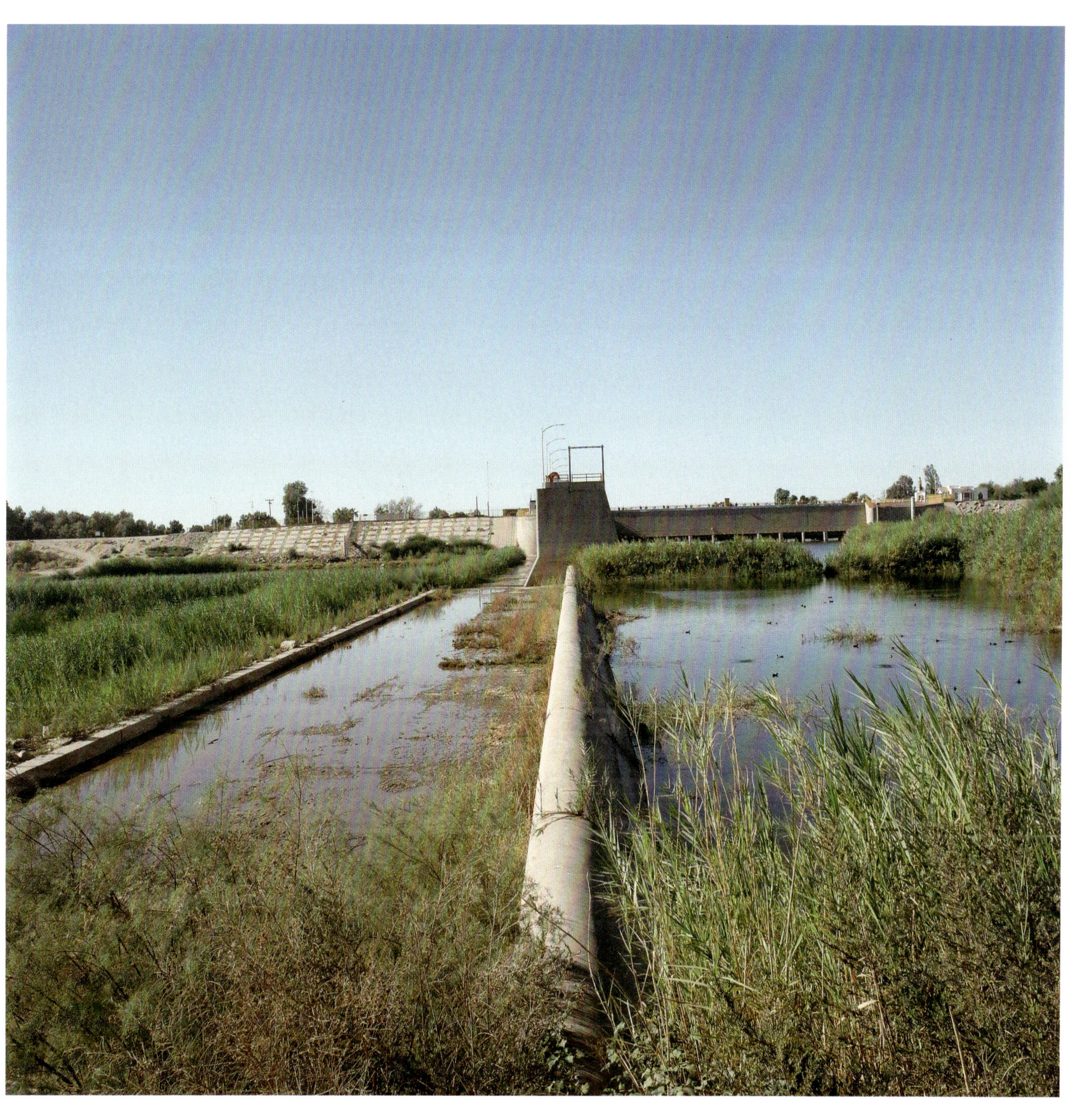

Morelos Dam,
Arizona and Mexico.

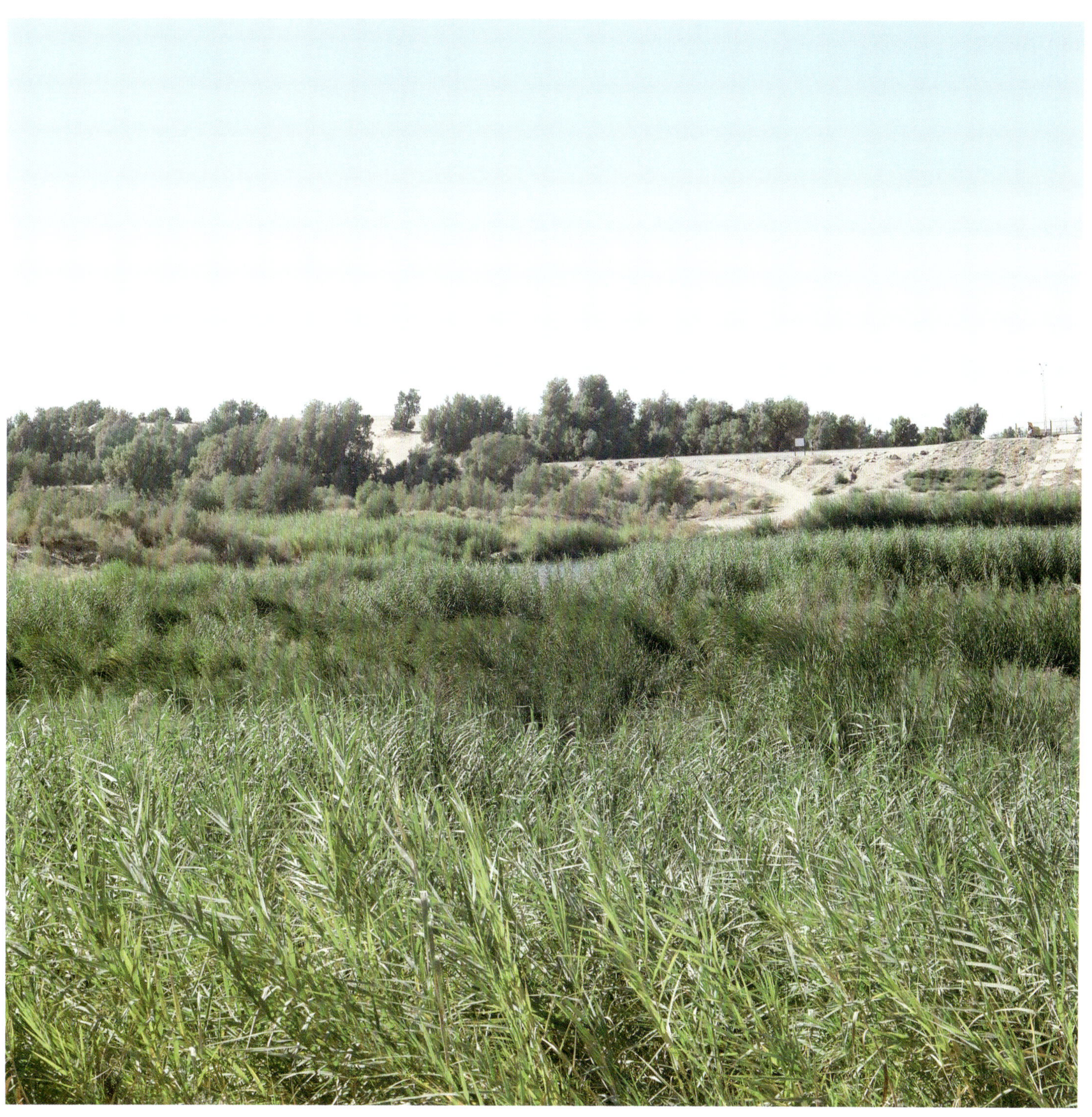

Colorado River
release toward
Mexico-US border.

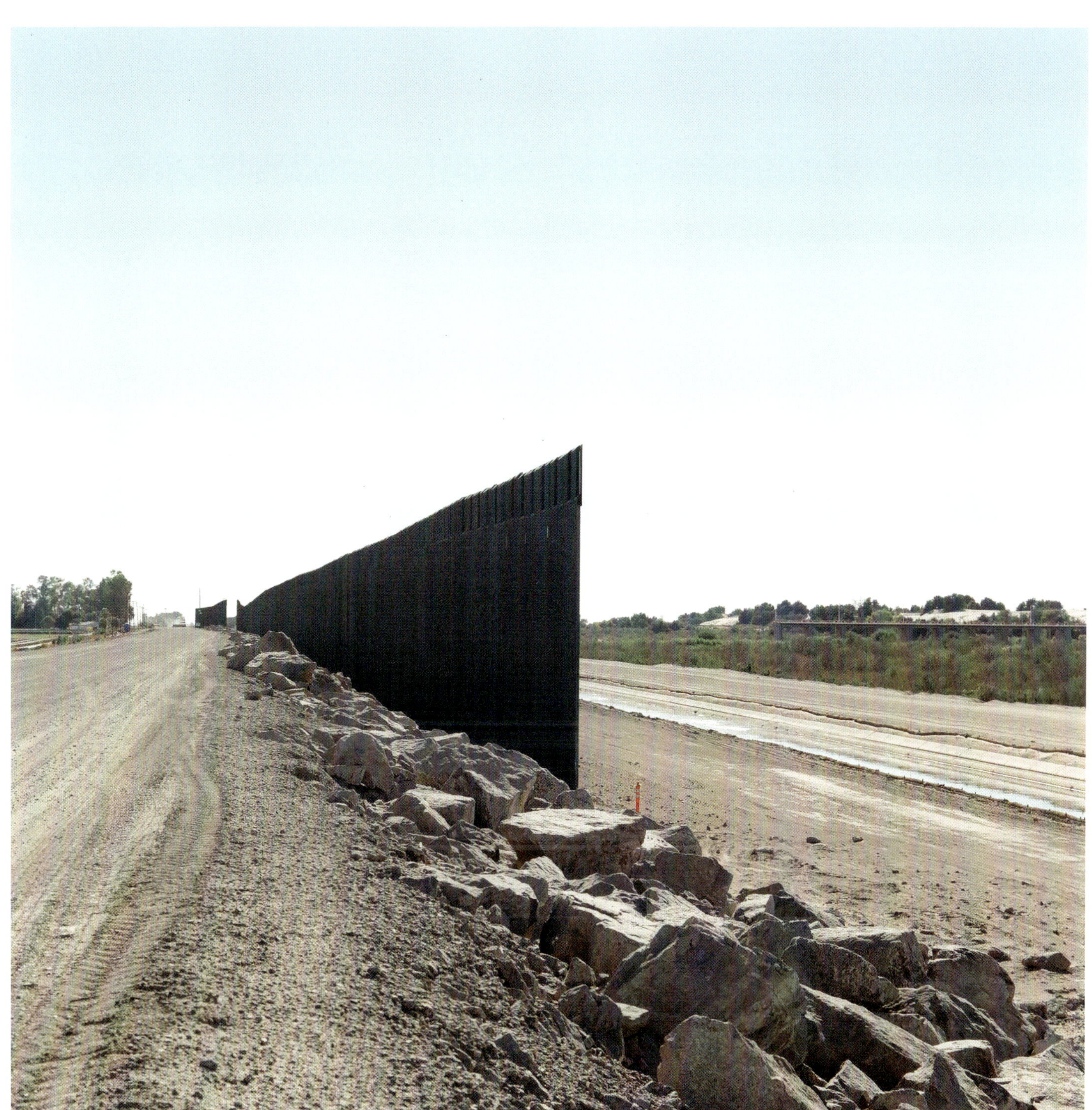

Border wall with
Morelos Dam in
distance.

There is no shortage of water in the
desert but exactly the right amount, a
perfect ratio of water to rock, of water
to sand, insuring that wide, free, open
generous spacing among plants and
animals, homes and towns and cities,
which makes the arid West so different
from any other part of the nation. There
is no lack of water here, unless you try to
establish a city where no city should be.

—Edward Abbey, *Desert Solitaire:*
A Season in the Wilderness

Q&A WITH DEBBIE BENTLEY
AND PHOTOGRAPHER LINDA CONNOR

LC: Photographing the Colorado River and main stem dams was a massive undertaking! Was there some sort of a personal aha moment that prompted you to take on this project?

DB: Yes. While I was researching and photographing my Salton Sea project in 2018, I traveled to Pilot Knob, near Winterhaven, California. This is the site of the 1905 cut into the Colorado River, which breached its banks, sending the river's full flow into the Salton Sink for two years. This was the birth of the Salton Sea. After spending more than a year shooting the rivers feeding the Salton Sea from Mexico, I began to take an interest in the All-American Canal and its origins in the Colorado River. In fact, during the work at the Salton Sea, I started researching the Colorado River, and the interconnected system of dams along its main stem, and the impact these dams have made on the overallocated and endangered Colorado River.

But my interest is deeper and more personal, as well. I was born and raised in Colorado. I saw and experienced the river and these spaces my entire life. I developed an affection for rivers in general, having spent many hours fishing Colorado rivers with my grandfather.

The project goal then became to provide a visual reference of the sheer size and length of the main stem of the Colorado River and explain the complexity of the system of dams along the route. Each dam impacts the river significantly as it flows from headwaters to Mexico. Additionally, given the current aridification of the western and southwestern US, I wanted to present images taken over time, paired with historical images to increase awareness. Much information is shared in the press, etc. related to the concerning situation at Lake Mead and Lake Powell, and much data is shared. Data, however, can't be visualized in the way a photograph can present it. This is an important component of environmental/eco art and photography in general.

LC: How many dams and diversions are on the main stem again?

DB: There are fifteen currently, with one in Colorado under construction. Soon to be a total of sixteen.

LC: So, these are just on the main stem? Are there dams on tributaries, as well?

DB: Yes. Over 100 dams have been built on the Colorado River and its tributaries.

LC: Going back to the Salton Sea work, it seems to be the genesis of your current project, *Dammed*. What prompted the Salton Sea work? It's a pretty unusual place in many ways! Did you go there with a project in mind? Or, like many people who make the trip, [were you] just curious?

DB: Actually, the first time I saw the Salton Sea was on a family vacation! We were escaping the winter in the warmth of Palm Springs for a few days. While exploring, we went to the Salton Sea. I really didn't know much about it, but after seeing it in obvious decline, littered with dead fish, I wanted to learn more about the lake and how it became that way. In spite of its decline, I saw a truly sublime, melancholic beauty in that place. I became interested in learning more. I was also interested in how the Colorado River played its part in the lake's creation. Honestly, I always ask questions and learn more about every place I go. Inquiring minds want to know, right?

LC: Yes, they do! From a personal perspective, what was one of the most memorable moments you experienced while working on *Dammed*?

DB: At the time the photography for the project began, I was living in California. As I mentioned earlier, I am from Colorado and have returned to live in my home state. I began the project at the end—on the lower Colorado, as this was logistically easier to accomplish at the time. I saw the river as it was released from dam after dam, with less and less flow, until its final diversion to Mexico at Morelos Dam. The entire route of the lower Colorado is desert: always the same; dry, and hot in the summer and cold in the winter. When we moved back to Colorado, the shooting began on the upper Colorado, and the headwaters of the Colorado River.

I stood in the meadow at La Poudre Pass and looked at the pure, untouched beginning of this river I had seen as it became nearly dead in Mexico. It made me cry.

All the experiences in the past two-plus years of shooting have been even more memorable thanks to my husband, Mike. We traveled all these miles together—quite the adventure of finding the river and making images. He laughingly referred to the travels as "Driving Miss Debbie."

Throughout the entire project, we camped near or at dam sites and used that as a home base for shooting. The project itself became something of a family affair. Mike and I and sometimes our youngest son, Jeremy, camped and explored the river and its relationship to the land and humans. We boated and fished on Lake Havasu, Lake Mead, and Lake Powell. We rented all-terrain vehicles in the desert; we walked on and across dams. Mike "threw a line in" at many locations along the Colorado River. I put my hands into its cool, clear waters in Rocky Mountain National Park.

We drove many, many miles and followed the river. Of course, the furriest part of the family, Bella the Wonder Dog, tagged along!

LC: In contrast to some of these more pleasant experiences, what would you say were some of the most disturbing things you encountered over the course of this investigation?

DB: I'd have to say a couple of things come to mind. When shooting at Hoover Dam and Lake Mead in 2022, it was so hot my digital Hasselblad camera and phone shut down completely in the 118 degree heat. Fortunately, I shoot both film and digital, so I was able to make images on film. That said, a large amount of my film also suffered emulsion degradation. That particular year was even hotter than previous years—an ongoing trend in the West and Southwest, and indeed the world.

I think one of the most glaring examples of just how low the water levels at Lake Powell really are was looking down at the canyon walls near Antelope Point Marina. The launch was closed, and looking over the sheer side to the water so far below was mind-blowing. To the left of the closed launch, a kayak rental company was hauling kayaks by hand up and down roughly 100 feet of canyon slope to launch into Powell.

LC: Are you planning any future projects combining the Salton Sea work and the Colorado River work?

DB: Possibly. I have done some work on the agricultural areas supplied by Colorado River waters, so that might be a direction to tie water issues and agriculture in the Colorado River Basin. I recently did photography follow-ups at the Salton Sea for the fifth year after the work in 2018. This could be joined to further-focused work on perhaps Glen Canyon and Hoover.

LC: As one photographer to another—there are often aspects of any project that present difficulty. Some things just don't go as planned. Were there any such aspects over the course of the Colorado River project?

DB: Oh boy, yes. I think the worst was in the initial photography at Morelos Dam. I use a Hasselblad 500C/M for all landscape and environmental photography and projects. Armed to the teeth with plenty of film rolls and newly serviced magazine backs, we hit the road to Morelos Dam at the border of Arizona and Mexico and up the river to Imperial Dam. Many, many images. Many magazine backs leaking light. Probably a third of all the work was not usable.

This is when I decided to shoot double fisted, so to speak. Digital and film Hasselblad.

LC: I'm curious. How did you get your start in photography?

DB: I had somehow acquired my grandfather's [Kodak] Pony 135 [Model] C after he passed away, as well as my grandmother's Argoflex. I'd enjoyed taking pictures as a child but hadn't picked up anything more than a disposable point-and-shoot for years. One day, I just felt like throwing a roll of film in "Grandpa" and that started a new direction for me. I actually shot exclusively with "Grandpa" for years! Lots of trial and error, patience, and learning.

When I began to make images with medium format, something just clicked. It is the weapon of choice for all my eco/environmental work.

REFERENCES

Bures, Sarah and Michael Elizabeth Sakas. 2023. "Indigenous Tribes Were Pushed Away From the Colorado River. A New Generation Is Fighting to Save It." CPR.org. May 10. Accessed 2023. https://www.cpr.org.

Daily, Vail. 2022. "Don't call it a 'drought': Climate Scientist Brad Udall Views Colorado River Crisis as the Beginning of Aridification." *Steamboat Pilot & Today*, August 25.

Davis, Wade. 2013. *River Notes*. Washington, DC: Island Press.

Deems, J.S., et al. 2013. "Combined Impacts of Current and Future Dust Deposition and Regional Warming on Colorado River Basin Snow Dynamics and Hydrology." *Hydrology and Earth System Sciences 17* 4401-4413. doi:10.5194/hess-17-4401-2013.

Grand Valley Water Users Association. n.d. "A Brief History of Grand Valley Water Users Association." *GVWUA*. Accessed 2023. https://gvwua.com.

Hiltzik, Michael. 2010. *Colossus*. New York, New York: Free Press, a division of Simon & Shuster, Inc.

Imperial Irrigation District. n.d. "All-American Canal." *Imperial Irrigation District.* Accessed 2020. https://www.iid.com/water.

—. n.d. "Imperial Dam." *Imperial Irrigation Dam.* Accessed 2023.

—. n.d. "Senator Wash." *Imperial Irrigation District.* Accessed 2020.

Kaur, Anumita. 2023. "The Breakthrough Deal to Protect the Colorado River, Explained." *The Washington Post*, May 23. https://www.washingtonpost.com/climate-environment/2023/05/23/colorado-river-deal-water-cuts-explained/

Kwon, Karen and Jennifer Gimbel. 2021. *Quenching Thirst in the Colorado River Basin*. Educational, Fort Collins: Colorado Water Center.

Lee, Katie. 1998. *All My Rivers Are Gone*. Boulder, Colorado: Johnson Printing.

Lohan, Tara. 2020. "'Megadrought' and 'Aridification' - Understanding the New Language of a Warming World." *The Revelator*, June 8. https://therevelator.org/author/taralohan/.

Macrotrends. n.d. *Phoenix Metro Area Population 1950–2023*. https://www.macrotrands.net/cities.

National Archives. n.d. *The Hoover Dam*. Accessed 2023. https://hoover.archives.gov.

National Park Service. 2021. *Effects of the Grand Ditch*. Informational, National Park Service. http://www.nps.gov.

Northern Water. 2023. "Chimney Hollow Reservoir Project." *Northern Water.*

—. n.d. "Lake Granby." https://www.northernwater.org.

—. n.d. "Northern Water Shadow Mountain." *Northern Water.* https://www.northernwater.org.

—. 2023. "Water for Growth Through Windy Gap." *Northern Water.*

Owen, David. 2017. *Where The Water Goes*. New York, New York: Riverhead Books, an imprint of Penguin Random House, LLC.

Porter, Eliot. 1968. *The Place No One Knew*. New York, New York: Sierra Club & Ballantine Books.

Reisner, Marc. 1993, Revised. *Cadillac Desert*. New York, New York: Penguin Books.

Runyon, Luke. 2022. "Lower Colorado River Reservoir Evaporation the Focus of New Analysis." *KUNC*. October 26. Accessed 2023. http://www.kunc.org.

Swanson, Conrad. 2023. "What Part Do Native American Tribes Play in Fixing the Colorado River Shortage?" *The Denver Post*, January 4. http://www.denverpost.com.

The Colorado River Basin States Representatives of Arizona, California, and Nevada. 2023. "Letter to Camille Calimlim Touton, Commissioner." May 22.

U.S. Census Bureau. n.d. "1940 Census."

U.S. Department of the Interior, Bureau of Reclamation. 1965. *Lake Powell Jewel of the Colorado*. Promotional Piece, Washington, DC: U.S. Government Printing Office.

U.S. Department of the Interior, Bureau of Reclamation. 2014. *Law of the River*. Information, U.S. Department of the Interior, Bureau of Reclamation.

Udall, B. and J. Overpeck. 2017. "The Twenty-First Century Colorado River Hot Drought and Implications for the Future." *Water Resources Research, 53* 2404-2418. doi:10.1002/2016WR019638.

Udall, B.H, E. Kuhn, J. Fleck, and D. Kanzer. 2018. "How Refusal to Accept Inconvenient Science Contributed to the Over-Development of the Colorado River." *American Geophysical Union, Fall Meeting 2018*.

United States Bureau of Reclamation. n.d. *Parker Dam*. U.S. Department of the Interior.

—. 2022. "Annual Lake Moovalya Drawdown in January for Maintainence Activities."

United States Bureau of Reclamation. 2023. "July 2023 Most Probable 24-Month Study." Monthly Study.

—. n.d. *Lower Colorado Dams Office*. Accessed 2023.

—. n.d. "Palo Verde Diversion Dam." *Projects & Facilities*. Accessed 2023. https://www.usbr.gov.

—. n.d. "Projects & Facilities." *Colorado–Big Thompson Project*. Accessed 2022. http://www. usbr.gov.

—. n.d. "Projects & Facilities." *Grand Valley Project*. Accessed 2021. https://www.usbr.gov.

—. n.d. "Projects and Facilities." *Granby Dam*. https://www.usbr.gov.

—. n.d. "The Mexican Water Treaty of 1944." *Reclamation and Arizona*. Accessed 2023. https://www.usbr.gov.

—. n.d. *Upper Colorado Region*. Accessed 2021. http://www.usbr.gov.

United States Bureau of Reclamtion. n.d. "Laguna Diversion Dam." *Projects & Facilities*. Accessed 2019. http://www.usbr.gov.

Upper Colorado River Alliance. n.d. "Windy Gap Reservoir Modification." *UCRA*. Accessed 2023. http://ucra.us/windy-gap.

ACKNOWLEDGMENTS

This project would not have been possible, nor as much of an adventure, without my husband, Michael. We followed the river together, stem to stern, and all the river's turns in between. He has always been my greatest supporter, hands down.

Looking forward to many more great adventures "Driving Miss Debbie."

Special thanks to Linda Connor for her insights and suggestions over the entire course of this project.

Ever and always, mentor and friend.

Onward!

This book is dedicated to my mother, Marilyn, who passed from this life during the making of the final work.

She will be so greatly missed.

Ma, GMa and GGMa.